Communications in Computer and Information Science 1262

Commenced Publication in 2007
Founding and Former Series Editors:
Simone Diniz Junqueira Barbosa, Phoebe Chen, Alfredo Cuzzocrea,
Xiaoyong Du, Orhun Kara, Ting Liu, Krishna M. Sivalingam,
Dominik Ślęzak, Takashi Washio, Xiaokang Yang, and Junsong Yuan

Editorial Board Members

More information about this series at http://www.springer.com/series/7899

Önder Babur · Joachim Denil ·
Birgit Vogel-Heuser (Eds.)

Systems Modelling and Management

First International Conference, ICSMM 2020
Bergen, Norway, June 25–26, 2020
Proceedings

 Springer

Editors
Önder Babur
Eindhoven University of Technology
Eindhoven, The Netherlands

Joachim Denil
University of Antwerp
Antwerp, Belgium

Birgit Vogel-Heuser
Technical University of Munich
Munich, Germany

ISSN 1865-0929   ISSN 1865-0937   (electronic)
Communications in Computer and Information Science
ISBN 978-3-030-58166-4   ISBN 978-3-030-58167-1   (eBook)
https://doi.org/10.1007/978-3-030-58167-1

This Springer imprint is published by the registered company Springer Nature Switzerland AG
The registered company address is: Gewerbestrasse 11, 6330 Cham, Switzerland

Preface

Objectives and Scope

Model-based approaches promote the use of models and related artefacts, such as simulation environments and experimental platforms, as central elements to tackle the complexity of building software-intensive systems. With the widespread use for large and diverse settings (including large ecosystems and multidisciplinary systems of systems such as embedded, cyber-physical, automation, production, medical, aerospace, and enterprise systems), the complexity, size, multiplicity, and variety of those artefacts has increased. This leads to challenges in the development and management of these heterogeneous systems, and calls for advanced modeling and model management approaches, along with supporting analytics techniques for the entire lifecycle of such systems. At the International Conference of Systems Modelling and Management (ICSMM), we aim to address these problems and propose novel solutions, promoting cross-fertilization across various modeling communities. The scope ranges from industrial reports and empirical analyses in the problem domain to novel cross-disciplinary approaches, e.g., exploiting techniques from model-based software/systems engineering, systems architectures, modeling and simulation, automated production systems, engineering design, data analytics, and machine learning. The topics of interest (non-exclusive) is as follows:

- Systems modeling and management for software-intensive systems such as embedded, cyber-physical, medical, and automotive systems
- Identification of open research challenges for systems modeling and management
- Empirical/case studies and industrial experiences for systems modeling and management
- Methods, tools, and datasets for systems modeling and management
- Multi-level/-paradigm/-disciplinary modeling, large-scale consistency checking, and (co-)evolution management for model-based systems
- Modeling and (co-)simulation for complex heterogeneous systems
- Modeling across different phases of system life cycle
- Model interoperability, synthesis, and linking of heterogeneous modeling artifacts, repositories, and toolchains
- Model repositories and mining for heterogeneous systems
- Data analytics and machine/deep learning for analyzing, adapting, and managing model-based systems
- Using models for problem exploration and decision making for the whole system life cycle
- Distributed computing and big data applications for systems modeling and management
- Clone, pattern, and aspect mining for systems models
- Visualization of large scale heterogeneous model-based systems

– Variability mining and management of model-based systems and model-driven product lines
– Intelligent techniques for automating modeling tasks
– Building and composing systems model management and analytics workflows, modeling-as-a-service for engineering complex systems

Submissions and Reviewing Process

We welcomed submissions of the following types:

– Full and short research papers: full papers (max. 16 pages without references) presenting mature research results on systems modeling and management, and short papers (max. 8 pages without references) corresponding to work in progress or early results. These should be original papers not previously or simultaneously submitted elsewhere.
– Extended abstracts: short manuscripts (max. 4 pages without references) for new ideas, experience reports from practitioners, tools for systems modeling and management, and so on. These were presented in lightning talk sessions and do not form part of the proceedings.

In the open call for papers, we received 20 submissions, one of which was desk-rejected with respect to the scope. Each submission was reviewed single-blind by exactly three Program Committee (PC) members. After several rounds of discussion we agreed to accept 10 full papers and 3 short papers, based on their relevance to the conference scope and the reviews provided by PC members.

Conference Proceedings

While the conference didn't take place physically or virtually (due to the COVID-19 situation), we invited the authors to either provide pre-recorded video presentations, or personally present their papers next year at ICSMM 2021 (to co-locate with STAF 2021). The conference proceedings, along with the video presentations where applicable, are published in this Springer *Communications in Computer and Information Science* (CCIS) volume. Further, we plan to invite extended versions of the papers for a special issue in the journal *Innovations in Systems and Software Engineering* (ISSE).

Outlook

We consider ICSMM 2020 as a solid foundation for a promising series of conferences for modeling communities. We hope to realize the actual networking and cross-fertilization potential next year by holding a physical conference.

Acknowledgements

We are very thankful to all PC members for the quality of their reviews and their contribution in the discussions, as well as the publicity and web chairs for their support in the organization. We further thank INCOSE and SysML consortium for their interest in the conference.

July 2020

Önder Babur
Joachim Denil
Birgit Vogel Heuser

Organization

Steering Committee

Mark van den Brand	Eindhoven University of Technology, The Netherlands
Bernhard Rumpe	RWTH Aachen, Germany
Hans Vangheluwe	University of Antwerp, Belgium
Manuel Wimmer	Johannes Kepler University Linz, Austria

Program Chairs

Önder Babur	Eindhoven University of Technology, The Netherlands
Joachim Denil	University of Antwerp, Belgium
Birgit Vogel-Heuser	Technical University of Munich, Germany

Program Committee

Ezio Bartocci	Technical University Wien, Austria
Moharram Challenger	University of Antwerp, Belgium
DeJiu Chen	KTH Royal Institute of Technology, Sweden
Federico Ciccozzi	Mälardalen University, Sweden
Loek Cleophas	Eindhoven University of Technology, The Netherlands
Romina Eramo	University of L'Aquila, Italy
Robert Heinrich	Karlsruhe Institute of Technology, Germany
Heiko Koziolek	ABB Corporate Research, Germany
Benjamin Kruse	Stevens Institute of Technology, USA
Ivan Kurtev	Altran, The Netherlands
Chris Paredis	Clemson University, USA
Alfonso Pierantonio	University of L'Aquila, Italy
Michel Reniers	Eindhoven University of Technology, The Netherlands
Miroslaw Staron	Chalmers University of Technology, Sweden
Bedir Tekinerdogan	Wageningen University & Research, The Netherlands
Mamadou Traore	University of Bordeaux, France
Daniel Varro	McGill University, Canada
Andreas Wortmann	RWTH Aachen, Germany
Alois Zoitl	Johannes Kepler University Linz, Austria

Publicity Chair

Moharram Challenger	University of Antwerpen, Belgium

Web Chair

Weslley Torres   Eindhoven University of Technology, The Netherlands

Additional Reviewer

Arda Göknil   University of Luxembourg, Luxembourg

Contents

Methods, Techniques and Tools

Verification and Validation

Applying Dynamic Programming to Test Case Scheduling for Automated Production Systems

Kathrin Land$^{(\boxtimes)}$, Birgit Vogel-Heuser, and Suhyun Cha

Chair of Automation and Information Systems, Technical University of Munich,
Garching near Munich, Germany
{kathrin.land,vogel-heuser,suhyun.cha}@tum.de

Abstract. In today's practice, the engineering lifecycle of the manufacturing systems is getting shorter due to frequent requirement changes. Since the manufacturing systems are required to have both – higher availability from a productivity viewpoint and reliability from a safety viewpoint. To check and meet these requirements, quality assurance, typified by testing is one of the significant engineering steps. Though existing test cases can be reused during testing, there also appears a selection problem out of a vast amount of test cases. Especially, it gets more important when the time is extremely limited, e.g. in commissioning and start-up process that is a mandatory process of manufacturing systems or in regression testing. In the previous work, we have presented approaches regarding how to define and determine the utility of test cases. In this paper, we present an efficient test case scheduling approach by applying an optimization algorithm, so called "dynamic programming". Considering a physical setup time of the mechatronics system within the approach, it becomes more applicable to the practice. Through the numerical experiment results, we also show the superiority and the scalability of the approach in comparison to two different straight-forward scheduling approaches.

Keywords: Test scheduling · Dynamic programming · Test prioritisation model

1 Introduction and Motivation

Automated production systems (aPS) are characterised by long life cycles. To obtain the availability and reliability of aPS and to adapt to changing customer requirements, they are subject to changes during their life cycle [1]. The changes made to the system and the demanded system quality are validated through testing. Based on the type of change and the testing phase, this includes test types that range from unit tests of a component (hardware and software) to system integration tests.

Regarding testing processes in aPS engineering, there are two major challenges in current practice as far as efficiency is concerned. First, a vast amount of test cases makes

---

Electronic supplementary material The online version of this chapter (https://doi.org/10.1007/978-3-030-58167-1_1) contains supplementary material, which is available to authorized users.

Ö. Babur et al. (Eds.): ICSMM 2020, CCIS 1262, pp. 3–20, 2020.
https://doi.org/10.1007/978-3-030-58167-1_1

testing more complicated as the test engineer has difficulties to manage all test cases in a clear manner. Nowadays model-based testing approaches are developed and applied to come up with user requirement systematically. These approaches usually yield a vast amount of test cases through automatic generation from the managed specification of the complex user requirement [2]. At the same time, as the second reason, testing processes are required to be done as fast as possible due to the limited testing resources, especially time [1]. In current practice, test cases are often still executed for the first time on-site during the plant commissioning. This is also due to the integration of separately delivered machines during commissioning which interfaces could not be tested. During the commissioning and on-site adjustments, customers urge to start production as early as possible, which leads to high time pressure for the test engineers [3].

Conclusively, the tester has to select just an excerpt out of the vast amount of test cases for the test execution. Though this final test runs decide the quality of the overall system, selecting test cases to be executed is often done manually depending on the tester's experience and knowledge [3]. This might lead to a non-optimal test case selection for the given testing phase and the system under test. To assist the tester in selecting, the utility of each test case could be defined by different criteria like the requirement-[2] or code-coverage [4] of the test case. Based on these utility values, the test cases can be judged regarding their worthiness to execute in a specific test scenario. On the assumption that all test cases are graded with a proper and reasonable utility value, the test engineer can easily select the test cases within a short period of time with the highest utility values. However, for the test case selection, the duration to execute each test case and the time to set up the system between two test case executions has to be regarded. If a test case with a high utility value has a relatively high execution duration, several test cases with lower utility values but shorter durations in combination might be more useful regarding the testing. So in order to find the optimal schedule, the test engineer has to consider the test execution times, the setup times between test cases as well as the utility values of the test schedules. This leads to an optimization problem to maximize the overall utility of the test schedule within the limited test execution time. In order to solve this optimization problem, suitable scheduling algorithms have to be applied. The scheduling approach shall hereby compute the optimal solution within a reasonable amount of time so that it is applicable to test case scheduling for aPS. Therefore, in this paper, dynamic programming is investigated regarding its suitability for test case scheduling for aPS while considering aPS-specific constraints.

The remainder of this paper is structured as follows: Sect. 2 provides an overview of related work on testing of automated production systems and scheduling approaches, especially dynamic programming for scheduling. Section 3 further explains the adaption of the dynamic programming approach to test case selection while considering the utilities of the different test cases as well as their execution times. In this section, the dynamic programming approach is already shortly compared to the two other, contrary scheduling approaches – permutation-based and utility-based. The dynamic programming approach is then adapted in Sect. 3.4 so that challenges in testing aPS, more precisely the setup times between different system states and test cases, are considered. In the following Sect. 4, the dynamic programming approach is evaluated and its performance is compared to the other two approaches in terms of computational time and overall utility of the resulting test plan. The paper is concluded in Sect. 5, which also provides an outlook on future work.

2 Related Work on Test Case Selection and Scheduling

Test scheduling to increase efficiency is a widely researched topic. It is especially researched in computer science (e.g. [5]) and applied in terms of various test case prioritisation techniques. However, test case scheduling for aPS is hardly considered and pure-software-related prioritisation techniques are not directly applicable to the industrial environment due to the essential difference: physical hardware and mechatronic effects. Scheduling techniques for aPS are mainly researched in production planning (e.g. [6] or [7] for aPS) and there also already exist approaches for Test Case Scheduling for system-on-chip design (e.g. [8]). In this section, some related works are introduced regarding the test scheduling for aPS. On the other hand, scheduling is a comparably mature topic especially in computer science. Some of the relevant and comparable approaches are also shown mainly concerning dynamic programming. The final subsection defines some terminologies that are used throughout this paper.

2.1 Test Case Selection and Prioritisation – The Utility Value

Evaluating test cases and reusing them in the regression testing perspective mainly focuses on selection and prioritisation of test cases [9]. Test case selection and prioritisation is regarded as one of the major issues to achieve a certain level of quality efficiently for aPS validation and re-validation [1, 10]. Especially due to the vast amount of test cases, which might be generated automatically, test case prioritisation gains importance in industry. There are several approaches in literature and industry to estimate the utility of a test case to detect faults in a specific testing scenario. Yoo and Harman [10] provide an overview on different test selection and prioritisation approaches for software tests with focus on regression testing. For aPS, Ulewicz et al. [3] presented a test case selection method considering the changes within the control software by evaluating the test case and the possible impact of the changed code [11]. In this case, code traceability and the test case coverage are within the main focus of the research regardless of the limitation of the test resource in terms of time. Efficient test case selection method with regards to the product line is presented in [12]. They aim for a test suite minimisation to sort out duplicate or less important test cases. Further approaches prioritise based on system models [13] or results from static code analysis [4, 11] e.g. code coverage. All these approaches prioritise the test cases in order to detect faults as early as possible during the testing process. According to [14], the chance to detect faults and thus the utility of a test case can be best estimated if a combination of several of the aforementioned prioritisation criteria is considered. This utility indication per test case assists the human tester in selecting a subset of test cases for a limited test execution time. In this paper, an already estimated utility value per test case due to the combination of different criteria is assumed.

The test efficiency regarding the available time for testing can be further increased by test scheduling. Especially for automated production systems there is a setup time necessary between the test case executions. The setup time varies depending on the pre-and post-conditions of each test case and reduces the available testing time without yielding more benefits. So if the test cases are ordered in a specific row so that the setup time is minimized, more test cases can be executed within the same amount of time. However, test scheduling related approaches are hardly found for aPS. Recently, Land et al. [15] have considered the utility of the test cases including various aspects and have started to consider the time limitation and test scheduling within the time limitation to achieve the optimal set of test cases and its order for the maximum utility within the available testing time. Though the need to maximize the overall utility for the limited available test execution time is considered, the scheduling algorithm performance, especially regarding its computational time and scalability, is not yet regarded.

2.2 Scheduling Strategies in Computer Science or Mathematics

In computer science and mathematics there are several typical scheduling approaches, especially for the application to production planning and job shop scheduling. The most conventional, static scheduling approaches are first-in-first-out (FIFO) or earliest-deadline-first (EDF) [16]. However, they are not applicable to test case scheduling as all test cases are assumed to be known from the start and there is no harsh deadline for a specific test case given. Other static approaches would be to schedule the test cases only based on their descending utilities (utility-based approach) or to schedule them based on their execution times e.g. shortest test case duration first, in order to achieve a maximum overall utility of the test run in a limited or minimum time. As such scheduling algorithms are fast to be calculated, their performance for test case scheduling lacks depending on the test cases. For example if the test cases are scheduled based on their execution time, this might result in a low overall utility of the whole test run if the shortest test cases have low utility values. In order to obtain the optimal schedule, another possible approach would be to calculate all possible test plan permutations. The optimal schedule is thus determined by comparing the overall utilities for each of the possible test plan permutations. From the set of all possible permutations of the test cases, a subset of permutations could be achieved which are possible to be executed within the given time. The optimal test case schedule is then obtained by comparing all resulting overall utilities to each other. As this approach is time consuming and scales factorial with an increasing number of for example test cases, other approaches with a similar performance but less computational time are needed. In mathematics and computer science, dynamic programming is a common approach to facilitate and fasten the scheduling task [6].

Dynamic programming is a mathematical optimisation function developed by Richard Bellmann [17]. It determines the optimal solution for a complex objective function by the combination of several solved sub problems. The equation is further known for solving the so-called knapsack optimisation problem. In this paper, the objective function would be to maximize the overall utility of a test plan within a limited time frame. This approach is promising as it is assumed to have a high performance with a reasonable and scalable computational time. Bellman proved that his dynamic programming approach satisfies recursive relations. The Bellman equation states that the value of the initial state must correspond to the (discounted) value of the expected next state plus the expected reward on the way there. Thus, the optimal schedule can be found by maximizing the value function for all states.

Banias [18] applied dynamic programming to test case selection and prioritisation for software testing and defines the optimisation problem to maximise the sum of utility values of the selected test cases within the given testing time. Further, Spieker et al. [19] proposed a reinforcement learning approach for test case selection and prioritisation. They therefore considered the execution time per test case as well as the last execution result and the failure history of the test case. Reinforcement learning is based on the dynamic programming by Bellman. Hence, Spieker et al. adapted it to test case scheduling. However, the two mentioned approaches focus on the field of computer science and thus did not deal with constraints of aPS. Constraints to be considered when testing aPS are manual test execution, temporarily available testing resources, setup times to set up preconditions of a test case from post conditions of the previously run test case or influences of the hardware on the testing process, especially upon test case failure. This paper focuses the two last-mentioned points. Tahvili et al. [20] suggested an approach that considers how the test cases and their results influence each other. Based on this information, they can provide a dynamic rescheduling. Even though Tahvili et al. focused on software tests, the approach could be adapted to the test cases and each of their post conditions aka end states as the end state of one test case influences the setup time to the next test case. Allahverdi et al. [6] compare different existing scheduling approaches as dynamic programming and even consider setup times and costs between the considered jobs. Nevertheless they do not consider the applicability to test case scheduling nor the domain of automated production systems. Petrenko et al. [21] applied mathematical scheduling methods to chain test fragments in an order so that the time between the test fragments is minimised. However, the test fragments are selected manually by test engineers based on their knowledge and all selected test fragments were scheduled. No maximal available testing time nor utility values maximisation per test run given the corresponding testing scenario were considered.

2.3 Basic Terms and Definitions

This subchapter shortly introduces the terms, which are essential to understand the following concept.

- **Test (Case) Schedule/Test Plan:** Arranged selection of test cases for test execution
- **Test Planning Time:** Time to plan test execution e.g. by calculating best test case schedule. This should be minimized to enable dynamic (re)scheduling during test case execution.
- **Test Execution Time:** Time that is available for the test execution itself (without Test planning Time)
- **Available Testing Time** = Test Planning Time + Test Execution Time
  In order to use most of the available testing time for the test case execution, the test planning time has to be minimized. Thus, the computational time per scheduling algorithm is an important criterion to rate the different approaches.
- **Utility:** The utility of a test case indicates its expected performance due to several different criteria.
- **Overall Utility:** Sum of the utility values of all test cases within the test schedule.

3 Optimize Test Case Scheduling for APS

3.1 Consideration of Setup Time for Test Case Scheduling

A test case is described by specific preconditions that must be fulfilled in order to run the test case, by the testing procedure itself and expected post-conditions. In aPS, these pre- and post-conditions can be described as two states (one for each) and the testing procedure is a possible transition between those two states. In order to set up a specific state, so called setup time is required for aPS. These setup times are not negligible due to the involvement of physical components that have to be moved. Hence, the setup times between the test cases have to be considered and minimized while planning the test run in order to maximize the possible overall utility [15].

3.2 Utility-Based and Permutation-Based Test Case Scheduling

A straight-forward scheduling approach is the utility-based scheduling. For the utility-based scheduling, test cases are sorted according to their descending utility values. Starting with the test case that is first in the resulting list, meaning the test case with the highest utility value, all test cases are planned into the schedule until the available test execution time is spent. Therefore, the execution duration per test case as well as the setup time to establish the preconditions of the test case have to be considered so that they do not exceed the remaining available test execution time. The following equation depicts the utility-based scheduling. The variable *isChosen* states whether the test case was chosen for the schedule. For that, *isChosen* can take the values one or zero. For all chosen test cases, their durations and setup times are added together. With this scheduling approach, test cases with the highest utilities are favoured despite the possibility that they might take very long so that no other test cases can be executed. As this approach only considers the utilities in descending order and not specifically the test execution duration or the setup times, the test cases are usually not in an order so that the setup time is minimized. Hence, a lot of valuable available test execution time (aTET) would be wasted on establishing preconditions instead of executing test cases.

$$\sum_{n=1}^{\#TCs}(duration_n + setup(currentState, startState_n)) * isChosen_n \leq aTET$$

In order to find the optimal test schedule regarding the overall utility with minimized setup times, all possible permutations of test cases (without duplicates within test schedule) can be calculated. The permutation-based approach analyses all possible test execution queues and determines the one with the highest overall utility within the given test execution time. Land et al. [15] used this permutation-based scheduling to demonstrate the benefit of arranging the test cases in a time efficient manner. However, the permutation-based approach is quite brute-forced as calculating and comparing all possible test execution orders requires a lot of computational time. Specifically, the computational time increases factorial with the number of possible test cases and the available testing time. The computational time of the permutation-based approach can be described by O(n!) with n as number of test cases. It can be shortened if not all test case combinations but only the feasible ones within the available test execution time are calculated. For example if there are three test cases, there are $3! = 6$ possible test schedules (e.g. abc). If one test case (e.g. test c) consumes the whole available test execution time, the following test case permutation calculation can be terminated. Thus there are only three possible test schedules (ab, ba or c) left. So the number of possible test schedules and computational time necessary to determine them increases with the available test execution time. Even despite this termination condition, the scalability of its computational time is unsuitable for industrial applications. Especially when considering dynamic rescheduling during test execution, the test planning time using this algorithm would exceed the test execution time which neglects its benefits regarding the time efficiency in the resulting test plan.

In order to obtain a superior test schedule in a reasonable amount of time, dynamic programming can be used. Hence, the following subsections show how dynamic programming and the Bellman equation [17] can be applied to test case scheduling, especially regarding the setup times which are essential for planning test execution on aPS.

3.3 Application of Dynamic Programming to Test Scheduling Without Setup Times - Test Case Selection

The Bellman equation is a mathematical optimisation approach that linearizes recursive or exponential problems. It assumes that an optimal solution for a specific point in time t can be found by combining optimal sub-solutions. To optimize the test case scheduling problem without considering the setup times, the Bellman equation is stated as follows:

$$\max_{tc} OU(t) = u(tc) + OU(t - duration(tc))$$

OU(t) describes the overall utility of the test run for a specific point in time t. OU(t) shall be maximized. Therefore, the available test execution time t is split into the time that is needed to execute a specific test case tc (i.e. duration(tc)) and the remaining time. Based on the previous assumption, the optimal solution of OU(t) can be derived by the optimal solution of the overall utility for an earlier point in time. So in order to derive the optimal test case selection, the utility of each test case is added to the overall utility of the timeslot that remains after planning the corresponding test case. As the optimal solution of all earlier points in time can be saved separately, the optimisation problem becomes a linear problem which is scalable for an increasing number of test cases and higher available test execution times. Originally, Bellman equation is a recursive function. Its computational time can be decreased by saving all intermediate optimal solutions OU(t-duration(tc)). The table-based approach is shown in the following Table 1. In the upper half of the table, an exemplary test set of three test cases with different test execution durations and utility values is given. For each point in time t (leftmost column of the table), the optimal overall utility is determined. For $t = 1$, only test case **c** can be executed. Hence, the resulting overall utility OU(1) is u(c) = 2. For $t = 2$, either test case **a** or test case **c** can be executed. As test case **a** has a higher utility, it is selected as the optimal test schedule for this point in time. Upon selecting test case **c**, $\tau = 1$ would remain to be further planned. However, it is assumed that multiple executions of the same test case within the same test plan does not yield additional benefits. Hence, OU(1) is not added to u(c) as each test case can be chosen just once per test case schedule. For t = 3, if test case **a** is planned, τ = 1 remains. As OU(τ = 1) is 2, the maximal overall utility for t = 3 is 5 as both test cases a and c can be selected for the test schedule which is considered more useful than selecting only test case **b** with utility 4. As all intermediate results for OU are saved and can be read from the table for each time slot, the dynamic programming approach according to Bellman scales linearly. As no setup times are considered in this equation, the order of the test cases is flexible. However, as setup times are essential in the test scheduling for aPS, the Bellman equation has to be adapted accordingly.

Table 1. Application of Bellman equation for an exemplary set of three test cases. (−: test case cannot be executed; +, τ: test case can be executed and remaining time is τ). Utility per test case is added to $OU(\tau = t - duration(tc))$ and max is saved in column "max OU(t)".

tc						
t	Test case tc	a	b	c	max OU(t) $= u(tc) + OU(\tau)$	Selected Test Cases
	Duration d(tc)	2 min	3 min	1 min		
	Utility u(tc)	3	4	2		
1	min	−	−	+, τ = 0	2	c
2	min	+, τ = 0	−	+, τ = 1	3	a
3	min	+, 1	+, τ = 0	+, 2	5	a, c
4	min	+, 2	+, 1	+, 3	6	b, c

3.4 Adapting Dynamic Programming for Scheduling with Setup Times

In test case scheduling for automated production systems (aPS), the order of the test cases is important. For example the laboratory plant xPPU was considered in [15], which consists of about 70 sensors and 30 actuators. The plants main part is a crane to transport work pieces between production modules. The setup time between two test cases varies based on the system states before and after each test case execution e.g. the crane position at one of the modules conveyor, stack and stamp. The following Table 2 gives an overview of the setup times between the three different system states. The setup times can be extracted e.g. based on the transition time between two states if the plant behaviour is modelled as state chart. The setup matrix is no symmetrical matrix as not every path from one state to another is directly reversible.

In order to apply dynamic programming to this optimization problem, the varying initial state depending on the previously executed test case has to be considered. Therefore, an overall utility per state, in which the test schedule starts, has to be calculated. All per state overall utilities are then saved in the corresponding state table. The number of state tables hereby relates to the number of (test start- and end-) states within a system. The equation to optimize the overall utility per test case is as follows:

$$\max_{state} OU(t, tc) = u(tc) + OU(t - duration(tc) - setup(endstate(tc), state))$$

Table 2. Left: Exemplary Setup-Matrix; Right: Start and End State of Test Cases of Table 1.

Setup Times between states in min			
to from	S1	S2	S3
S1	0	3	1
S2	2	0	1
S3	1	1	0

Test case	Start State	End State
a	S1	S1
b	S1	S2
c	S2	S3

This equation calculates the highest overall utility per test case OU(t, tc). It is the utility of the test schedule that starts with a particular test case tc. Therefore, the utility of that test case is added to the overall utility for the point in time given by the remaining time τ. This is as it was with the original Bellman equation that was applied in chapter 3.3. But to consider the setup time, the remaining time τ is calculated not just by the difference of the available execution time and the test case duration. It is further reduced by the setup time between the state after the test case execution (*endstate(tc)*) and the next state. This setup time is read from the setup matrix in Table 2. The remaining time is calculated for all system states and the overall utility for that state is read from the state table. All resulting utilities are compared and the maximal overall utility per test case OU(t, tc) is determined and saved. This is done for all test cases per point in time. Afterwards, the table with the overall utilities per state has to be updated so that they can be used in the next iteration of the overall utility per test case calculation. The maximal overall utility per state can be calculated by the following equation:

$$OU(t, state) = \max($$
$$\max_{state} OU\,(t, tc)\,of\,(\forall tc|(startstate(tc) = state),$$
$$OU\,(t - 1, state),$$
$$\max(OU(t - (setup\,(state, oState))), oState)$$
$$)$$
$$with\,\{\,oState \in \forall states|oState \neq state\}$$

The overall utility per state per point in time OU(t, state) is the maximum of one of three possible schedules. The optimal schedule and overall utility is either

1. the highest of the overall utilities of one of the test cases that starts in this state or
2. the overall utility of the previous point in time of that state or
3. the highest of the utilities of the other states for the specific point in time reduced by the setup time that is needed to switch to that state from the current state. *oState* hereby represents any state except the current state.

The following tables show the exemplary application of the equations and the resulting tables for the intermediate results. Therefore, the exemplary test set introduced in Table 1 and the setup times given in Table 2 are assumed. In Table 3, the overall utility per test case OU(t, tc) is determined and saved. It is calculated with the previously introduced equation for $OU(t, tc)$. In the table, the remaining time Δt_{Sx} per test case indicates the line to be read of Table 4 of state Sx. Table 4 presents all saved overall utility values per state $OU(t, state)$. The entries in the state table are extracted to determine the overall utility per starting test case $OU(t, tc)$. For example take test case **a** and the point in time $t = 4$ min: τ_{S3} is 1 min, so that in Table 4, the saved schedule for state S3 for point in time $t = 1$ min is extracted and added to test case **a**. This leads to the optimal schedule "**a, c**" with overall utility 5 for test case **a** as initial test case. After the overall utilities for all test cases for a specific point in time is calculated, the state table (cf. Table 4) has to be updated. The overall utility values per state per point in time OU(t,state) are calculated and saved in the state table.

Table 3. Test Case Table to save intermediate results of OU(t, tc) – maximal OU(t, tc) is printed bold, saved and considered for updating the State Table (cf. Table 4).

tc						
t	a		b		c	
	τ	OU(t, a); schedule	τ	OU(t, b); schedule	τ	OU(t, c); schedule
1 min	–	0; –	–	0; –	+, $\tau_{S1} = -1$ $\tau_{S2} = -1$ $\tau_{S3} = 0$	– – **2; c**
2 min	+, $\tau_{S1} = 0$ $\tau_{S2} = -3$ $\tau_{S3} = -1$	**3; a** – –	–	0; –	+, $\tau_{S1} = 0$ $\tau_{S2} = 0$ $\tau_{S3} = 1$	– – **2; c**
3 min	+, $\tau_{S1} = 1$ $\tau_{S2} = -2$ $\tau_{S3} = 0$	**3; a** – –	+, $\tau_{S1} = -2$ $\tau_{S2} = 0$ $\tau_{S3} = -1$	– **4; b** –	+, $\tau_{S1} = 1$ $\tau_{S2} = 1$ $\tau_{S3} = 2$	2; c 2; c **2; c**
4 min	+, $\tau_{S1} = 2$ $\tau_{S2} = -1$ $\tau_{S3} = 1$	3; a – **5; a, c**	+, $\tau_{S1} = -1$ $\tau_{S2} = 1$ $\tau_{S3} = 0$	**−6: b, c** – –	+, $\tau_{S1} = 2$ $\tau_{S2} = 2$ $\tau_{S3} = 3$	3; a 2; c **3; a**

Table 4. State Table to save intermediate optimal solutions per state OU (t, state)

state \ t	S1	S2	S3
1 min	-	2; c	-
2 min	3; a	2; c	2; c
3 min	4; b	2; c	3; a
4 min	6; b, c	5; c, a	4; b

In the following calculation examples, the determination of OU(t, state) for the marked cell within Table 4 is shown exemplary in order to have a better understanding of the proposed equation. The marked cell contains the overall utility and the schedule for state S1 for the point in time $t = 3$ min. In this case, the two test cases **a** and **b** that start in state S1 are considered and their overall utility values for the time $t = 3$ are compared. These values are read from Table 3. The resulting overall utility 4 and schedule "b" is compared to the overall utility of S1 for $t = 2$ according to Table 4 (which is 3; a). The result is further compared to the overall utility values of all other states for the remaining time τ. Therefore, the available time t is reduced by the setup time to get into each other state. In case of state S2, the setup time is the same as the available time so that there is no schedule possible. For S3, the remaining time is 2, hence the overall utility value and schedule "2; c" can be read from the corresponding cell. After comparing all of these overall utility values and possible schedules, the resulting optimal schedule is **b** with an overall utility of 4.

$$
\begin{aligned}
\mathbf{OU(t} = 3, \mathbf{S1}) = \max(\ & \\
& \max(OU(3, tc = a), OU(3, tc = b)), \\
& OU(3 - 1 = 2, S1), \\
& \max(OU(3 - 3 = 0, S2), OU(3 - 1 = 2, S3))\ ) \\
= \ & \max(\max(3,\ 4),\ 3,\ \max(-,\ 2)) \\
= \ & \mathbf{4}\ \text{with resulting schedule} : \mathbf{b}
\end{aligned}
$$

The tables with the overall utility per state per point in time are also usable for a dynamic rescheduling during the test execution. Dynamic rescheduling might be necessary upon a test case failure if the system is for example in another state than expected. Further, the test execution time per test case is not reliably predictable, especially not in case of a test case failure, so that the remaining test execution time could also differ. In such cases, the new best schedule given the circumstances (state and remaining time) can be read directly from the state tables.

4 Evaluation of Dynamic Programming Approach for Test Case Scheduling Considering Setup Times

4.1 Introduction of Evaluation Example Test Set

For the evaluation, several exemplary test sets were considered. To compare the computational time and the resulting test schedules, thirty test sets were generated. The computational time of the permutation-based approach is expected to increases factorial with an increasing number of test cases as all possible permutations of test cases have to be calculated. This leads to a high computational time even for small and medium numbers of test cases. Hence for the comparison of the different scheduling approaches, each of the thirty test sets consists of only ten test cases. With this, a computation of the different scheduling approaches can be made in a reasonable amount of time. Also, the subset of ten test cases is assumed to be enough to demonstrate the characteristics of the different approaches. The utility values and the execution times of the test cases were generated based on the standard normal distribution. This results in utility values that vary between one and five and execution times that vary between one and ten minutes. The start and end states are uniformly distributed.

The test cases were scheduled with the three different approaches – permutation-based, utility-based and with the dynamic programming approach. In order to compare the different approaches, the best schedule per point in time was determined. The approaches were applied to a total available testing time from one to sixty minutes. The evaluation considered an excerpt of a test model with four different test states (pre- and postconditions of the test cases) for the test scheduling and the setup time determination. Therefore, the previously introduced setup matrix in Table 2 was assumed.

4.2 Implementation and Application of Scheduling Algorithms

In order to compare the adapted dynamic programming approach for test case scheduling to the other two approaches, they were all implemented and plotted in Matlab. The pseudocode is as follows:

Pseudocode to calculate highest utility starting with a specific test case tc_k for a certain point in time t_i:

```
Δtime = tᵢ - duration (tcₖ)
If Δtime < 0: not executable
If Δtime = 0: testTable (tᵢ,tcₖ) = tcₖ
If Δtime > 0:
   // Append optimal solution for remaining time Δtime
   testTable (tᵢ,tcₖ) = tcₖ
   for each state {
      remainingTime = Δtime - setup(endstate(tcₖ), state s))
      schedule = tcₖ + stateTable (remainingTime, state s)
      testTable (tᵢ,tcₖ) = max (testTable (tᵢ,tcₖ), schedule)
   }
```

Pseudocode to save best schedule for given time slot in state table:

```
for each state s {
COMPARE
 utility of previous best schedule for s in stateTable
TO
 utilities of all schedules in testTable for test
 cases that start in state s
TO
 utility in stateTable of all other states for time (testtime
- setup(state s, other_state))
SAVE test schedule with highest utility
}
```

4.3 Discussion of Evaluation Results

There are three points to discuss from the result of this numerical experiment. First, the computational time of the scheduling approaches are compared (Fig. 1) Second, the overall utility values of the dynamic scheduling approach and the utility-based approach are compared to the results of the permutation-based approach which resembles the optimal test schedule and thus the highest achievable overall utility (Fig. 2). Third, the scalability of the dynamic programming approach is investigated (Fig. 3).

The following Fig. 1 displays an excerpt of the change of the computational time in comparison to the time that is set for the test case execution. The utility-based approach has a short computation time as it merely sorts the test cases according to their utility values. Conversely, the permutation-based approach calculates every possible test schedule. Thus, its computation time is very high, so that even for a small two-digit number of test cases, it does not schedule in an acceptable time (calculation takes several hours to days). If the test time is sufficient to schedule all test cases, the algorithm generates n! permutations for n test cases. Due to that, the computation time of the permutation-based algorithms show an factorial incline as shown in Fig. 1. The permutation-based algorithm is implemented so that it generates and compares only permissible test plans that do not exceed the test time. As it does not calculate all permutations, its computational time is reduced. However, it still increases factorial. This means that the computational time of the algorithm depends not only on the number of test cases, but also on the test time. As the test time increases, the computational time for the permutation algorithm also increases significantly (Fig. 1). The graph comparison in Fig. 1 also indicates that the permutation-based approach is faster than the dynamic programming approach for a small number of test cases and short available testing time. Hence, the crossing point between the two graph lines shows the trade-off between the two approaches so that the most suitable approach for a specific testing scenario can be selected.

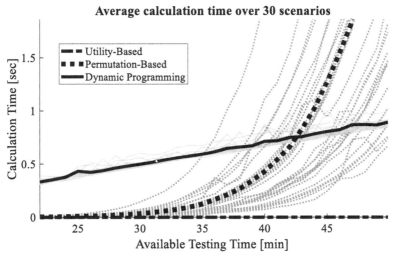

Fig. 1. Excerpt: Comparison of Computational Time for 30 scenarios of test sets of ten test cases that were generated with standard normal distribution. Permutation-based Scheduling has high computational time in comparison to other two scheduling approaches.

As shown in Fig. 1, the permutation-based approach requires a long computational time. However, it is able to select the test schedule with the highest achievable overall utility for a specific available testing time. Thus its results are considered to be the optimal test schedule solution for the next evaluation point. The utility-based approach has a mixed test efficiency, which depends strongly on the utility values of the different test cases. For example, the utility values of the test cases could randomly reflect the ideal execution order, resulting in a very good test efficiency. However, this is usually not the case and the utility-based approach has a rather poor test efficiency in mechatronic systems. The three approaches were compared regarding the overall utility of their test schedule results. As the permutation-based approach is assumed to determine the highest overall utility, the results of the other two approaches were compared to it. Figure 2 represents the difference between the resulting overall utility values. For each of the thirty test scenarios, the resulting overall utilities of each approach were subtracted from the highest achievable value and the corresponding graphs were plotted. The bold lines represent the average difference in the overall utility values between the approaches. The resulting graphs (cf. Figure 2) clearly show that the dynamic programming approach is close to the x-axis. Hence, its performance is close to the performance of the permutation-based approach whereas the average utility values of the utility-based approach show a higher deviation from the x-axis and thus from the optimum.

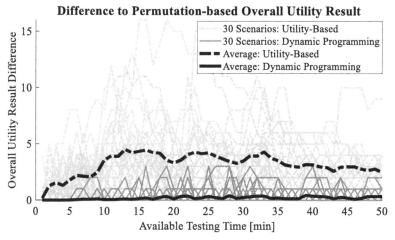

Fig. 2. Deviation of the overall utility values compared to the permutation approach for 30 scenarios of test sets of ten test cases: Dynamic Programming approach performance close to permutation-based approach and better than utility-based approach performance.

The first two evaluation points revealed that the dynamic programming approach and the permutation-based approach show a similar performance in determining the optimal overall utility and corresponding test schedule. Dynamic programming is hardly inferior compared to the permutation-based approach. In the timing performance, it is better scalable especially for the longer timing due to its linearity. In the following graph (Fig. 3) the scaling of the dynamic programming approach for an increasing number of

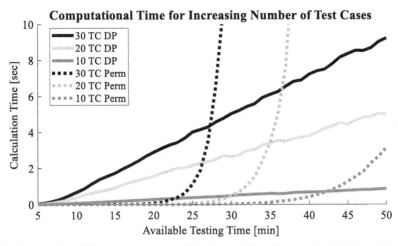

Fig. 3. Computational Time for increasing Number of Test Cases – Scalability of Dynamic Programming approach (DP) and permutation-based approach (Perm) for 10/20/30 test cases (TC)

test cases is analysed in comparison to the scalability of the permutation-based approach. The incline of the dynamic programming approach increases because the number of columns within the test table to be read and written in order to calculate the optimal schedule per test case per time unit raises. This is also reflected in the Bellman equation:

$$\max_{tc} OU(t) = u(tc) + OU(t - duration(tc))$$

To determine the test schedule with the highest overall utility, the equation is calculated per test case. Therefore, the utility per test case is added to the optimal schedule for the remaining time which can both be read from the aforementioned tables. Hence, the computational time for the dynamic programming approach only scales with the number of test cases, which is linear. The dynamic programming approach was chosen and applied based on this assumption, which is confirmed by the results in Fig. 3.

In case of failure during test execution, a dynamic scheduling strategy is needed that does not require a high computational time as otherwise it would lead to time loss. The dynamic programming approach is especially suitable for dynamic test scheduling due to the already calculated lookup tables for the different time slots. If for example a test case takes more execution time than expected due to a failure, the schedule that was planned in advance might not be feasible anymore. Instead of calculating a new optimal schedule for the remaining time, the optimal test plan for this time slot and for the current state can be read from the lookup tables. A test case failure could lead to a blockage that prevents the majority of other test case executions so that the lookup tables are not applicable. However in this case, a new calculation can be done within a reasonable amount of time.

5 Conclusion and Future Work

The time to test automated production systems is limited especially in regression test-ing. Hence, the test cases to be executed (additional to mandatory test cases) have to be selected carefully. Assuming that each test case has a utility value for example based on its error detection rate, an indicator for a reasonable test case selection is given. However, to run a test on an automated production system (aPS), the system has to be set into a specific state. This requires a setup time which cannot be neglected. Thus, a time efficient test case schedule is necessary so that the time that is wasted by setting up the system between two test cases is minimized. This leads to an optimization problem where the sum of all utility values per test case shall be maximized within the limited available time while considering aPS constraints like the setup times between the test cases. As other approaches like calculating all possible permutations of test cases is time consuming and does not scale well for an increasing number of test cases, dynamic programming is applied to the test case scheduling problem in this paper. Therefore, the dynamic programming approach and the corresponding Bellman equation are adapted so that the setup times between the test cases are considered. The resulting equation as well as the time efficient solution with tables for intermediate schedule results were pre-sented. Finally, the approach was compared to two other approaches – utility-based and permutation-based scheduling – to evaluate the performance of the dynamic programing approach regarding the resulting test schedule utility and the computational time needed to derive it. The dynamic programming approach turned out to have nearly the same performance than the permutation-based approach within a reasonable amount of time.

Future works are twofold. First, stochastic test execution time should be considered. Since the many behaviours of aPS by nature requires human interaction for usual manu-facturing or fault handling processes, there exist various types of uncertainty regarding the test execution time which might result in the different result of the test scheduling. The approach should be extended to achieve more correct result by adding the human interaction model for different cases. Second, further scheduling approaches such as meta-heuristics with more constraints shall be analysed and compared regarding their suitability for test case scheduling for aPS. Depending on the industrial use case, other scheduling approaches might turn out to be more time efficient or can be applied easier than dynamic programing. Hence, a thorough analysis of the superiority of this app-roach is planned to be evaluated in different realistic, industrial settings. In future, a suggestion of the optimal test schedule strategy per testing use case, requirements and edge values of the system would be beneficial. Further, not only test execution time optimisation but also other scheduling goals such as human interaction time or resource usage minimisation shall be considered in a joint approach.

References

1. Vogel-Heuser, B., Fay, A., Schaefer, I., Tichy, M.: Evolution of software in automated produc-tion systems: challenges and research directions. J. Syst. Softw. **110**, 54–84 (2015). https://doi.org/10.1016/j.jss.2015.08.026
2. Sinha, R., Pang, C., Martinez, G.S., Kuronen, J., Vyatkin, V.: Requirements-aided automatic test case generation for industrial cyber-physical systems. In: 20th International Conference on Engineering of Complex Computer Systems (ICECCS), pp. 198–201 (2015)

3. Ulewicz, S., Vogel-Heuser, B.: Industrially applicable system regression test prioritization in production automation. IEEE Trans. Autom. Sci. Eng. **15**(4), 1839–1851 (2018). https://doi.org/10.1109/TASE.2018.2810280
4. Simon, H., Friedrich, N., Biallas, S., Hauck-Stattelmann, S., Schlich, B., Kowalewski, S.: Automatic test case generation for PLC programs using coverage metrics. In: IEEE 20th Conference on Emerging Technologies & Factory Automation (ETFA), pp. 1–4 (2015)
5. Elbaum, S., Rothermel, G., Kanduri, S., Malishevsky, A.G.: Selecting a cost-effective test case prioritization technique. Softw. Qual. J. **12**(3), 185–210 (2004). https://doi.org/10.1023/B:SQJO.0000034708.84524.22
6. Allahverdi, A., Ng, C.T., Cheng, T.C.E., Kovalyov, M.Y.: A survey of scheduling problems with setup times or costs. Eur. J. Oper. Res. **187**(3), 985–1032 (2008). https://doi.org/10.1016/j.ejor.2006.06.060
7. Keddis, N., Javed, B., Igna, G., Zoitl, A.: Optimizing schedules for adaptable manufacturing systems. In: IEEE 20th Conference on Emerging Technologies & Factory Automation (ETFA), pp. 1–8 (2015)
8. Chakrabarty, K.: Test scheduling for core-based systems using mixed-integer linear programming. IEEE Trans. Comput.-Aided Des. Integr. Circ. Syst. **19**(10), pp. 1163–1174 (2000). https://doi.org/10.1109/43.875306
9. Engström, E., Runeson, P.: A qualitative survey of regression testing practices. In: Ali Babar, M., Vierimaa, M., Oivo, M. (eds.) PROFES 2010. LNCS, vol. 6156, pp. 3–16. Springer, Heidelberg (2010). https://doi.org/10.1007/978-3-642-13792-1_3
10. Yoo, S., Harman, M.: Regression testing minimization, selection and prioritization: a survey. Softw. Test. Verif. Reliab. **22**(2), 67–120 (2012). https://doi.org/10.1002/stv.430
11. Angerer, F., Grimmer, A., Prahofer, H., Grunbacher, P.: Configuration-aware change impact analysis (T). In: 30th IEEE/ACM International Conference on Automated Software Engineering, pp. 385–395 (2015)
12. Baller, H., Lity, S., Lochau, M., Schaefer, I.: Multi-objective test suite optimization for incremental product family testing. In: IEEE Seventh International Conference on Software Testing, Verification and Validation (ICST), pp. 303–312 (2014)
13. Estevez, E., Marcos, M.: Model-based validation of industrial control systems. IEEE Trans. Ind. Inf. **8**(2), 302–310 (2012). https://doi.org/10.1109/TII.2011.2174248
14. Parejo, J.A., Sánchez, A.B., Segura, S., Ruiz-Cortés, A., Lopez-Herrejon, R.E., Egyed, A.: Multi-objective test case prioritization in highly configurable systems: a case study. J. Syst. Softw. **122**, 287–310 (2016)
15. Land, K., Cha, S., Vogel-Heuser, B.: An approach to efficient test scheduling for automated production systems. In: IEEE 17th International Conference on Industrial Informatics (INDIN), pp. 449–454 (2019)
16. Pinedo, M.: Scheduling: Theory, Algorithms, and Systems. Springer, Heidelberg (2016). https://doi.org/10.1007/978-3-642-46773-8_5
17. Bellman, R., Dreyfus, S.: Dynamic Programming, 1st edn. Princeton University Press, Princeton (2010)
18. Banias, O.: Test case selection-prioritization approach based on memoization dynamic programming algorithm. Inf. Softw. Technol. **115**, 119–130 (2019). https://doi.org/10.1016/j.infsof.2019.06.001
19. Spieker, H., Gotlieb, A., Marijan, D., Mossige, M.: Reinforcement learning for automatic test case prioritization and selection in continuous integration. In: Proceedings of the 26th ACM SIGSOFT International Symposium on Software Testing and Analysis, pp. 12–22 (2017)

20. Tahvili, S., Pimentel, R., Afzal, W., Ahlberg, M., Fornander, E., Bohlin, M.: sOrTES: a supportive tool for stochastic scheduling of manual integration test cases. IEEE Access **7**, 12928–12946 (2019). https://doi.org/10.1109/ACCESS.2019.2893209
21. Petrenko, A., Dury, A., Ramesh, S., Mohalik, S.: A method and tool for test optimization for automotive controllers. In: 2013 IEEE Sixth International Conference on Software Testing, Verification and Validation Workshops, pp. 198–207 (2013)

A Model-Driven Mutation Framework for Validation of Test Case Migration

Ivan Jovanovikj[(✉)], Nils Weidmann, Enes Yigitbas, Anthony Anjorin,
Stefan Sauer, and Gregor Engels

Department of Computer Science, Paderborn University, Paderborn, Germany
{ivan.jovanovikj,nils.weidmann,enes.yigitbas,
anthony.anjorin,stefan.sauer,gregor.engels}@upb.de

Abstract. Software testing is important in software migration as it is used to validate the migration and ensure functional equivalence which is a key requirement. Developing new test cases for the migrated system is costly and, therefore, the migration of existing test cases is an attractive alternative. As the migrated test cases validate the whole migration, their migration should be clearly validated as well. Applying mutation analysis to validate test case migration is a promising solution candidate. However, due to the diversity of the migration context, applying mutation analysis is quite challenging for conceptual and especially for practical reasons. The different types of test cases combined with the different technologies used, make the application of existing, mostly code-based and mutation score-oriented, mutation tools and frameworks barely possible. In this paper, we present a flexible and extensible model-driven mutation framework applicable in different migration scenarios. We also present a case study, where our mutation framework was applied in industrial context.

Keywords: Software migration · Software testing · Mutation analysis

1 Introduction

Software migration is a well-established strategy to reuse software and results in a software system that runs in a new environment. The main requirement that must be fulfilled by the migrated system is functional equivalence with the original system. Software testing is a well-known strategy used in software migration. As developing test cases is an expensive and cumbersome activity, existing test cases can be used which requires their co-migration along with the system, as depicted in Fig. 1. Hence, their migration has to be validated as well. This means that, similarly to the system migration, functional equivalence must hold for the migrated test cases. In other words, the migrated test cases still have to assert the same expected system behavior as the original test cases.

Electronic supplementary material The online version of this chapter (https://doi.org/10.1007/978-3-030-58167-1_2) contains supplementary material, which is available to authorized users.

© Springer Nature Switzerland AG 2020
O. Babur et al. (Eds.): ICSMM 2020, CCIS 1262, pp. 21–29, 2020.
https://doi.org/10.1007/978-3-030-58167-1_2

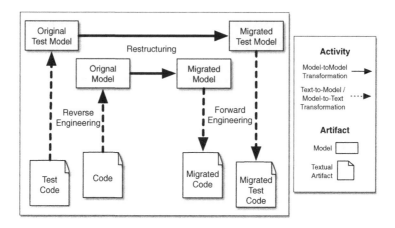

Fig. 1. Model-driven co-migration of test cases

The problem of validating test case migration is similar to the problem of validating test case refactoring as both activities tend to keep asserted behavior unchanged. In the case of test refactoring, mutation analysis [4] has been applied as validation strategy. This has inspired us to apply the same technique as a validation strategy for test case migration. The initial idea was presented in [2] and defines different mutation scenarios. The scenarios differ regarding the artifact being mutated, either the original or the migrated system, or the original or the migrated test cases, or even the transformation leading to the migrated system and the migrated test cases could be mutated. This initial analysis has shown that proper tool support is a must for any of the scenarios. However, the high diversity that a software migration context is characterized by, makes the application of existing mutation tools and frameworks difficult.

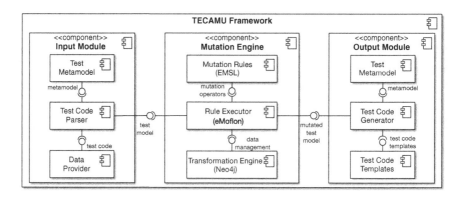

Fig. 2. The architecture of the TECAMU framework

Furthermore, as software migration is dependant on the actual situation in which it is performed, it must be situation-specific. As a consequence, the validation method for the test case migration, in our case based on mutation analysis, also has to be situation-specific. Hence, the mutation framework has to provide high flexibility and extensibility so that it is applicable in any given situation. Furthermore, as most of the migration frameworks are model-based, the mutation framework has to provide means to specify mutation operators on a higher level of abstraction and not just directly on the code level. Moreover, the mutation framework should provide an easy and intuitive way for the specification of mutation operators.

To address the aforementioned problems, we introduce the Test Case Mutation (*TECAMU*) framework, a flexible and extensible model-driven mutation framework. It is a component-based framework, consisting of three main components, *Input Module*, *Mutation Engine*, and an *Output Module*, as shown in Fig. 2. The *Input Module* deals with providing the proper data for the main component, the *Mutation Engine*, which provides means to specify mutation operators and apply mutation on the input data. The *Mutation Engine* component relies on the *eMoflon* framework and the *Neo4J* database. The *Output Module* deals with the generation of the mutated code. The component-based architecture guarantees easy adaptation of the framework to any situation.

The structure of the rest of the paper is as follows: In Sect. 2, the underlying model-driven solution architecture is described. Afterwards, Sect. 3 presents the process used for realizing test case mutation. Then, Sect. 4 briefly describes the implementation of the framework. In Sect. 5, the instantiation of the framework is shown based on a case study from an industrial context. Finally, in Sect. 6, we discuss related work and at the end, in Sect. 7, we conclude our paper and give an outlook on future work.

2   Solution Architecture

The solution architecture of the *TECAMU* framework is depicted in Fig. 2 and shows the three main components of the framework, *Input Module*, *Mutation Engine*, and *Output Module*.

The leftmost component, namely the *Input Module*, as the name suggests, handles the input data, i.e., the test cases that have to be mutated. It consists of three components, namely *Test Metamodel*, *Test Code Parser*, and *Data Provider*. The *Test Code Parser* requires the metamodel of the test cases that have to be parsed. The *Test Metamodel* component provides the particular metamodel to the parser, as shown in Fig. 2. The test cases are provided by the *Data Provider* to the *Test Code Parser*. The *Input Module* component provides the parsed data, in terms of a test model, to the main component of the mutation framework, namely the *Mutation Engine*.

The *Mutation Engine* component is based on the *eMoflon* transformation framework, which is a tool suite for applying Model-Driven Engineering (MDE) and provides visual and formal languages for (meta)modelling and model management[1]. It consists of three components, *Mutation Rules*, *Rule Executor*, and *Transformation Engine*. The *Mutation Rules* component is responsible for the specification of the mutation operators in terms of mutation rules which are basically model transformation rules. The specified mutation rules can be executed by the *Rule Executor* and completely relies on *eMoflon*. This requires the mutation operators as well as the outcome of the *Test Code Parser* component, namely the test model. Having this input, the *Rule Executor* applies the rules and mutates the test model, i.e., the test cases which are part of the test model. Regarding the execution, the application of the mutation rules can be configured. By default, each mutation rule is applied on the first match in a test case. For efficient execution, the transformation rules are executed to the *Transformation Engine* which relies on *Neo4J*, which is a graph database that exchanges data with via Cypher queries[2]. Once the mutation rules are executed, i.e., the mutation of the test model is performed, the mutated test model is used by the *Output Module*.

The *Output Module* component consists of three main components, *Test Metamodel*, *Test Code Generator*, and *Test Code Templates*. The central component is the *Test Code Generator* component, which is concerned with the generation of the executable mutated test cases. It requires the test metamodel as well as the test code templates so that the test code generation can be performed.

3   Process

Figure 3 shows the underlying mutation process of the *TECAMU* framework. The horseshoe model as a common representation in the area of reengineering is used to visualize the model-driven approach. In general, the process consists of three main activities, *Test Model Discovery*, *Mutation*, and *Test Code Generation*. Beside the activities, we distinguish between two types of artifacts, models and textual artifacts. Lastly, we have also visualized the tools, i.e., the framework components introduced in the previous section, necessary for the automation of the whole process.

In the first activity, i.e., *Test Model Discovery* (shown on the left-hand side of Fig. 3), *Test Model* is extracted out of the *Test Code* by using the previously introduced *Test Code Parser*. Having the outcome of this activity, i.e., the *Test Model* which conforms to *Test Metamodel*, the actual model mutation can be performed. For the *Mutation* activity, first of all, a set of relevant *Mutation Rules* has to be specified in terms of model transformation rules specified in *EMSL*[3], a uniform language for model management. Then, the *Mutation Engine*, takes the *Mutation Rules* and executes them against the previously obtained

---

[1] https://emoflon.org/.

[2] https://neo4j.com/developer/cypher-query-language/.

[3] https://emoflon.org/.

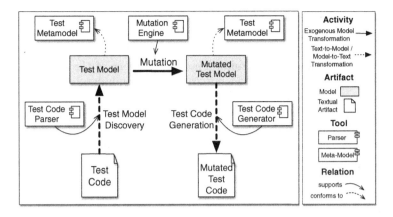

Fig. 3. The mutation process of the TECAMU framework

Test Model. The outcome of the *Mutation* activity is a *Mutated Test Model*, which also conforms to the *Test MetaModel*.

In the third and the last activity of the mutation process, namely the *Test Code Generation* activity, based on the *Mutated Test Model*, and the *Test Code Templates*, the *Test Code Generator* generates executable mutated test cases, i.e., *Mutated Test Code*.

4   Implementation

The *TECAMU* framework was implemented as a composition of three different *Eclipse* plugins which correspond to the three main components shown in Fig. 2. Such an architecture enables flexibility and extensibility towards supporting mutation for different types of testing frameworks as well as mutation of different types of systems.

Firstly, the plugin corresponding to the *Input Module* component, was implemented to support the two main activities of the *Test Model Discovery* process, namely the parsing and the understanding activities. The parsing activity firstly parses the code and the test code and extracts an abstract syntax tree. In the case of *JUnit*[4] test cases, this means that firstly, a suitable Java parser is necessary (e.g., *JDT* Parser). Having the abstract syntax tree, a more concrete model can be obtained by applying model-to-model transformation as part of the understanding activity. When considering, *JUnit*, a suitable metamodel is necessary to enable this activity. As outcome of the understanding activity, a test model is obtained in terms of a *JUnit* test model or if necessary, a more general representation is possible in terms of *xUnit* metamodel.

The main component, namely the *Mutation Engine*, was realized also as an Eclipse plugin, which highly relies on the *eMoflon* framework. Among others,

---

[4] https://junit.org/junit5/.

eMoflon has its own language for specifying model transformation rules, namely the *EMSL* (*eMoflon* Specification Language). Consequently, the rules in the *Mutation Rules* component are specified in *EMSL*. *Rule Executor* also provides means to execute the specified rules. The management of the data is realized by the *Transformation Engine*, which is *Neo4J*[5], a graph database management system, which provides a high scalability for model management tasks [7]. The outcome of this plugin is the mutated test model, e.g., a *JUnit* test model.

The last Eclipse plugin realizes the *Output Module* component. The central component, i.e., the *Test Code Generator*, is realized with the help of *Xtend*[6], a statically typed programming language being placed on top of Java known for developing code generators. The generator needs the *Test Code Templates*, which are defined as *Xtend* templates and are dependent on the target framework, i.e., the testing framework for which the mutated executable test cases have to be generated. Furthermore, the generator needs the *Test Metamodel* which in the concrete implementation is an *xUnit* metamodel. The outcome of the *Test Case Generation* activity and at the same time of the whole mutation process is the *Mutated Test Code*, which in the concrete example are *JUnit* test cases.

5   Case Study

The *TECAMU* framework was applied in an industrial context, where the problem of enabling cross-platform availability of the well-known Eclipse Modeling Framework (EMF)[7] was addressed [6]. EMF is highly accepted in practice and generates Java code from platform independent models with embedded Object Constraint Language (OCL)[8] expressions. As feature complete Ecore and OCL runtime APIs are not available for other platforms like Windows, MacOS, Android etc., a migration to CrossEcore [6], a multi-platform enabled modeling framework, was performed. In order to ensure that the migration of the OCL implementation was performed successfully, around 4000 OCL test cases were reused by applying our solution for automatic co-migration of test cases [3].

To further ensure that the migrated test cases were correctly migrated, we applied the *TECAMU* framework. In the following, we explain the scenario, where the original OCL JUnit test cases were mutated. Before showing how we applied the framework, firstly we explain the structure of the test cases that had to be mutated. An OCL test case tests a specific part of the OCL implementation by executing and asserting a particular OCL expression, e.g., filtering or casting a given collection. The OCL implementation in EMF is in a *Just-In-Time (JIT)* manner, i.e., the OCL statements are being interpreted. Consequently, the OCL statements in the corresponding test cases are also being interpreted. This means that they also contain native string-based OCL expressions as shown in Fig. 4 written in *JUnit*. The particular test case tests the append functionality, i.e., it

[5] https://neo4j.com/.

[6] https://www.eclipse.org/xtend/.

[7] https://www.eclipse.org/modeling/emf/.

[8] http://www.omg.org/spec/OCL/2.4/.

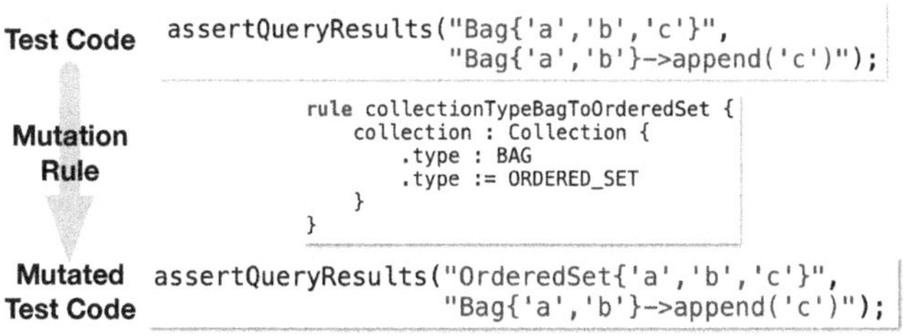

Fig. 4. OCL mutation operators specified as transformation rules

checks whether the execution of the `append('c')` function on the `Bag{'a','b'}` collection, results in `Bag{'a','b','c'}`, which is the expected result. The assert function `assertQueryResults()`, compares the values of the expected result and the particular OCL functionality which are specified as strings.

So, for this particular example, we instantiated the process shown in Fig. 3, with concrete actions, artifacts, and tools. Namely, first of all, we had to develop the *Test Case Parser* and the *Test Metamodel*. In this particular case, we used the JDT Parser[9] to parse the test code and then we developed model transformations to obtain the test model conform to the *xUnit* metamodel. Having the test model, we had to develop meaningful mutation operators. As the original test cases were testing the OCL functionality, we had to define mutation operators that will change the semantics of the OCL expressions, contained in the test cases, either as the action to be performed or the expected result to be checked. For this reason, an additional parser for the string-based OCL expressions was also developed. Having the OCL expressions interpreted, we then developed a set of OCL mutation operators in terms of model transformation rules. Based on the general groups of mutation operators like method-level or class-level operators, we have developed OCL language-specific mutation operators. For example, as shown in Fig. 4, the `collectionTypeBagToOrderedSet` rule, swaps a `Collection` of a `type BAG` to `ORDERED_SET`. Once the mutation operators were defined, we could apply them on the test cases. Figure 4 shows a mutation example, with the previously introduced test case and mutation rule. As could be seen in the example, the first occurrence of `Bag` was changed to `OrderedSet`. In this concrete case study, we could see that our framework could be used to perform mutation analysis of test cases in a model-driven way. As each component of the framework can be exchanged, the validation approach could be used for different situations and for mutation of different artifacts: system code, test code or even their corresponding transformations, i.e., migrations.

6   Related Work

In the area of mutation analysis, there are already existing tools and frameworks which provide an automated and configurable way to perform mutation analy-

---

[9] https://www.eclipse.org/jdt/.

sis. Regarding Java, there are lot of well-established mutation frameworks like PIT^{10}, $MuJava^{11}$, $Javalanche$ [5] and others. Also, regarding C#, there are well established mutation frameworks such as $VisualMutator^{12}$, $NinjaTurtles^{13}$ and others. The identified frameworks provide a lot of different features and also an efficient way to do code-based mutation by specifying language specific mutation operators. The approach presented in [1], introduces the concept of model-based mutation testing. However, as we deal with the domain of situation-specific (test case) migration, a mutation framework that also addresses situativity is necessary [3]. Also, as we have seen in the examples, inside the test cases, another language, like OCL, could be embedded, and the expressions specified using that language have to be mutated. In such cases we need a framework which provides a high level of flexibility and extensibility. Furthermore, most of the test cases focus on the mutation of the system. As we already have mentioned, in our approach we have also foreseen a migration of test cases and that is a feature which is not explicitly supported by the existing frameworks. Even if we consider a reuse of some of the frameworks, its barely doable as most of them do not provide a proper API to do that or they become obsolete as development or support no longer exist. All in all, as the main intention is to apply the mutation analysis-based validation approach in different situations, it is important to be able to replace all components of the framework, and this was difficult or impossible for existing frameworks.

Hence, we decided that the development of a framework which provides a high level of flexibility and extensibility, and an easy way to specify mutation operators was the solution to go with.

7   Conclusion and Future Work

In this paper, we have presented the $TECAMU$ framework, a model-driven mutation framework, which provides a high level of flexibility and extensibility, and an easy way to specify mutation operators in terms of model transformation rules. The presented framework has a component-based architecture, which makes it flexible and adaptable to any situation at hand. Namely, any component could be exchanged with a new component or it could be customized so that it is suitable for the given situation. Also, if necessary, a new component which addresses processing of embedded languages for example, could be easily integrated to the existing components. The mutation operators, which are often specific to the domain of the migration, can be easily specified in terms of transformation rules specified with $eMoflon$. Currently, the mutation framework is in an experimental phase and evaluation regarding its effectiveness (e.g., identified false positives and false negatives) or efficiency (e.g., time needed for generating a set of mutants) is performed as ongoing work.

---

[10] http://pitest.org/.
[11] https://cs.gmu.edu/~offutt/mujava/.
[12] https://visualmutator.github.io/web/.
[13] http://www.mutation-testing.net/.

References

1. Belli, F., Budnik, C.J., Hollmann, A., Tuglular, T., Wong, W.E.: Model-based mutation testing-approach and case studies. Sci. Comput. Program. **120**(C), 25–48 (2016)
2. Jovanovikj, I., Yigitbas, E., Anjorin, A., Sauer, S.: Who guards the guards? On the validation of test case migration. In: Softwaretechnik-Trends, Proceedings of the 20th Workshop Software-Reengineering & Evolution (WSRE) & 9th Workshop Design for Future (DFF) (2018)
3. Jovanovikj, I., Yigitbas, E., Grieger, M., Sauer, S., Engels, G.: Modular construction of context-specific test case migration methods. In: Proceedings of the 7th International Conference on Model-Driven Engineering and Software Development, MODELSWARD 2019, pp. 534–541 (2019)
4. Lipton, R.J., Sayward, F.G.: Hints on test data selection: help for the practicing programmer. Computer **11**(4), 34–41 (1978)
5. Schuler, D., Zeller, A.: Javalanche: efficient mutation testing for java. In: Proceedings of the the 7th Joint Meeting of the European Software Engineering Conference and the ACM SIGSOFT Symposium on the Foundations of Software Engineering, pp. 297–298. ACM (2009)
6. Schwichtenberg, S., Jovanovikj, I., Gerth, C., Engels, G.: Poster: crossecore: an extendible framework to use ECORE and OCL across platforms. In: 2018 IEEE/ACM 40th International Conference on Software Engineering: Companion (ICSE-Companion), pp. 292–293, May 2018
7. Weidmann, N., Anjorin, A., Fritsche, L., Varró, G., Schürr, A., Leblebici, E.: Incremental bidirectional model transformation with emoflon: : Ibex. In: Proceedings of the 8th International Workshop on Bidirectional Transformations Co-located with the Philadelphia Logic Week, Bx@PLW 2019, pp. 45–55 (2019)

Towards Consistency Checking Between a System Model and Its Implementation

Robbert Jongeling[1]([✉]) [ID], Johan Fredriksson[2], Federico Ciccozzi[1] [ID],
Antonio Cicchetti[1] [ID], and Jan Carlson[1] [ID]

[1] Mälardalen University, Västerås, Sweden
{robbert.jongeling,federico.ciccozzi,
antonio.cicchetti,jan.carlson}@mdh.se
[2] Saab AB, Järfälla, Sweden
johan.fredriksson@saabgroup.com

Abstract. In model-based systems engineering, a system model is the central development artifact containing architectural and design descriptions of core parts of the system. This abstract representation of the system is then partly realized in code. Throughout development, both system model and code evolve independently, incurring the risk of them drifting apart. Inconsistency between model and code can lead to errors in development, resulting in delayed or erroneous implementation. We present a work in progress towards automated mechanisms for checking consistency between a system model and code, within an industrial model-based systems engineering setting. In particular, we focus on automatically establishing traceability links between elements of the system model and parts of the code. The paper describes the challenges in achieving this in industrial practices and outlines our envisioned approach to overcome those challenges.

Keywords: Model-based systems engineering · Consistency checking · Agile model-based development

1 Introduction

The engineering of complex systems requires a team of engineers, each having specific expertise and working on different artifacts. A commonly investigated challenge is the management of consistency between the many different artifacts describing various aspects of the same system; for instance, consistency between a system model and code in model-based systems engineering (MBSE). There is empirical evidence indicating that inconsistency feedback improves the performance of software engineers in scenarios where the code needs to be updated after a change in the model [14]. Furthermore, the literature is rich in approaches that deal with consistency between artifacts, each considering a set of requirements identified as necessary for industrial adoption; they are discussed in Sect. 4. However, few studies apply their approaches to industrial settings. In this paper, we

This research is supported by Software Center https://www.software-center.se.

O. Babur et al. (Eds.): ICSMM 2020, CCIS 1262, pp. 30–39, 2020.
https://doi.org/10.1007/978-3-030-58167-1_3

report on a work in progress towards creating and evaluating an approach for checking the structural consistency between a system model and its corresponding implementation.

2   MBSE in the Industrial Setting Under Study

There are many different ways in which MBSE is adopted in industry. We do not discuss them all, but describe in this section how the MBSE paradigm is practiced in the industrial setting we study in this paper. Nevertheless, note that the proposed approach in Sect. 3 is not limited only to the industrial setting described in this paper. The outlined MBSE way-of-working within the studied setting is based on well-established standards such as the INCOSE systems engineering handbook [24], Friedenthal's "a practical guide to SysML"[8], and the ISO42010 standard [10]. Hence, our findings are expected to be generalizable beyond the scope of this specific scenario under study.

Several system engineers and around a dozen software engineers are involved in a collaborative effort to design and implement those systems. In this collaboration, the system engineers are mostly concerned with capturing the intended system design in a system model. This model is the core development artefact and contains the structural and functional design of the system. The functionality is decomposed into function blocks and then further implemented by smaller components. The model also captures the allocation of those components to either software or hardware. Note that the refinement of the system model into implementation is a manual effort, the system model does not contain enough detail to automatically generate code from it.

2.1   Overview of the System Model

The system model is described using SysML diagrams. Each function block is represented by a block in a block definition diagram (BDD) containing a combination of system components, supplemented by an interface described by SysML Full ports. Each system component is described by a block in the internal block diagram (IBD) corresponding to the function block it is contained in. A system component contains attributes, operations, and signal receptions in the form of three proxy ports (for input, output, and test). Each operation defined in the system component is defined with an activity diagram. Furthermore, each system component contains a state machine defining its behavior. A schematic overview of these meta-elements is shown in Fig. 1.

We are primarily interested in checking the consistency between the software realization of system components as defined in the system model, and the code implementing it. In the system model, the software realization consists of software blocks. They are defined in BDDs and then elaborated in IBDs, which define interfaces between different software blocks and the protocols by which messages are sent between them. Like function blocks, both software blocks and hardware blocks also define their own interfaces as SysML full ports.

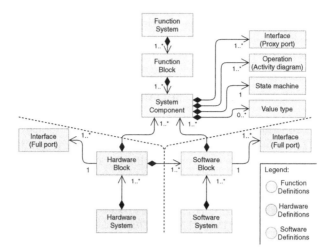

Fig. 1. Simplified overview of meta-elements composing a system model. Not depicted are the native, foreign, and test interfaces of function blocks.

2.2   Motivation for Consistency Checking

Development based on inconsistent artefacts can cause delays in development or worse, can cause the eventual implementation to be erroneous. For example, when the code violates interface definitions in the system model, some refactoring might be required to obtain the desired system. The longer such an inconsistency goes unnoticed, the more other code could be created that relies on it and therefore needs to be refactored upon eventual discovery of the inconsistency. Inconsistencies therefore need to be identified as early as possible and resolved before it causes harm. But complete consistency is also not possible, nor desirable, since the development should also not be inhibited. Awareness of inconsistencies soon after their introduction allows developers to decide the best course of action [12]. Therefore, we aim to detect, but not automatically repair, introduced inconsistencies between the system model and its corresponding implementation.

In the industrial setting under study, software engineers typically do not view the system model directly. Rather, changes to the system model are gathered by system engineers and presented to software engineers during handover meetings. These presentations, together with documents generated from the system model, serve as the primary input for software engineers to work on the implementation. At the same time, the system engineers have a limited view on what parts of the system model are implemented where in the code. The lack of traceability between system model and code complicates collaborative development, a lot.

Among other things, this lack of traceability inhibits development in shorter cycles [11]. The main concern, though, is the lack of impact analysis and thereby the potential late discovery of errors. Indeed, system engineers have, in this setting, limited support to assess the impact of potential changes in the system model to related code, and late discovery of errors may induce large repair efforts. Hence, we aim to improve the communication between system engineers and software engineers, by providing inconsistency feedback to them both during their development activities.

2.3   Challenges

A model-code consistency checking approach requires two ingredients: i) traceability or navigation between model and code elements, determining which part of the model is realized by which part of the code, and ii) consistency rules that express what it means for elements to be consistent [20]. The first challenge to identifying inconsistencies is the scale of the system model under consideration, which implies that manually creating traceability links is not feasible. Automating this task yields numerous other challenges. We have summarized them in Table 1, and will detail them in the remainder of this section.

Table 1. Challenges to consistency checking in our industrial use-case.

Model	Size
	Distribution over many diagrams
	Addresses multiple concerns
Code	Spread out over different repositories
	Names *mostly* similar to model
	Variety in implementation of same concepts
Evolution	Existing model and code base
	Model and code evolve throughout project
	Way-of-working should not be hindered
	Model aims to capture end product, code captures current state

Model. The SysML system model in this case study consists of BDDs, IBDs, state machines, and activity diagrams. In total, a model of a complex system can consist of hundreds of system components defined across dozens of diagrams. The corresponding code-base is similarly large, consisting of dozens of code files and make files across several repositories. To establish traceability between the model and the code, we must first determine which parts of the model are implemented in the code. The number of required traceability links scales with the number of model elements. Furthermore, navigating the model and code base to find the appropriate elements is a labor-intensive task.

As described, the model addresses several concerns and not all of them are reflected in the code, as for instance the allocation of system components to hardware. Hence, our approach should only attempt to identify code elements realizing model elements that are expected to be realized in the code.

When comparing model and code elements, some amount of inconsistency is to be expected, since the system model typically aims to describe the final product, whereas the code naturally always represents the current state of the implementation. Our goal is not to ensure complete consistency all the time, but rather to indicate inconsistency as something that might signal problems in an early stage.

Code. The implementation of the system model is spread out over a large number of code files. Among these are also additional artefacts such as make-files, required for building the system, that could be utilized to find dependencies that might not be described in the system model. A common software engineering practice is to organize such a project by creating several repositories to separate common, re-used functionality from components describing functionality for specific systems. This division is only shown at the software level and is not represented in the system model. Consequently, some additional effort is required to locate the implementation corresponding to given model elements, in order to create traceability links.

To trace elements between the artefacts, we cannot rely solely on the names of the elements. Partially, this is due to the complexity and separate evolution of system model and implementation code. The names are not purposefully obfuscated, but names of code elements diverge from names of model elements. This can happen, among other reasons, due to coding standards, typical use of abbreviations, or simply the impossibility of having spaces within names of code elements. In this way a model element "Hardware Monitor" can become "hw_mon" in the code.

Evolution. It is also important to note that both a system model and a large code base already exist and are evolved separately throughout system development. We are not starting from scratch, but rather aim to introduce traceability links between the existing development artefacts. Beyond aforementioned scaling concerns, this also means that any proposed approach should not inhibit existing development processes.

3   Approach

In this section, we outline our envisioned approach to automatically establishing traceability links between model elements and code, within the described development scenario. We plan to extend this approach to report on the level of consistency between the linked artifacts, too.

3.1   Automatically Discovering Traceability Links.

In establishing traceability links, we can distinguish between two stages: initial creation and maintenance throughout development. Below, we describe our envisioned approach to these two stages while keeping in mind the challenges as outlined in Table 1.

Creating Traceability Links in an Existing MBSE Project. As described in Sect. 2, we target traceability between those parts of the system model that have a corresponding representation in the code. In the described setting, there is a high naming consistency between for example C++ *namespaces* and SysML interfaces. As another example, state machines contained in system components are typically implemented in distinct classes in the code, where each state is expected to correspond to a method inside these classes. The patterns are typical, but not necessarily followed throughout the implementation. Hence, we cannot rely on them exclusively but require some additional input.

We outline here our plan to match model elements despite their differences, following the previously mentioned example of linking "Hardware Monitor" to "hw_mon". A dictionary is established for the translation of common abbreviations to their full form. In this way, "hw" and "mon" can be understood as "hardware" and "monitor" respectively. On top of that, some rewrite rules are created to transform naming from models and code into a common format. An example need for such rules is to remove spaces from all names of model elements. Using these rules, we can translate "hardware monitor" to "hw_mon". Finally, name comparisons should be case insensitive. Now, we can link "Hardware Monitor" to "hw_mon".

By applying these rules, some elements may be mapped directly, because after rule application, their name is identical. However, also collisions might occur where several names are all equal or very similar. To deal with this, we envision our approach as going through the model "top-down", i.e., starting from function blocks and following the model hierarchy down to the functionality defined in it. In this way, we aim to drastically narrow the search scope for elements to be matched. Since we have knowledge of which types of model elements are likely matched to which types of code elements, we can furthermore be more confident to suggest correct links. We follow the hierarchy as outlined in Fig. 1. In the next step, we look at matching C++ *namespaces* to interfaces described as SysML full ports. Most model elements lower in the hierarchy are then expected to be found within the linked namespace. In cases where this does not yield a result, we plan to apply the name similarity approach to a wider set of artifacts.

Maintaining Traceability Links When Artifacts Evolve. To be useful, a set of discovered traceability links needs to be updated throughout the evolution of the system. Newly implemented functionality should be reflected by additional traceability links. Removed or refactored functionality can lead to obsolete or outdated links that need to be discarded or updated. Hence, we envision an updating mechanism to be executed after a newly committed change to the model or code.

Changes can break existing links, for example due to the renaming of one of the linked elements. In this case, we cannot automatically assume that the traceability link should be kept, so instead we reapply the discovery stage for the affected function block. We believe that, in our setting, it is better than updating the link automatically, because a rename might indicate also the following of a new system design. In other settings, the other alternative may be preferable.

4 Related Work

Despite the recognition of the importance of consistency [10] and the large body of work on consistency checking topics, few empirical evaluations and industrial applications have been published [4]. Indeed, model synchronization is still considered a challenge to industrial adoption of MDE. Selic identifies the scale of industrial applications as one of the main challenges to overcome for a model synchronization approach to be applicable. In particular, the number of consistency links can be huge and then the effort to maintain them will be very high and thus at constant risk of being neglected in favor of more pressing issues [22].

We focus in this work not on automatically synchronizing the model and code, but rather on identifying inconsistencies arising during development and providing modelers and developers with insights into them. Many formalisms have been proposed for capturing consistency rules. From languages like OVL [15] and EVL [16], to graph pattern matching approaches [9], to triple-graph grammars [21] and triple-graph patterns [7]. It should be mentioned that some of these approaches go further than merely identifying inconsistencies and additionally aim to repair. Devising another such approach is not the focus of this paper. Instead, we focus on the first required ingredient for consistency checking. Given an existing system model and corresponding implementation, we aim to automatically create traceability links between elements of the system model and parts of the code.

In further discussing the related work, it is important to note that we are not considering *requirements* traceability. Rather, we discuss here some approaches dealing with traceability between heterogeneous artifacts. For example, linking (parts of) artifacts using XML [23]. Or more formal approaches, such as "semantically rich" links [18], meaning that the links are formalized and can be automatically validated. Dependencies between different artifacts can also be explicitly modeled to enable inconsistency detection and a better overall management of the development process [19]. Building on top of that, another approach proposes modeling the development process to better identify and handle emerging inconsistencies [5]. This approach seems most appropriate when applied from the beginning of a new development project. Whereas in our case, we want to identify inconsistencies in already existing system model and corresponding code base.

Other types of approaches consider applying information retrieval methods to discover traceability links, although such methods are prone to reporting a large number of false positives [17]. In our work, we hope to limit these by combining the purely syntactic name information with the semantic information of model element types. For example, in the studied setting, a class name is not likely matched with the name of a state in a state machine; rather, that state would be matched to a function name. The revision history of development artifacts can be utilized as well to detect traceability links by assessing what elements have been changed together in the past [13]. In our scenario, this approach is less suitable, since there is a clear separation between development of the system model and the code.

The concept of megamodeling is aimed at establishing links between models and model elements [6]. Megamodeling proposed a global modeling management framework, aimed at applying modeling techniques to numerous, large, complex artifacts distributed throughout a development setting and expressed in disparate modeling languages [3]. An example implementation is the tool AM3[1], which supports the automatic generation of traceability links based on existing model transformations. In the remainder of our work we will benefit from the concepts explored in megamodeling, particularly in the area of maintaining traceability links throughout the system's evolution.

It is clear that automated ways of obtaining traceability links are valuable to MBSE or any software development projects [1]. Furthermore, means to be notified of violations of architectural consistency are desired [2]. Nevertheless, few approaches of automating the discovery of traceability links have been studied in industrial settings.

5 Conclusion and Future Work

In this paper, we have discussed a work in progress towards checking consistency between a system model and code in a large scale industrial MBSE setting. We have outlined the state-of-practice and argued that consistency checking would be beneficial for both system engineers and software engineers. Although we have not yet implemented and rolled out consistency checks, we have identified challenges to its implementation and ideas to overcome them. These are summarized in Table 1 and are related to the system model, code, and the development process. In conclusion, establishing traceability links between system model and code in a real industrial setting is far from a trivial task.

The continuation of this work consists of three phases. In the first phase, we plan to implement automated support for discovering traceability links between elements of the system model and the implementation code. This will build further on the envisioned approach as briefly outlined in Sect. 3. We expect to add additional means of discovering links once we get to the implementation phase. The second phase consists of ensuring the semi-automated maintenance of traceability links when the model or code evolves. For some cases, this may be trivial once a link has been established and therefore there indeed is a code element corresponding to the model element. For more elaborate structural checks, like possible interface violations in the code, however, it remains necessary to evaluate the discovered links. In the final phase, we aim to calculate, given these traceability links, the structural consistency between the linked elements. And then, we aim to visualize the discovered consistency within the system model.

---

[1] https://wiki.eclipse.org/AM3

References

1. Aizenbud-Reshef, N., Nolan, B.T., Rubin, J., Shaham-Gafni, Y.: Model traceability. IBM Syst. J. **45**(3), 515–526 (2006). https://doi.org/10.1147/sj.453.0515
2. Ali, N., Baker, S., O'Crowley, R., Herold, S., Buckley, J.: Architecture consistency: state of the practice, challenges and requirements. Empirical Softw. Eng. **23**(1), 224–258 (2018). https://doi.org/10.1007/s10664-017-9515-3
3. Allilaire, F., Bézivin, J., Bruneliere, H., Jouault, F.: Global model management in eclipse GMT/AM3 (2006)
4. Cicchetti, A., Ciccozzi, F., Pierantonio, A.: Multi-view approaches for software and system modelling: a systematic literature review. Softw. Syst. Model. 18(6), 1–27 (2019). https://doi.org/10.1007/s10270-018-00713-w
5. Dávid, I., Denil, J., Gadeyne, K., Vangheluwe, H.: Engineering process transformation to manage (in) consistency. In: Proceedings of the 1st International Workshop on Collaborative Modelling in MDE (COMMitMDE 2016), pp. 7–16 (2016)
6. Favre, J.M.: Towards a basic theory to model model driven engineering. In: 3rd Workshop in Software Model Engineering, wisme, pp. 262–271. Citeseer (2004)
7. Feldmann, S., Kernschmidt, K., Wimmer, M., Vogel-Heuser, B.: Managing inter-model inconsistencies in model-based systems engineering: application in automated production systems engineering. J. Syst. Softw. **153**, 105–134 (2019). https://doi.org/10.1016/j.jss.2019.03.060
8. Friedenthal, S., Moore, A., Steiner, R.: A Practical Guide to SysML: The Systems Modeling Language. Morgan Kaufmann (2014)
9. Herzig, S., Qamar, A., Paredis, C.: An approach to identifying inconsistencies in model-based systems engineering. Proc. Comput. Sci. **28**, 354–362 (2014). https://doi.org/10.1016/j.procs.2014.03.044
10. ISO/IEC/IEEE: ISO/IEC/IEEE 42010:2011(E) Systems and software engineering - Architecture description. Technical report, December 2011. https://doi.org/10.1109/IEEESTD.2011.6129467
11. Jongeling, R., Carlson, J., Cicchetti, A.: Impediments to introducing continuous integration for model-based development in industry. In: 2019 45th Euromicro Conference on Software Engineering and Advanced Applications (SEAA), pp. 434–441. IEEE (2019). https://doi.org/10.1109/SEAA.2019.00071
12. Jongeling, R., Ciccozzi, F., Cicchetti, A., Carlson, J.: Lightweight consistency checking for agile model-based development in practice. J. Object Technol. **18**(2), 11:1–20 (2019). https://doi.org/10.5381/jot.2019.18.2.a11, the 15th European Conference on Modelling Foundations and Applications
13. Kagdi, H., Maletic, J.I., Sharif, B.: Mining software repositories for traceability links. In: 15th IEEE International Conference on Program Comprehension (ICPC 2007), pp. 145–154. IEEE (2007). https://doi.org/10.1109/ICPC.2007.28
14. Kanakis, G., Khelladi, D.E., Fischer, S., Tröls, M., Egyed, A.: An empirical study on the impact of inconsistency feedback during model and code co-changing. J. Object Technol. **18**(2), 10:1–21 (2019). https://doi.org/10.5381/jot.2019.18.2.a10
15. Kolovos, D., Paige, R., Polack, F.: The epsilon object language (EOL). In: European Conference on Model Driven Architecture-Foundations and Applications, pp. 128–142. Springer (2006). https://doi.org/10.1007/11787044_11
16. Kolovos, D., Paige, R., Polack, F.: Detecting and repairing inconsistencies across heterogeneous models. In: 2008 1st International Conference on Software Testing, Verification, and Validation, pp. 356–364. IEEE (2008). https://doi.org/10.1109/icst.2008.23

17. Lucia, A.D., Fasano, F., Oliveto, R., Tortora, G.: Recovering traceability links in software artifact management systems using information retrieval methods. ACM Trans. Softw. Eng. Methodol. (TOSEM) **16**(4), 13-es (2007). https://doi.org/10.1145/1276933.1276934

18. Paige, R.F., et al.: Rigorous identification and encoding of trace-links in model-driven engineering. Softw. Syst. Model. **10**(4), 469–487 (2011). https://doi.org/10.1007/s10270-010-0158-8

19. Qamar, A., Paredis, C.J., Wikander, J., During, C.: Dependency modeling and model management in mechatronic design. J. Comput. Inf. Sci. Eng. **12**(4) (2012). https://doi.org/10.1115/1.4007986

20. Riedl-Ehrenleitner, M., Demuth, A., Egyed, A.: Towards model-and-code consistency checking. In: 2014 IEEE 38th Annual Computer Software and Applications Conference, pp. 85–90. IEEE (2014). https://doi.org/10.1109/COMPSAC.2014.91

21. Schürr, A.: Specification of graph translators with triple graph grammars. In: International Workshop on Graph-Theoretic Concepts in Computer Science, pp. 151–163. Springer (1994). https://doi.org/10.1007/3-540-59071-4_45

22. Selic, B.: What will it take? A view on adoption of model-based methods in practice. Softw. Syst. Model. **11**(4), 513–526 (2012). https://doi.org/10.1007/s10270-012-0261-0

23. Service, G., Nentwich, C., Capra, L., Emmerich, W., Finkelstein, A.: Xlinkit: aconsistency checking and smart link generation service. ACM Trans. Internet Technol. **2** (2001). https://doi.org/10.1145/514183.514186

24. Walden, D.D., Roedler, G.J., Forsberg, K., Hamelin, R.D., Shortell, T.M.: Systems Engineering handbook: A Guide for System Life Cycle Processes and Activities. John Wiley & Sons (2015)

Applications

Towards Model-Driven Digital Twin Engineering: Current Opportunities and Future Challenges

Francis Bordeleau[1], Benoit Combemale[2], Romina Eramo[3(✉)],
Mark van den Brand[4], and Manuel Wimmer[5]

[1] Ecole de Technologie Superieur, Universite du Quebec, Quebec, Canada
`francis.bordeleau@etsmtl.ca`
[2] University of Toulouse, CNRS IRIT, Toulouse, France
`benoit.combemale@irit.fr`
[3] University of L'Aquila, L'Aquila, Italy
`romina.eramo@univaq.it`
[4] Eindhoven University of Technology, Eindhoven, The Netherlands
`m.g.j.v.d.brand@tue.nl`
[5] CDL-MINT & Johannes Kepler University Linz, Linz, Austria
`manuel.wimmer@jku.at`

Abstract. Digital Twins have emerged since the beginning of this millennium to better support the management of systems based on (real-time) data collected in different parts of the operating systems. Digital Twins have been successfully used in many application domains, and thus, are considered as an important aspect of Model-Based Systems Engineering (MBSE). However, their development, maintenance, and evolution still face major challenges, in particular: (*i*) the management of heterogeneous models from different disciplines, (*ii*) the bi-directional synchronization of digital twins and the actual systems, and (*iii*) the support for collaborative development throughout the complete life-cycle. In the last decades, the Model-Driven Engineering (MDE) community has investigated these challenges in the context of software systems. Now the question arises, which results may be applicable for digital twin engineering as well.

In this paper, we identify various MDE techniques and technologies which may contribute to tackle the three mentioned digital twin challenges as well as outline a set of open MDE research challenges that need to be addressed in order to move towards a digital twin engineering discipline.

Keywords: Heterogeneous modeling · Modeling languages · Digital twins

1 Introduction

The complexity of the new generation of systems developed in the context of IoT, Industry 4.0, digital transformation, high-tech systems, and smart systems

© Springer Nature Switzerland AG 2020
O. Babur et al. (Eds.): ICSMM 2020, CCIS 1262, pp. 43–54, 2020.
https://doi.org/10.1007/978-3-030-58167-1_4

(e.g., ranging from smart buildings over smart cities to smart mobility) triggers a set of major challenges, both from a technical and a business perspective. Organizations developing systems in these application domains must constantly be looking for ways to improve the quality and efficiency of their processes, systems, and products (in terms of different factors like costs, and energy consumption) and reduce development, operations, and maintenance cost. Moreover, these systems must be able to adapt to constantly evolving (open) contexts and environments [21].

The very essence of this new generation of systems requires maximizing the use of data collected throughout the system life cycle, which need to be processed, organized and structured to help managing and improving the systems.

Digital Twins have been emerging in various engineering disciplines since the beginning of this millennium to better manage systems based on (real-time) data collected in different parts of the systems. They have been already successfully used in many application domains and are now considered as an important aspect of Model-Based Systems Engineering (MBSE) [10]. While they were initially developed solely for physical systems (e.g., space systems at NASA [30] and industrial systems such as Industry 4.0 manufacturing components), they are now used for many other types of systems, including cyber-physical (e.g., a car or robotic system), socio-cyber-physical (e.g., a smart building, city, enterprise), or natural (e.g., a cell) systems. One of their key characteristics is that they allow leveraging the benefits provided by software (digital) technologies for the design, development, analysis, simulation, and operations of non-digital systems.

While their benefits have been demonstrated in many contexts, their development, maintenance, and evolution, trigger major challenges. In this paper, we focus on three main challenges: (i) the use and integration of a set of heterogeneous models that are required to address the different aspects and disciplines of a system, (ii) the synchronization of the digital twin with runtime data, and (iii) the co-development and management of the evolution of digital twins by teams of engineers.

In the last decades, the Model Driven Engineering (MDE) community has addressed many issues and challenges that are currently faced by other engineering disciplines in the development and evolution of complex systems based on digital twins. Among other things, the MDE community has developed solutions for the creation and evolution of modeling artifacts, support for collaborative development of large distributed teams, agile development, management of models linked to runtime systems, integration of heterogeneous models, etc. MDE is now considered a mature engineering discipline with a huge body of knowledge [13] that provides a broad range of modeling languages (e.g., UML [31], SysML [18], BPMN [3], Modelica [19], BIM [16], XES [1]), tools and methodologies addressing different development aspects.

The main objectives of this paper are to: (i) discuss how different techniques and technologies developed by the MDE community can contribute to resolve the three main challenges previously identified; and (ii) identify a set of open research challenges, related to MDE, that need to be addressed to support the development and evolution of digital twins - potentially leading to a digital twin engineering discipline.

2   Digital Twins and MDE

In this section, we describe the concept of digital twin from an MDE perspective, provide concrete examples of digital twins in different application domains (smart building/city, high tech, and smart enterprises), and discuss the three main digital twin challenges based on the given examples.

2.1   Digital Twins and Their Relationship to MDE

A digital twin is defined as a virtual representation (or replica) of an actual system that it is continuously updated with real-time system data throughout its life cycle and, at the same time, allows to interact with and influence the system (cf. Fig. 1 for an illustration). A system can be associated with a set of (one or more) digital twins, each defined for a specific purpose.

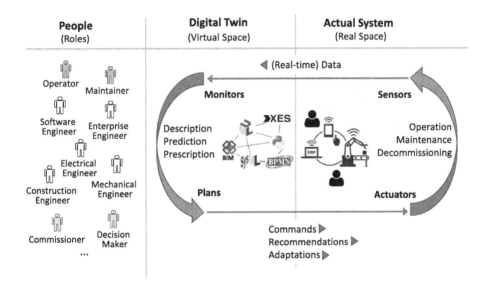

Fig. 1. Digital twin from an MDE perspective.

From a systems engineering perspective, digital twins can provide many important benefits. For example, a digital twin can be developed to enable real-time monitoring of actual systems and processes, provide timely analysis of data to intercept problems before they arise, prevent downtime, improve performance, schedule preventive maintenance to reduce/prevent faults, support decision making, plan for future upgrades and new developments, provide a mechanism to develop the control software before finalizing the physical artifact, or simulate "bad-weather behaviour" in a safe way while the system is running.

The concept of digital twin is intimately linked to models and MDE. Each digital twin is defined in terms of one or more models of the system, or part of it [26]. The type of models used depends on the type of system and the purpose of the digital twin. For instance, models may be used for descriptive, predictive, and prescriptive purposes. Also, since the different aspects typically involve different engineering disciplines, the development of digital twins involves the definition, combination, and management of a set of heterogeneous models from various disciplines and require the involvement of teams of engineers collaborating on the development of the digital twins, and models (cf. the people swim lane of Fig. 1 for some examples).

Data play a central role in digital twins (cf. real-time data stream from the actual system to the digital twin in Fig. 1). Digital twins "connect" models with the runtime data provided by the different sensors and measurement devices of the system with dedicated monitors. It is this connection between the models and system data that constitutes the essence of a digital twin and that enables reasoning about different aspects of a systems based on actual system data (often referred to as digital shadow). In digital twins, models are not only important for the design of the system, but also for the interpretation and analysis of the data, as well as for investigating different design or operation alternatives.

2.2 Examples of Digital Twins

Smart Buildings and Smart Cities. Digital twins can be used to manage and optimize many features of smart buildings and smart cities. As a concrete example, a digital twin was developed to help manage (reduce) the energy consumption of the Vienna Airport[1] to keep it under a certain threshold to avoid the necessity of building a new power line which would require a very high investment, and to avoid planning mistakes that would only become visible in the operation of the physical airport. The core of the Vienna Airport digital twin was built using Building Information Modeling (BIM) [16] and uses building physics simulations to reason about the energy balance of the airport.

A digital twin can use data collected from the city infrastructure to analyze and improve a smart city from several points of view [28]. For instance, it can be used to plan, inspect, and validate different aspects of a city before it is built. As an example, the new capital of the Indian state of Andhra Pradesh, was presented in [36] as the first entire city born with a digital twin. In this case, the digital twin collects data (via sensors, drones or other IoT and Industrial IoT tools) and uses a set of models to perform advanced analytics, Machine Learning (ML) and Artificial Intelligence (AI) to gain real-time insights about the physical asset's performance, operation or profitability.

---

[1] Virtual Airport City Vienna: https://simlab.tuwien.ac.at/virtual-airport-city-vienna/.

High-Tech Systems. In [29], a model driven approach is presented by means of a domain specific language to create digital twins in an efficient way. The concepts of wafer handler, the component in a wafer scanner that takes care of moving wafers from storage to source for exposure, are captured in a domain specific language. The goal of the digital twin of the wafer handler was to test the control software outside a clean room and to test bad weather without causing physical damage to the equipment itself. It also allowed to experiment with other set-ups and to test the performance of these set-ups.

Digital Enterprise. Enterprise modeling, such as the specification of organizational models, workflow models, business models, is used since decades and especially since the emergence of enterprise architecture. However, new advances in data processing allows for real-time monitoring of enterprises not only on a technology level but on the business level as well. Connecting runtime data to the enterprise design models allows for real-time monitoring, conformance checking, and optimizations. In particular, the analysis of runtime data by process mining techniques [34] allows to extract knowledge from historical data and to close the gap from the technological and business perspectives. Thus, organizations are starting to use so-called enterprise digital twins to coordinate the dependencies between people, business processes, and IT.[2]

2.3 Digital Twin Challenges

To be successful, digital twins need to be properly planned, resourced, and managed like any other software product. Based on the analysis of digital twins in different contexts and application domains, including the examples described in Subsect. 2.2, we focused on the integration and management of heterogeneous models as a key aspect. In particular, we identified three main challenges to which MDE can contribute:

1. **Systematically managing heterogeneous models.** In order to capture the different technical and domain aspects of a system, the creation of digital twins requires the development and combination of models from different engineering disciplines. As a result, a main challenge relates to the management of a collection of heterogeneous models to ensure their consistency.
2. **Bi-directional synchronization with the actual system.** The essence of digital twins is based on their ability to exploit runtime information to improve the management of a system. To achieve this, bi-directional communication and synchronization must be establish between the digital twin and the system. A main challenge consists in providing scalable solutions to support this bi-directional communication and synchronization throughout the life cycle of the system.
3. **Collaborative development throughout the system life-cycle.** The development and evolution of digital twins, and of the heterogeneous models

---

[2] https://www.softwareag.com/info/innovation/enterprise_digital_twin/default.html.

that they are based on, require the collaboration of many engineers that can work simultaneously on different parts of the digital twins, and associated models. For this reason, it is essential that the development environment provides proper support for collaborative development.

3   MDE Contributions to Digital Twin Challenges

In this section, we discuss how MDE techniques and technologies can contribute to the three digital twins challenges described in the previous subsection.

3.1   MDE Contribution to the Management of Heterogeneous Models

As actual systems grow in complexity, also their virtual counterparts need to capture these multiple aspects of the system. Thus, they have to move from digital representations of single entities to models of interconnected components. In software engineering, there is the common trend of having multiple models describing different aspects of the software. Especially complex software systems are mostly built using several (modeling) languages. To deal with such situations, various model management tools have been developed, such as the Epsilon [23], over the last decade.

Families of languages have been proposed such as UML [31]. In such families, multiple modeling formalisms are brought together supported by multiple development methodologies, e.g., RUP (Rational Unified Process) and development environments, e.g., Papyrus, are developed to support the creation of such models.

From a software point of view, a digital twin must be able to integrate a collection of heterogeneous models, and take care of the orchestration and interaction of the models. This is very similar to the development of modern software systems. In order to ensure that the integrated models make sense from a systems engineering point of view, it is essential that the models are consistent with respect to behaviour, exchanged data, units, etc. A modeling language like SysML, the systems engineering extension of UML, supports both hardware and software development. Engineers are thus faced with the difficult task of relating information presented in different models. Although existing modeling tooling performs well on this point, establishing and ensuring the consistency between heterogeneous models is a new area to explore [14]. It involved identification of similar concepts both syntactically and semantically, and the definition of possibly complex composition operators with various possible semantics (e.g., consistency, refinement, or coordination). Addressing this challenge will support the following critical aspects of developing digital twins: communication across teams working on different aspects and engineering disciplines, coordination of work across the teams, well-defined management of the teams to ensure product quality, and a broader engagement of the final users in the loop [9]. Based on these observations, it is important to ensure that modeling concepts are semantically well understood.

3.2 MDE Contribution to the Bi-directional Synchronization Between Digital Twins and Actual Systems

To enable bi-directional synchronization between digital twins and actual systems, support is required for the following steps: (*i*) extracting the relevant information from the raw runtime data provided by the system, (*ii*) enabling the digital twin models to use the information extracted from the runtime data, and (*iii*) enabling the information produced by the digital twin models to be fed into the system during execution.

This set of issues has been addressed by the MDE community in the context of Models@run.time [6,8]. Models@run.time have been developed to extend the use of software models produced during the design phase to the runtime environment with the goal of providing effective mechanisms to help reasoning about the system based on information generated by the system during its execution. Moreover, Models@run.time provide a view on a running software system that can be used for monitoring, analyzing, fixing design errors, exploring new design alternatives, or adapting it through a causal connection between a model and the system. However, having one single model@run.time that reflects a running system is not practicable when dealing with complex software systems. From a digital twin point of view, multiple and potentially diverse models@run.time are typically required to capture different system concerns [5,35]. Furthermore, the models associated with a digital twin need to be continuously updated with runtime data throughout the system life-cycle to reflect its status (regarding different aspects like performance, energy consumption, health, and maintenance) [4].

3.3 MDE Contribution to the Collaborative Development of Digital Twins

For decades, software development is considered as a collaborative effort, and thus, has become place and time independent. This has been facilitated by introducing advanced means of communications, but also tools to store different versions of software systems and to allow developers to work simultaneously on one single software system. Over the years, the collaborative development technologies and tools initially developed for code (i.e., text-based files) have been adapted for models. This includes the use of version control technologies that somehow constitute the foundation of collaborative development, but also the use of tools to compare different versions of a model to identify differences and to support the resolution of conflicts and the merge of the different versions. Work on this topic includes [12,24] and tools like EMFCompare [2,33]. As a result, current MDE tools allow storing of models, performing model comparison and merge, and keeping track of changes in order to deal with co-development and model evolution. These ingredients are necessary to be able to work in a collaborative way on models. The traditional engineering disciplines have a more individual or sequential way of working and the classical tooling to support the development of models is often lacking modern support to develop models in a collaborative way as well as dedicated model evolution support. However, for realizing the vision of digital twins, these features are highly needed in order to incrementally improve systems based on digital twin updates as well as to rollback to previous versions or explore possible future versions. Finally, collaboration support is needed across engineering discipline borders which may also require dedicated collaboration models supported by tool chains in order to organize work. The availability of powerful tooling for these aspects is a prerequisite to facilitate proper systems engineering in general and digital twin development in particular.

4   Open Research Challenges

In this section, we discuss a set of open research challenges that arise from the MDE contributions in the context of digital twins presented in the previous section.

Modeling Languages for Digital Twins. Because of the specific nature of the application domains in which digital twins are used, the use of a Domain-Specific Modeling Languages (DSML) may be an option to consider. Many language workbenches have been developed and used successfully in different application domains in the last decade, e.g., EMF[3], the GEMOC Studio [11], MPS[4], Rascal [22] or Monticore [25]. However, in spite of the benefits they provide, the use of DSML requires an upfront cost (in terms of time and effort) to identify the set of domain concepts to be included in the DSML, and to define and formalize the relevant abstractions of the language. In addition, legacy languages may be already in use for decades which are not yet fully digitalized. Finding a good mix, both in terms of number of languages and formalization is a major challenge for each domain.

Architectural Framework for Digital Twins. One open research challenge relates to the development of a framework for digital twins that would allow reducing the cost of building a digital twin. This framework should be defined in terms of a basic architecture, and set of language concepts and services, for instance for integrating existing heterogeneous models, that can be adapted and extended for specific digital twin developments. Among other things, the framework must enable the connection of the digital twin with system data on concrete platforms.

Openness and Sustainability. To deal with the evolution of the systems and their environment, digital twins must be open to the addition of new models or data as they become available. The research challenge here consists in developing digital twin architectures and frameworks that support such open environment

---

[3] https://www.eclipse.org/modeling/emf/.
[4] https://www.jetbrains.com/mps/.

and which provides advanced composition operators to enable the integration of new models and data while the system is running. In this research challenge, it is also important to consider the impact on current model management solutions which have to provide more dynamic features to deal with runtime aspects of the model [27]. How this may be realized for long-living systems running for several decades gives this challenge an extra twist.

Uncertainty. Research on uncertainty modeling has emerged in the MDE community over the last years. Some recent work allows supporting the explicit modeling of uncertainty in design models, e.g. [7]. However, these concepts have not been integrated in current runtime modeling approaches yet. One research challenge consists in integrating the concept of uncertainty with runtime environments and digital twins to better deal with variations in received data, errors, changing operational conditions, and human behaviour. The identification of components that contribute to uncertainty and to which level is another research challenge.

Design Space Exploration. Digital twins should enable the exploration of different versions and variants of the same system at the virtual level, the granularity of the models may be different depending on the tasks to be performed. While there are already several approaches to perform design space exploration by using search or simulation techniques, it is less clear if these approaches are applicable in current digital twin scenarios with respect to responsiveness and scalability. The research challenge is to efficiently perform the simulations in relation to the exploration in order to make informed decisions, specially if uncertainty is involved about future states of the system.

Inconsistency Management. If multiple models from different domains are involved in the creation of a digital twin, a certain level of consistency between the individual models is required, but at the same time, inconsistencies must be also acceptable and highlighted at certain times [17]. Hence, while model management and inter-model consistency approaches are crucial, the main challenge is to be able to integrate models that are created by means of other tools, e.g., technical drawings. However, model exchange and interoperability in tool chains is still a major issue [15,32] and novel techniques may be required to process truly heterogeneous models.

Models and Data. Finally, the complementarity and duality of models and data in the specific context of digital twins must be addressed, in order to perform, for example, model optimization based on data obtained from digital twins and real machines. Especially, the efficient representation of historical data in models would allow for new temporal reasoning capabilities based on temporal models [20].

5   Conclusion

In this paper, we outlined how the current state of the art in MDE that can contribute to main challenges in the domain of digital twins. For this, we identified three major contributions for engineering digital twins: model management approaches for dealing with heterogeneous models, models@runtime for synchronizing the digital twin with the actual system, and collaborative modeling based on model versioning systems.

Next to and based on these contributions, we also identified a number of research challenges related to the development of digital twins. The systems engineering community may re-use the techniques, tools and methodologies developed within the MDE community, instead of starting from scratch. At the same time, they have to be adapted to this new context in order to be useful for systems engineers in the particular fields.

References

1. Acampora, G., Vitiello, A., Di Stefano, B., Van Der Aalst, W.M., Günther, C.W., Verbeek, E.: IEEE 1849TM: the XES standard: the second IEEE standard sponsored. IEEE Comput. Intell. Mag. 4–8 (2017)
2. Addazi, L., Cicchetti, A., Rocco, J.D., Ruscio, D.D., Iovino, L., Pierantonio, A.: Semantic-based model matching with EMFcompare. In: Tanja Mayerhofer, B.S., Pierantonio, A., Tamzalit, D. (eds.) 10th Workshop on Models and Evolution, pp. 40–49. CEUR-WS, October 2016
3. Allweyer, T.: BPMN 2.0. BoD (2010)
4. Bencomo, N.: The role of models@run.time in autonomic systems: keynote. In: Proceedings of the IEEE International Conference on Autonomic Computing (ICAC), pp. 293–294 (2017)
5. Bencomo, N., Bennaceur, A., Grace, P., Blair, G.S., Issarny, V.: The role of models@run.time in supporting on-the-fly interoperability. Computing **95**(3), 167–190 (2013)
6. Bencomo, N., Götz, S., Song, H.: Models@run.time: a guided tour of the state of the art and research challenges. Softw. Syst. Model. **18**(5), 3049–3082 (2019)
7. Bertoa, M.F., Moreno, N., Barquero, G., Burgueño, L., Troya, J., Vallecillo, A.: Expressing measurement uncertainty in OCL/UML datatypes. In: Pierantonio, A., Trujillo, S. (eds.) ECMFA 2018. LNCS, vol. 10890, pp. 46–62. Springer, Cham (2018). https://doi.org/10.1007/978-3-319-92997-2_4
8. Blair, G., Bencomo, N., France, R.B.: Models@ run. time. Computer **42**(10), 22–27 (2009)
9. Bordeleau, F., Combemale, B., Eramo, R., van den Brand, M., Wimmer, M.: Tool-support of socio-technical coordination in the context of heterogeneous modeling. In: Proceedings of MODELS 2018 Workshops, co-located with ACM/IEEE 21st International Conference on Model Driven Engineering Languages and Systems (MODELS 2018), pp. 423–425 (2018)
10. Borky, J., Bradley, T.: Effective Model-Based Systems Engineering. Springer, Heidelberg (2019)

11. Bousse, E., Degueule, T., Vojtisek, D., Mayerhofer, T., DeAntoni, J., Combemale, B.: Execution framework of the GEMOC studio (tool demo). In: van der Storm, T., Balland, E., Varró, D. (eds.) Proceedings of the 2016 ACM SIGPLAN International Conference on Software Language Engineering, Amsterdam, The Netherlands, 31 October–1 November 2016, pp. 84–89. ACM (2016)
12. Brosch, P., Seidl, M., Wieland, K., Wimmer, M., Langer, P.: We can work it out: collaborative conflict resolution in model versioning. In: Wagner, I., Tellioğlu, H., Balka, E., Simone, C., Ciolfi, L. (eds.) ECSCW 2009. Springer, London (2009). https://doi.org/10.1007/978-1-84882-854-4_12
13. Burgueño, L., et al.: Contents for a model-based software engineering body of knowledge. Softw. Syst. Model. **18**(6), 3193–3205 (2019)
14. Cheng, B.H.C., Combemale, B., France, R.B., Jézéquel, J.M., Rumpe, B.: On the globalization of domain-specific languages. In: Combemale, B., Cheng, B., France, R., Jézéquel, J.M., Rumpe, B. (eds.) Globalizing Domain-Specific Languages. LNCS, vol. 9400. Springer, Cham (2015). https://doi.org/10.1007/978-3-319-26172-0_1
15. Combemale, B., DeAntoni, J., Baudry, B., France, R.B., Jézéquel, J., Gray, J.: Globalizing modeling languages. Computer **47**(6), 68–71 (2014)
16. Eastman, C., Teicholz, P., Sacks, R., Liston, K.: BIM Handbook: A Guide to Building Information Modeling for Owners, Managers, Designers, Engineers and Contractors. Wiley Publishing, Hoboken (2008)
17. Feldmann, S., Kernschmidt, K., Wimmer, M., Vogel-Heuser, B.: Managing inter-model inconsistencies in model-based systems engineering: application in automated production systems engineering. J. Syst. Softw. **153**, 105–134 (2019)
18. Friedenthal, S., Moore, A., Steiner, R.: A Practical Guide to SysML: Systems Modeling Language. Morgan Kaufmann Publishers Inc., San Francisco (2008)
19. Fritzson, P., Engelson, V.: Modelica — a unified object-oriented language for system modeling and simulation. In: Jul, E. (ed.) ECOOP 1998. LNCS, vol. 1445, pp. 67–90. Springer, Heidelberg (1998). https://doi.org/10.1007/BFb0054087
20. Gómez, A., Cabot, J., Wimmer, M.: *TemporalEMF*: a temporal metamodeling framework. In: Trujillo, J.C., et al. (eds.) ER 2018. LNCS, vol. 11157, pp. 365–381. Springer, Cham (2018). https://doi.org/10.1007/978-3-030-00847-5_26
21. Kienzle, J., et al.: Toward model-driven sustainability evaluation. Commun. ACM **63**(3), 80–91 (2020)
22. Klint, P., van der Storm, T., Vinju, J.: EASY meta-programming with rascal. In: Fernandes, J.M., Lämmel, R., Visser, J., Saraiva, J. (eds.) GTTSE 2009. LNCS, vol. 6491, pp. 222–289. Springer, Heidelberg (2011). https://doi.org/10.1007/978-3-642-18023-1_6
23. Kolovos, D., Rose, L., Paige, R., Garcia-Dominguez, A.: The Epsilon Book. Eclipse (2010)
24. Kolovos, D.S., Di Ruscio, D., Pierantonio, A., Paige, R.F.: Different models for model matching: an analysis of approaches to support model differencing. In: 2009 ICSE Workshop on Comparison and Versioning of Software Models, pp. 1–6. IEEE (2009)
25. Krahn, H., Rumpe, B., Völkel, S.: MontiCore: modular development of textual domain specific languages. In: Paige, R.F., Meyer, B. (eds.) TOOLS EUROPE 2008. LNBIP, vol. 11, pp. 297–315. Springer, Heidelberg (2008). https://doi.org/10.1007/978-3-540-69824-1_17

26. Kritzinger, W., Karner, M., Traar, G., Henjes, J., Sihn, W.: Digital twin in manufacturing: a categorical literature review and classification. IFAC-PapersOnLine, **51**(11), 1016–1022 (2018). 16th IFAC Symposium on Information Control Problems in Manufacturing INCOM 2018
27. Mazak, A., Wimmer, M.: Towards liquid models: an evolutionary modeling approach. In: Proceedings of the 18th IEEE Conference on Business Informatics (CBI), pp. 104–112 (2016)
28. Mohammadi, N., Taylor, J.E.: Smart city digital twins. In: 2017 IEEE Symposium Series on Computational Intelligence (SSCI), pp. 1–5 (2017)
29. Nagy, I., Cleophas, L.G., van den Brand, M., Engelen, L., Raulea, L., Mithun, E.X.L.: VPDSL: a DSL for software in the loop simulations covering material flow. In: Proceedings of the 17th IEEE International Conference on Engineering of Complex Computer Systems (ICECCS), pp. 318–327 (2012)
30. Piascik, R., Vickers, J., Lowry, D., Scotti, S., Stewart, J., Calomino, A.: Technology area 12: Materials, structures, mechanical systems, and manufacturing road map. Technical report, NASA Office of Chief Technologist (2010)
31. Rumbaugh, J., Jacobson, I., Booch, G.: Unified Modeling Language Reference Manual. 2nd edn. Pearson Higher Education (2004)
32. Silva Torres, W., van den Brand, M., Serebrenik, A.: Model management tools for models of different domains: a systematic literature review. In: Proceedings of the 13th Annual IEEE International Systems Conference (2019)
33. Toulmé, A.: Presentation of EMF compare utility. In: Eclipse Modeling Symposium (2006)
34. van der Aalst, W.M.P.: Process Mining - Data Science in Action, 2nd edn. Springer, Heidelberg (2016)
35. Vogel, T., Giese, H.: Requirements and assessment of languages and frameworks for adaptation models. CoRR, abs/1805.08679 (2018)
36. Weekes, S.: The rise of digital twins in smart cities. Smart Cities World (2019)

Reusable Data Visualization Patterns
for Clinical Practice

Fazle Rabbi[1,2(✉)], Jo Dugstad Wake[3], and Tine Nordgreen[4,5]

[1] Department of Information Science and Media Studies, University of Bergen,
Bergen, Norway
Fazle.Rabbi@uib.no
[2] Department of Computer Technology, Electrical Engineering and Science,
Western Norway University of Applied Sciences, Bergen, Norway
[3] NORCE Norwegian Research Centre, Bergen, Norway
Jo.Wake@norceresearch.no
[4] eMeistring, Bjørgvin DPS, Division of Psychiatry, Haukeland University Hospital,
Bergen, Norway
Tine.Nordgreen@uib.no
[5] Department of Clinical Psychology, University of Bergen, Bergen, Norway

Abstract. Among clinical psychologists involved in guided internet-facilitated interventions, there is an overarching need to understand patients symptom development and learn about patients need for treatment support. Data visualizations is a technique for managing enormous amounts of data and extract useful information, and is often used in developing digital tool support for decision-making. Although there exists numerous data visualisation and analytical reasoning techniques available through interactive visual interfaces, it is a challenge to develop visualizations that are relevant and suitable in a healthcare context, and can be used in clinical practice in a meaningful way. For this purpose it is necessary to identify actual needs of healthcare professionals and develop reusable data visualization components according to these needs. In this paper we present a study of decision support needs of psychologists involved in online internet-facilitated cognitive behavioural therapy. Based on these needs, we provide a library of reusable visual components using a model-based approach. The visual components are featured with mechanisms for investigating data using various levels of abstraction and causal analysis.

Keywords: Data visualization · Metamodeling · Model transformation · Visual analytics · Usability · Health informatics · Guided internet-delivered treatments · mHealth

1 Introduction

Digitalizing healthcare systems is considered a major means for dealing with the current challenges in healthcare [28]. Overall, the potential benefits of digitizing

Supported by Intromat (www.intromat.no).

healthcare include the increasing access to care and the improvement of service quality. These are essential requirements for making health systems responsive and sustainable. In addition, digitizing healthcare systems has the potential for enabling the transition from treatment to prevention. In this paper we present results from the ongoing research project Intromat (Introducing mental health through adaptive technology). Part of the project goals is to develop internet-delivered psychological prevention and treatment programs to people with mental health challenges or problems. One of the cases in the project is related to eMeistring, a routine care clinic that provides guided internet-facilitated cognitive behavioural therapy (iCBT) in secondary care for adults with anxiety and depression.

Each therapist in the eMeistring clinic is responsible for providing support and treatment to approximately 15 patients. As one of the benefits of internet-facilitated treatments is increased therapist capacity (ca 3 times more patients per therapist), the therapists are in need of user-friendly and effective IT support. The clinical management system currently in use is purely text-based, and the clinic is in need of dashboards for improving the conditions for online clinical practice for both therapists and patients. This can include better overview over patient activity in the system, easier access to patients symptom development, and indicators of patients who are in need of more support. These goals are also relevant to other healthcare practices; for example, healthcare professionals often do not get enough time to look into patients historical information. In order to improve the quality of service, healthcare professionals may be equipped with patient data analytics, including data visualizations. In this paper, we present the results from a study of clinical needs from healthcare professionals involved in guided iCBT, and present a list of reusable visual components. We have conducted interviews with the therapists working in the eMeistring treatment program to gather the requirements for a data support for therapists, and also built insight into patient needs. In this paper we focus on the usability and reusability issues of supporting clinical mental health practice within guided iCBT.

Our aim is to support clinical practice in guided iCBT by providing data visualisations to therapists showing patients activities. Activities are in this context mostly refer to what patients and therapists are engaged in while using digital treatment support systems. The underlying idea is that traces of digital activity, system-generated data can be used to raise awareness about important aspects for the clinical outcomes of mental health therapy. Again, these traces can be aggregated in the form of visualisations. Although there is a scarcity of this kind of work in guided iCBT, examples can be found in other fields. For instance, in educational research, the field of learning analytics focuses on data-driven ways of improving educational outcomes [24] by collecting and analysing traces of what learners leave behind in digital systems [23]. Charleer and colleagues [8] have studied learner dashboards for students and found that visualising student effort (i.e. produced materials, time spent etc.) is only helpful when it highlights how the effort contributes toward the intended learning outcomes of what is being studied. They furthermore find that solutions that empower students and increase their ability to reflect and make decisions, have a more positive effect on motivation, than for example automating the learning trajectory based on data. Corrin [10] and colleagues have studied how analytics can be integrated with a teacher's learning design, and argue the necessity of matching the data visualisations with the pedagogical intent of the teacher. CBT and education share the notion that one of the major change processes or facilitators of improvement is human learning.

Usability: In computer science, a common approach to assessing the value of an application is to evaluate its usability. Poor usability and lack of user-centered design have been described as two of the reasons for low engagement with mHealth apps [27]. In general, ICT with poor usability can lead to situations of low goal-achievement efficiency or the application not being used or being rejected. Usability studies are grounded not only in the social and behavioral sciences but also in the science of design [18]. Through the approach of research-trough design, it is possible to explore ideas to improve practices by building artefacts to support the practice at the same time as ensuring their relevance and validity [30]. This can be ensured by engaging with practitioners within the addressed field, in design of the digital artefacts. A recent review of usability practices in design of digital health applications [13] found that end users such as patients seldom are involved in the design of applications, although they are often involved in post-development evaluation. Here, we advance the state of art mHealth development practice by engaging therapists in the design of the digital environments that are being used to mediate guided iCBT.

Reusability: Model-driven software development may play a significant role in supporting digital health. In current practice, data analysts need to spend a vast amount of time processing data for analysis and producing effective reports. In this paper, we present a model-based approach to develop reusable visual components. With this approach, a data analyst will be able to incorporate visualizations for representing results throughout the process of data analysis. This technique allows the user to visualize data from various level of abstraction. For instance, it allows grouping of activities based on an ontological hierarchy, which permits data visualization from a higher level of abstraction. The visual components are equipped with temporal sliders which allows a user to perform causal analysis. Since our work is related to the topics of visual analytics [16], we clarify the fact that our focus for this paper is in the overlapping part of three research areas which include visual analytics and usability, digital health and model-based information system development (see the Venn diagram in Fig. 1). The paper is organized as follows: In Sect. 2 we provide an overview of the research methods that have been used while conducting this research; in Sect. 3 we present the findings from a case study from mental healthcare and present visual artefacts that have been developed; in Sect. 4 we propose a model based system for visual analytics; in Sect. 5 we present related works, and in Sect. 6 the paper is concluded.

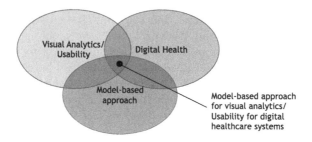

Fig. 1. The focus of this research

2   Methods

We have studied the practice of guided iCBT at a mental health clinic, in order to understand how to support the clinical and therapeutic practices with visualisations of relevant aspects of their activity. Additionally, we have been interested in how to improve the online environment for the patients, in particular in how to help motivate their persistent engagement with the therapy. The methods we have used include interviews and workshops with clinicians. Two to three therapists have taken part in a series of three collaborative workshops. The first two workshops focused on patient and therapist needs. Then a set of low-fidelity drafts for data visualisations were created. In the following workshops, the therapists provided feedback on the perceived usability and value of the visualisations. These feedback were used to improve the draft designs. A final usability and design workshop has been planned to be carried out with all therapists who work at the clinic. The primary focus of this research activity is the investigation of the design requirements reflecting therapists' insight into the program for a better data-driven digital solution. The resulting data material are workshop notes and transcriptions. No personally identifiable information has been recorded, and all the notes and transcriptions are anonymised.

3   Case Study: A Mental Health Clinic for Guided Internet-Delivered CBT

Our exploratory study has taken place in collaboration with a mental health clinic – eMeistring – that offers guided online cognitive behavioural theory for the mental health problems of panic- and social anxiety, and depression. The effects of the CBT on the patients mental health are considered positive and long-lasting, also when compared to face-to-face therapy, in line with findings from recent scholarly literature [2,3,12,20,26]. There are issues with patient dropout, however, also in line with scientific literature findings on mHealth and online mental health therapy worldwide, see e.g. [14,21]. In the long run, our work is intended to contribute towards lowering the dropout rate, increasing the percentage of successful therapeutic outcomes, and enrich the opportunities for interaction between the patients and the therapists. At an individual patient level, we take as a starting point that there are particular conditions to counselling patients who therapists don't meet or see face-to-face, but only interact with through text in a web-based system, and that this activity can be scaffolded more or less ideally.

Patients are admitted to the clinic by their general practitioners' or other clinical specialist referral. It is also currently possible for patients to contact the clinic directly without a referral. The treatment program lasts 14 weeks, and consists of eight modules covering aspects of mental health problems and CBT. The main activities that the patients are engaged in are reading and reflecting on their mental health problems; completing assignments about the content of each module; and behavioural elements such as behavioural activation. Additionally, they complete self-assessment (MADRS) once a week. All activities except behavioural activation are mediated through a text-based clinical management system. The behavioural activation module is paper-based. Each patient is assigned a therapist, who assesses the patients' progress and provides personal feedback via messages every week. The therapist additionally assesses whether a module needs to be considered as completed by a patient, and, if yes, subsequently assigns the next module.

As mentioned the practice of online mental health therapy is based on different conditions than face-to-face therapy. For example, the interaction between the patient and the clinician in face-to-face therapy is very much temporally and spatially tied. There is a dedicated hour and place for the therapy, which encompasses the relationship between the clinician and patient. In guided iCBT, the patient-clinician and patient-therapy relations are in many ways sustained temporally, and can take place anywhere. One of the treatment strategies in use in the clinic is behavioural activation, which is a common strategy used for treating depression. Behavioural activation [9] is a sometimes standalone component of CBT and involves the "scheduling of pleasurable activities to increase contact with sources of positive reinforcement" [15, p.361]. Ideally, the therapist should be aware of the correlation between the patients' scheduled activities and symptoms, and in guided iCBT this involves making the data available.

Based on our exploration of the problem space in collaboration with therapist representatives from the clinic, we arrived at three main ways of how patients and therapists can be supported with activity data visualisations, and a number of proposals of how to concretely visualise relevant information. The visualisations are drafted as snippets, which easily can be integrated with the digital system in use by the therapists. The following needs are identified:

1. Supporting therapist insight into group of assigned patients
2. Supporting therapist insight into individual patient activity and development
3. Motivating patient persistence

Supporting Therapist Insight into Group of Assigned Patients. The therapists will presumably be in a better position to support the patient therapeutic process the more he or she knows about the patients needs, development and activities. This need can be exemplified by quotes such as "How do I choose the right person (to treat) first?", and "The least active patients are the least visible in the system". In the current version of the therapy management system, the traces of patient activity available to the therapists are messages sent between them, weekly self-assessment screening results, and patient diaries and responses to tests tied to each module (i.e. "what have you learnt in this module"). It is possible, however, to provide more detailed information, based on the data produced by patients and therapists while using the system. System needs exploration carried out with therapists for this project, revealed three main categories of therapists needs for insight into patients: 1) A way to prioritise who to help first of the patients; 2) To know about how each patient is progressing with the therapy; and 3) To know how much time and effort the therapist has spent on each patient during the therapy trajectory. The first need arises partly because the therapists do not have access to any kind of aggregated views of their patients in the system, and partly because the patients have individual needs for example for follow-up for the duration of the therapeutic process. The state of each patient must currently be assessed by reviewing direct responses to self-assessments and diaries etc. The same observation is the cause of the second need for information. The clinic experiences a high dropout rate (around 60% complete the therapy), a common phenomenon in iCBT [26], and has a stated goal of lowering this number. Currently, the therapists have access to the information provided above, in addition to whether the patient has completed a module or not. Insights into each patient activity will enable the therapist to intervene and assist with advice and encouragement, for example in cases where progress is not taking place as expected. The third and final category is insight into how much effort has been exerted by each patient, and is a way to learn about both how much progress can be expected for each patient, but also for the therapist to be able to self-reflect and adjust treatment strategies to ensure a constructive balance of efforts between each patient. Currently, the only source of feedback on this issue is personal memory.

Proposed Visualisation: Figure 2 represents a generated view of the progress and activity of each of the patients assigned to a therapist. It is intended to support making decisions about who of the patients to prioritise. The concentric circles each indicate one week of the program (14 in total). Each segment or "cake" in the circle indicates a patient. The colour in each segment indicates how far the patient has gotten since starting. The colour (red - gray - green) and colour grading for each patient indicates trends in the MADRS score, red is negative, green positive and gray indicates stable values. Visualising trends in MADRS scores is based on the previous work of Grieg et al. [11] about supporting guided iCBT with visual analytics. The black lines indicate how many of the modules each patient has submitted. Comparing with the background colour tells the therapist whether a patient is on, ahead or behind schedule. The thickness of the black line indicates how much time the patient has spent online in the system. The grey shadow behind each black line indicates how much time the therapist has spent on each person.

Although the visualisation has the advantage of presenting patient activity and progress data in a condensed way, there is a threshold to how many patients it can present at the same time. From a usability perspective we estimate that it will scale well up to 15 patients, before the information becomes too condensed. However if the number of patients increases for each therapist, we proposed an alternative solution where the same information is presented in a tabular format with patients listed vertically, and progress and significant events are presented horizontally. Due to the limitation of space, this alternative visualisation is not presented in the paper.

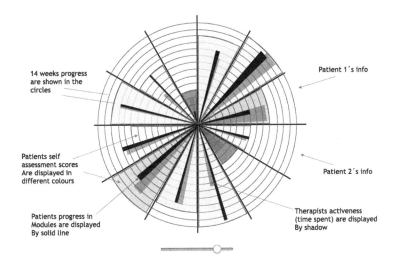

Fig. 2. Therapist overview of patients (Color figure online)

Supporting Therapist Insight into Patient Activity and Development. In addition to have an overview of all patients to be able to prioritise between them, therapists also have a need for insight into the activity and development of each individual patient. Currently, the insights are based on the patients' responses to the module tests, their patient diaries and the MADRS results. The patients additionally keep behavioural activation diaries, but this information is currently paper-based and outside the system they use. The idea is that by visualising the relevant information, the therapists will have better bases for making their therapeutic decisions, and additionally will have further opportunities to make interventions when patients are in danger of dropping out.

Proposed Visualisations: Figure 3 is a visualisation proposal that collects items from the patients behavioural activation diary and compares it with their MADRS scores, for therapists to see which activities works well and vice versa.

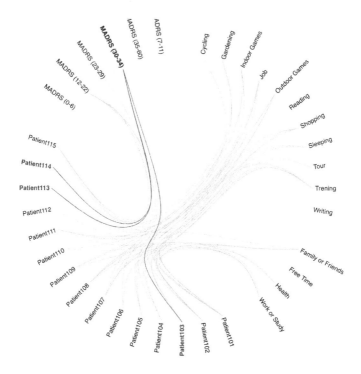

Fig. 3. Connection between patient activity and MADRS score

Fig. 4. Patient dropout warning list (Color figure online)

Additionally, the therapist have a need to see which of their patients are in danger of dropping out. Figure 4 is a draft for a list containing the patients assigned to a therapist who are behind on their modules. This can for example be generated by listing the patients who are behind a specified threshold of expected modules completed, or by listing all patients who are behind with their modules. The list contains a link to the patient page of the persons in question, along with indication of how much time they have spent in they system (green bar) and how many modules they are behind (red squares). To provide the therapist insight into how a patient works during the week, we have drafted a table where days of the week are indicated by letters vertically on the left, and hours of the day are displayed horizontally at the bottom. The green bars indicate when patients are online and working in the iCBT management system. The blue dot indicates that a module is completed. The email icons indicate when messages are sent (closed envelope) and read (open envelope). This could be further augmented with data about the platform used when accessing the system, as there are different conditions to system use for example when using mobile platforms compared to a PC. (The system can be accessed using any platform.)

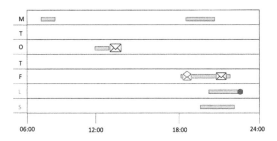

Fig. 5. Patients weekly activity

Motivating Patient Persistence. We have also aimed to increase the amount of visual feedback provided to each patient. The goal has been to increase the support offered to each patient, and to increase the likelihood of successful therapeutic outcomes. The needs of the patients, as expressed by the therapists can be exemplified as: "Am I doing too much, am I doing too little, am I on the right track?" and "What have I delivered, compared to what I am supposed to deliver?" The current source of feedback offered to the patient comes in form of qualitative assessment messages from the therapists. We aimed to provide more day-to-day and direct feedback based on the activity levels and kinds of the patient, and to increase the patient motivation to continue the therapy.

Proposed Visualisations: To support patients continued engagement with the CBT, we propose a refined version of a relatively simple and well known visualisation of progress - a progress bar. It compares actual progress with expected or planned progress, in addition to visualising the amount of messages to and from their therapist. This visualisation is also reported as interesting to therapists, to see if one particular patient is progressing as expected, in a simple way. The dots or arrows in the middle of the progress indicates total weeks of therapy. The colour shaded section (blue in v1 and gray in v2) indicates generic progress as expected, measured by counting weeks from the start. In Fig. 6 the actual patient progress is indicated with the vertical slider, and measured by completed modules. The messages are indicated with differently coloured dots, with the patient messages at the top and therapist messages at the bottom. In Fig. 7 the patients actual progress is illustrated with the yellow arrow, patient messages with a red speech bubble, and therapist messages with blue speech bubbles.

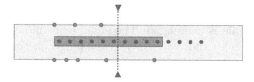

Fig. 6. Therapy progress bar for patients, v1 (Color figure online)

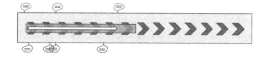

Fig. 7. Therapy progress bar for patients, v2 (Color figure online)

4   Model Based Approach for Reusable Visual Components

We propose to use domain specific models for dashboard components. Dashboard components i.e., visualizations, data analysis techniques are associated with an information model. In Fig. 8 we present the architecture of our system where we articulate the client server communication by means of an application programming interface (API). A library of model-based visual components are available in the server. When a client e.g., browser requests for a visual artefact, the server sends the scripts for rendering graphics in the client device. Server application fetches relevant data from existing healthcare database and transforms them into appropriate model for visualization. The server maintains the status of the visual component running at the client device. The server application is featured with the following:

- Support for abstraction by using ontologies [22];
- Support for cause analysis using data mining techniques

Besides these features, the visual components are equipped with temporal sliders which enables the user of the system to see the progression of events for a particular time period. The proposed architecture describes the design of our solution space. Figure 9 illustrates how model-driven engineering can be applied in various stages of implementing our system. The figure is adapted from [6] where the concept of extractor and injector were introduced. The idea of using an extractor is to represent the availability of appropriate software artefacts that are able to extract knowledge from a technical space and be able to inject such knowledge in another technical space (called injectors). The problem space consists of requirement specification and domain model which we have described in previous section. The library of visual components are developed by reverse engineering D3 js libraries. The domain model for visualization are specified using

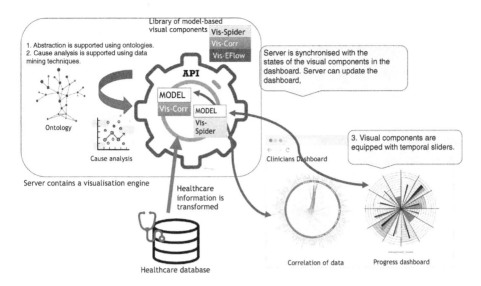

Fig. 8. Architecture design of model based dashboard system

graphs which are used for generating JSON code by applying model-to-model (M2M) transformation. In our approach the visual components can be adapted by model-to-text (M2T) transformation. We use M2M transformation for converting healthcare information into suitable data format for the visual components. As mentioned above, in our approach visual components are associated with domain model, Fig. 10(a) presents a domain model for the proposed spider-graph. We will refer to this visualization as Vis-Spider. Model transformation techniques can be used to extract this information from an existing health information system and instantiate this domain model with instances. This visual component needs to be connected with other parts of the system such as, the system should allow selecting a patient from the cake view and see the details of patients completion of modules or the correlation of patients symptoms with self-assessment score. The API at the server side mediates the communication between a variety of visual components. Figure 10(b) presents the domain model for visualizing event flow. We will refer to this visualization as Vis-EFlow. The events are associated with case-id (i.e., patients identification), time stamp (i.e., event time), activity and resource information. Many existing process mining tools use event logs that include these information [1]. In this domain model we have incorporated dimensional information for activities. This allows our event logs to be organized hierarchically. The incorporation of dimensional modeling in event logs permits us to group activities and view information from different perspective. The concept of dimensional modeling originated from data warehousing and business intelligence (DW/BI). Organizations embraced DW/BI techniques

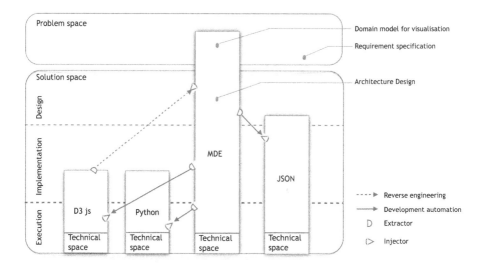

Fig. 9. Technical spaces and coverage

in order to handle large amount of information. Dimensional modeling allows us to incorporate following features:

- organization of large amount of data
- process raw data in various ways and turn them into useful information
- show correct information to the right person
- provide useful knowledge to help decision making.

The DW/BI systems emphasize collecting and processing raw data quickly, and turn them into useful information while preserving the consistency of the data [17]. It has been widely accepted by the BI community because of its simplicity and performance in presenting analytic data. In our approach we propose to use dimensional modeling for organizing healthcare information e.g., filtering and grouping events based on patients diagnosis, activities, etc. In our case, dimensional models packages the data in a format that allows simplicity for displaying understandable information to users and also supports developing efficient data analytic tools in terms of query performance. Our event-model allows us to change the level of abstraction in the event logs. We utilize this feature of dimensional modeling for specifying event flow analysis requirements. The purpose of this dimensional model is to provide an easy to use visualization for its user to investigate care flow from different context. We propose to use ontological hierarchies to provide hierarchical representation of healthcare information along each dimensional model. Traditionally, fact tables are used to store data at the lowest grain e.g., records about physical activity or events. Fact tables always use foreign keys to associate the records/events to

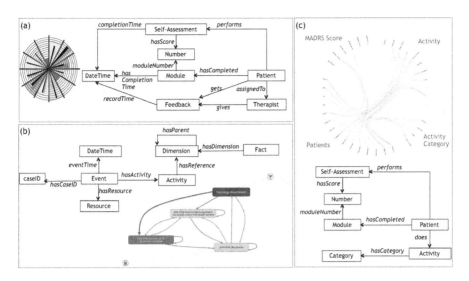

Fig. 10. Domain specific model for (a) Vis-Spider; (b) Vis-EFlow; (c) Vis-Corr

their dimensional models. Figure 11 shows a dimensional model where we incorporated healthcare ontologies e.g., SNOMED-CT, ICD-10 ontologies. Fragment of the SNOMED-CT ontology is shown in the figure that links a data from a dimensional model. In Fig. 10(c) we present a visualization called Vis-Corr to study correlation of patients activity and self-assessment score. Activities are recorded hourly by patients in a diary, as part of their behavioural activation. In eMeistring this visualization can be used to see how activities carried out by the patient correlate with their MADRS scores (or symptoms), or in other words which activities play a role in reducing the symptoms of depression. Since eMeistring allows patients to write free text for activities, the number of nodes representing activities could be very many in the visualization. To deal with this situation, we propose to use an activity ontology [29] which will allow hierarchical representation of activities in the visualization. The visualization with a temporal slider allows therapists to investigate the effects of various activities and their correlation with depression symptoms. In future we will incorporate a data mining technique which will extract patterns and visualize them with Vis-Corr. For example, the therapists would be able to see if activity-a and activity-b plays a major role in the reduction of depression symptoms. Many CBT treatments are based on the principle of behavior activation. However, therapists currently do not have a visual tool support to investigate how their patients are practicing them. Our proposed method will allow therapists to investigate more into this.

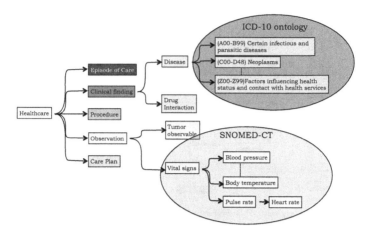

Fig. 11. A dimensional model for specifying data mining/visualization requirements in healthcare

5   Related Work

In [7] the authors proposed an architecture to support model driven software visualization. The visualization artefacts that they proposed are capable of representing the relationship and constraints of software components. In this paper we proposed a different technique to visualize healthcare information. We emphasized on utilizing a model driven approach for the construction of reusable visual components.

In [5] the authors presented a vision for the future of data-driven technology by means of incorporating IoT devices and visualizing healthcare information e.g., bio-markers for monitoring patients physical condition. They urged for the need of using such technology and visualization in healthcare. However they did not provide any information how such system can be developed or the software components can be reused. In this paper we provide a case study and present reusable visual components that can be reused in various healthcare settings.

Keim et al. [16], provided a conceptual framework of how visualization could fit into the phases of information life cycle. They argued for the importance of relevant information and provided a definition of visual analytics. They also provided a list of technical challenges for advanced visual analytics solutions. Our work fits well into the conceptual framework of visual analytics as presented by Keim et al. and in this paper we address several challenges such as infrastructure, visual representation and level of detail, data dimensionality.

In [4] the authors introduced the idea of using model-based approach for big data analysis to lower the amount of competences needed in the management of a big data pipeline and to support automation of big data analytics. They presented a methodology data analysis steps can be specified using declarative models. However in their approach, authors only considered using scatter plot chart.

Streit et al. in [25] presented a model-driven design approach for visual analysis of heterogeneous data from healthcare. They addressed the issue of how healthcare data from various sources can be linked and how visualization can be used for supporting investigation. They applied their design process to a biomedical use case where they considered visualizing medical data consisting of MR/CT/X-ray, Gene/Protein expression, lab results, disease database, etc. While our work overlaps with their approach in many aspects- in our work we focused on the mental healthcare domain and emphasized on constructing visualization that provides meaningful information for therapists providing internet based treatment. The visualization of data incorporated with an ontology as presented in our approach will facilitate healthcare workers to investigate data from various level of abstraction.

In [19], Medeiros et al. presented an ontology based process mining approach where they discussed about the necessity of relating elements in event logs with their semantic concepts. In their approach they linked event logs with the concepts from an ontology which enabled then to perform concept-based analysis. The idea of using semantics makes it possible to automatically reason or infer relationships of concepts that are related. They distinguished between the application of process mining in two different levels: instance level and conceptual level. They illustrated an example process model to repair telephones in a company. The process model includes three different ontologies: Task ontology, Role ontology and Performer ontology. The idea of using an ontology is for process mining presented in [19] is very similar to our approach. The idea of filtering based on ontological concepts and the idea of grouping nodes by a high level ontological concept is similar. However, in our approach we emphasize on various kinds of data visualization where ontology plays a major role for providing various level of abstraction for healthcare information. While in [19] the authors implemented their technique in ProM, our approach is more general and can be plugged in to several areas in the healthcare system.

Grieg [11] et al. presented an architecture for accessing healthcare data using HL7 FHIR and provided a methodology for visualizing healthcare information in various ways. Their visualization technique include a visualization of clinical observations and self-screening results for individual patients and/or a group of patients. A spider-chart was introduced for visualizing MADRS score of a patient which shows the progression of the symptoms in a single visualization. In their work authors provided an evaluation of the performance of accessing healthcare information using HL7 FHIR API. They pointed out the fact that such architecture based on HL7 FHIR APIs may have scalability problems as HL7 FHIR consists of lot of meta-data information. In our approach we provided an architecture which is more robust in a sense that visualizations are tied to a model. Healthcare information from a variety of sources can be transformed into appropriate format for visualization.

6   Conclusion and Future Work

This paper took a starting point in the potential of mHealth and guided Internet-delivered treatments in providing efficient treatment for mental health issues, and increasing overall access to mental healthcare. Through an identified need for, and a large potential in ICT to provide support for clinicians and patients involved in guided Internet-delivered treatments, we have created a set of low-fidelity prototypes for supporting online clinical practice and mental health therapy with visualisations of activity in the online systems used. The needs have been established in dialogue with representatives of clinical personnel working with guided Internet-delivered treatments, and has been crucial in understanding the practice that is addressed through our study. Particularly, we have drafted solutions for therapists to understand and have insight into their patients' activity and need for support, and to help prioritise how to use their time with the patients. We have also focused on what useful and valuable things can be learned about a guided Internet-delivered treatments patient from his or her online activity, and how can this be conveyed to the therapist, to make the therapy as efficient as possible. We have developed an example of how data from patients can be used to help the clinician learn about which of the activities that patients engage in behavioural activation, and how the data can form the basis for the therapist to give substantiated advice to the patient. This work will be tested in a clinical setting were increased quality of user experience and efficacy will be the main outcomes. In addition we will use this work in our industry-research-clinic collaborationship as the industry are offered user-centered tools that improve therapist workflow and increase patient outcomes.

In this paper we proposed to use a model-based approach for visual analytics. We presented how model-based artefacts such as ontology, dimensional models, meta-models could be composed for the construction of reusable visual components. The application of model-based approach for visual analytics will bring several benefits including the reduction of cost, ease of customization, support for model based analysis for the healthcare domain.

The next steps for this study is to validate the results achieved so far, and implement examples in practical settings. Validation involves gathering further usability data, focused on how the visualisation examples give meaning to a wider set of therapists, how understandable they are, and how actionable they are. It is also relevant to study how they can be integrated with the systems currently in use at the clinic. Based on usability and usefulness evidence, the examples should be implemented in practice at the clinic. Everyday use in clinical practice would allow measurement and assessment of long term effect on therapy efficiency and outcomes.

References

1. van der Aalst, W.: Process Mining: Data Science in Action, 2nd edn. Springer Publishing Company Incorporated (2016)

2. Andersson, G., Carlbring, P., Ljótsson, B., Hedman, E.: Guided internet-based CBT for common mental disorders. J. Contemp. Psychother. **43**, 223–233 (2013). https://doi.org/10.1007/s10879-013-9237-9
3. Andersson, G., Topooca, N., Havik, O., Nordgreen, T.: Internet-supported versus face-to-face cognitive behavior therapy for depression. Expert Rev. Neurother. **16**(1), 55–60 (2016). https://doi.org/10.1586/14737175.2015.1125783
4. Ardagna, C.A., Bellandi, V., Ceravolo, P., Damiani, E., Bezzi, M., Hebert, C.: A model-driven methodology for big data analytics-as-a-service. In: 2017 IEEE International Congress on Big Data (BigData Congress), pp. 105–112, June 2017. https://doi.org/10.1109/BigDataCongress.2017.23
5. Bhavnani, S., Sitapati, A.M.: Virtual care 2.0-a vision for the future of data-driven technology-enabled healthcare. Curr. Treat. Options Cardiovasc. Med. **21**, 1–13 (2019)
6. Brambilla, M., Cabot, J., Wimmer, M.: Model-Driven Software Engineering in Practice. 2nd edn. Morgan and Claypool Publishers (2017)
7. Bull, R.I., Storey, M., Favre, J., Litoiu, M.: An architecture to support model driven software visualization. In: 14th IEEE International Conference on Program Comprehension (ICPC 2006), pp. 100–106, June 2006. https://doi.org/10.1109/ICPC.2006.11
8. Charleer, S., Klerkx, J., Duval, E., De Laet, T., Verbert, K.: Creating effective learning analytics dashboards: lessons learnt. In: Verbert, K., Sharples, M., Klobučar, T. (eds.) EC-TEL 2016. LNCS, vol. 9891, pp. 42–56. Springer, Cham (2016). https://doi.org/10.1007/978-3-319-45153-4_4
9. Chartier, I.S., Provencher, M.D.: Behavioural activation for depression: efficacy, effectiveness and dissemination. J. Affect. Disord. **145**(3), 292–299 (2013). https://doi.org/10.1016/j.jad.2012.07.023
10. Corrin, L., et al.: Loop: a learning analytics tool to provide teachers with useful data visualisations. In: Proceedings of Ascilite 2015: 32nd Australasian Society for Computers in Learning in Tertiary Education Conference (ASCILITE 2015), pp. 409–413 (2015)
11. Grieg, N.A., Lillehaug, S.I., Lamo, Y.: A visual analytics dashboard to support ICBT therapists. In: Proceedings of the 17th Scandinavian Conference on Health Informatics, 12–13 Nov 2019, pp. 134–140, Oslo Norway (2019)
12. Hofmann, S., Asnaani, A., Vonk, I., Sawyer, A., Fang, A.: The efficacy of cognitive behavioral therapy: a review of meta-analyses. Cogn. Ther. Res. **36**(5), 427–440 (2012). https://doi.org/10.1007/s10608-012-9476-1
13. Inal, Y., Wake, J.D., Guribye, F., Nordgreen, T.: Usability evaluations of mobile mental health technologies: a systematic review study. J. Med. Internet Res. **22**(1), e15337 (2020). https://doi.org/10.2196/15337
14. Kannisto, K.A., Korhonen, J., Adams, C.E., Koivunen, M.H., Vahlberg, T., Välimäki, M.A.: Factors associated with dropout during recruitment and follow -up periods of a mHealth-based randomized controlled trial for mobile.net to encourage treatment adherence for people with serious mental health problems. JMIR mHealth **19**(2), e46 (2017)
15. Kanter, J.W., Puspitasari, A.J., Santos, M.M., Nagy, G.A.: Behavioural activation: history, evidence and promise. Br. J. Psychiatry **200**(5), 361–363 (2012). https://doi.org/10.1192/bjp.bp.111.103390

16. Keim, D., Andrienko, G., Fekete, J.-D., Görg, C., Kohlhammer, J., Melançon, G.: Visual analytics: definition, process, and challenges. In: Kerren, A., Stasko, J.T., Fekete, J.-D., North, C. (eds.) Information Visualization. LNCS, vol. 4950, pp. 154–175. Springer, Heidelberg (2008). https://doi.org/10.1007/978-3-540-70956-5_7

17. Kimball, R., Ross, M.: The Data Warehouse Toolkit: The Definitive Guide to Dimensional Modeling. 3rd edn. Wiley Publishing (2013)

18. Lindgaard, G.: Early traces of usability as a science and as a profession. Interact. Comput. **21**(5–6), 350–352 (2009). https://doi.org/10.1016/j.intcom.2009.03.006

19. Alves de Medeiros, A.K., van der Aalst, W.M.P.: Process mining towards semantics. In: Dillon, T.S., Chang, E., Meersman, R., Sycara, K. (eds.) Advances in Web Semantics I. LNCS, vol. 4891, pp. 35–80. Springer, Heidelberg (2008). https://doi.org/10.1007/978-3-540-89784-2_3

20. Nordgreen, T., Gjestad, R., Andersson, G., Carlbring, P., Havik, O.E.: The effectiveness of guided Internet-based cognitive behavioral therapy for social anxiety disorder in a routine care setting. Internet Interv. **13**, 24–29 (2018). https://doi.org/10.1016/j.invent.2018.05.003, http://www.sciencedirect.com/science/article/pii/S2214782918300204

21. Peiris, D., Miranda, J., Mohr, D.C.: Going beyond killer apps: building a better mHealth evidence base. BMJ Global Health **3**(1), e000676 (2018). https://doi.org/10.1136/bmjgh-2017-000676

22. Rabbi, F., Lamo, Y.: Development of an E-mental health infrastructure for supporting interoperability and data analysis. In: Rutle, A., Lamo, Y., MacCaull, W., Iovino, L. (eds.) 3rd International Workshop on (Meta) Modelling for Healthcare Systems (MMHS). pp. 59–66. No. 2336 in CEUR Workshop Proceedings, Aachen (2018). http://ceur-ws.org/Vol-2336/

23. Siemens, G., Long, P.: Penetrating the fog: analytics in learning and education. EDUCAUSE **46**, 30–32 (2011)

24. Siemens, G.: Learning analytics: envisioning a research discipline and a domain of practice. In: LAK 2012: Proceedings of the 2nd International Conference on Learning Analytics and Knowledge, pp. 4–8 (2012)

25. Streit, M., Schulz, H., Lex, A., Schmalstieg, D., Schumann, H.: Model-driven design for the visual analysis of heterogeneous data. IEEE Trans. Visual Comput. Graph. **18**(6), 998–1010 (2012). https://doi.org/10.1109/TVCG.2011.108

26. Titov, N., et al.: ICBT in routine care: a descriptive analysis of successful clinics in five countries. Internet Interv. **13**, 108–115 (2018). https://doi.org/10.1016/j.invent.2018.07.006

27. Torous, J., Nicholas, J., Larsen, M., Firth, J., Christensen, H.: Clinical review of user engagement with mental health smartphone apps: evidence, theory and improvements. Evid. Mental Health **21**(3), 116–119 (2018). https://doi.org/10.1136/eb-2018-102891

28. World Health Organization: What you need to know about digital health systems (2019). http://www.euro.who.int/en/health-topics/Health-systems/pages/news/news/2019/2/what-you-need-to-know-about-digital-health-systems. Accessed 17 Mar 2020

29. Woznowski, P., Tonkin, E., Flach, P.A.: Activities of daily living ontology for ubiquitous systems: development and evaluation. Sensors **18**(7), 2371 (2018)

30. Zimmerman, J., Forlizzi, J., Evenson, S.: Research through design as a method for interaction design research in HCI. In: Proceedings of CHI 2007, pp. 493–502 (2007)

A Model Based Slicing Technique for Process Mining Healthcare Information

Fazle Rabbi[1,2(✉)], Yngve Lamo[2], and Wendy MacCaull[3]

[1] Department of Information Science and Media Studies, University of Bergen,
Bergen, Norway
Fazle.Rabbi@uib.no
[2] Department of Computer Technology, Electrical Engineering and Science,
Western Norway University of Applied Sciences, Bergen, Norway
Yngve.Lamo@hvl.no
[3] Department of Computer Science, St. Francis Xavier University,
Antigonish, NS, Canada
wmaccaul@stfx.ca

Abstract. Process mining is a powerful technique which uses an organization's event data to extract and analyse process flow information and develop useful process models. However, it is difficult to apply process mining techniques to healthcare information due to factors relating to the complexity inherent in the healthcare domain and associated information systems. There are also challenges in understanding and meaningfully presenting results of process mining and problems relating to technical issues among the users. We propose a model based slicing approach based on dimensional modeling and ontological hierarchies that can be used to raise the level of abstraction during process mining, thereby more effectively dealing with the complexity and other issues. We also present a structural property of the proposed slicing technique for process mining.

Keywords: Healthcare systems · Ontology · Process mining · Slicing · Abstraction

1 Introduction

Today's vast amount of healthcare related information needs to be accessed easily and integrated intelligently to support better healthcare delivery. Systematic analysis of healthcare data can help to detect patterns so that healthcare providers can optimize their resource allocation and clinicians can optimize treatment plans for individuals leading to better health outcomes. To improve the quality of health services delivery, healthcare professionals are particularly interested to know what are the common pathways for patients, how can a process model be improved, and to what extent do existing systems follow clinical guidelines. However it is not easy to answer these questions as healthcare processes are

Partially funded by Intromat (www.intromat.no).

O. Babur et al. (Eds.): ICSMM 2020, CCIS 1262, pp. 73–81, 2020.
https://doi.org/10.1007/978-3-030-58167-1_6

highly dynamic, complex, sometimes ad-hoc, increasingly multidisciplinary [15], and involve numerous points of care and a variety of clinicians and treatment plans.

Data analysis techniques such as process mining present the opportunity to analyse healthcare information, from numerous viewpoints (i.e., contexts) such patient populations with specific diseases, ages, gender, incidences of comorbidity, or type of healthcare service setting (e.g., clinic, hospital, nursing home), home location (urban or rural), or procedures used, etc., in order to learn from this information. Process mining [4] techniques hold great potential to improve health services delivery.

van der Aalst presented four different analysis perspectives in [4] which include control-flow perspective, organizational perspective, case perspective, and time perspective. These perspectives are useful to derive useful insight with respect to ordering of activities, the roles of resources, the attributes related to a particular case, and the frequency and timing of events. However, this approach lacks an abstraction mechanism allowing health professionals to both mine relevant information from highly discipline specific data sources and also to process event data from often highly individualistic patient pathways in order to discover common pathways.

In this paper, we address some of the challenges of process mining and learning from the large amount and variety of healthcare information. We present a model based slicing technique for process mining which utilizes dimensional modeling and ontological representations of healthcare information. Ontologies are increasingly being used to standardize terminologies in healthcare and other areas. For example, the ICD-10 ontology [16] provides diagnostic codes for classifying diseases, including a wide variety of signs, symptoms, abnormal findings, etc., while SNOMED-CT [3] provides a comprehensive terminology for clinical health. Our proposed slicing technique proposes that we use graphical representations incorporating an easy-to-use graphical interface allowing health professionals to apply process mining on a variety of abstraction levels.

de Medeiros and van der Aalst [11], discussed the necessity of relating elements in event logs with their semantic concepts, allowing them to perform concept-based reasoning and analysis. They illustrated their ideas with an example process model to repair telephones in a company which included three different ontologies and implemented their technique in ProM. Our approach is similar; however, we illustrate the value and potential of using a graphical query language for specifying slicing requirements of process mining. The graphical query language uses dimensional modelling and ontology which makes it suitable for applying the slicing technique in the very complex healthcare domain.

Mans et al. [10], discussed the application of process mining in healthcare and provided an overview of frequently asked questions by medical professionals in process mining projects. The questions reflect the medical professionals' interest both in learning common pathways of different patient groups, to determine their compliance with internal and external clinical guidelines, and also in gathering information about the throughput times for treating patients.

The authors pointed out the need for accumulating data from different data sources claiming this to be a major challenge in healthcare. and urging the exploitation of ontology-based process mining approaches in the healthcare domain.

Bistarelli et al. presented a prototype tool called PrOnto in [6] which can discover business processes from event logs and classify them with respect to a business ontology. The tool takes an event log file as input and produces an UML based activity diagram in XML format. The aim is to raise the level of abstraction in process mining by utilizing business ontologies. They proposed an ontology representing the hierarchy of resources to define which level of abstraction will be used [6]. Here we use both dimensional models and ontologies to classify event logs allowing us to be more specific in one portion of the process model while being more generic in another portion of it. Our mining technique uses several pre-processing steps, allowing us to specify both context and level of abstraction.

The rest of this paper is organized as follows. Section 2 discusses the characteristics of and challenges of process mining in the healthcare domain. Section 3 presents data abstraction methods involving dimensional modelling, ontological hierarchies and graphical representations resulting in novel approaches to process mining. We study the structural property of our slicing technique in Sect. 4. Section 5 concludes the paper and gives directions for our future work.

2   Characteristics of and Challenges in Careflow Analysis

In this section, we briefly discuss several characteristics of healthcare data which make process mining so difficult. We argue that the current practice of process mining needs to be advanced by means of a rich information model in order to accommodate the requirements of the many and various stakeholders.

In many developed countries, the majority of the citizens use public healthcare services provided by a variety of service providers using a large number of software applications. For instance, Helse Vest IKT (HV-IKT) [2] an IT company in Norway that supplies equipment and services within the ICT area to specialist health services in the western part of Norway, has more than 1000 software systems to support the regional healthcare. As a result, healthcare data are often in silos and different standards are followed by different health facilities to code diagnosis, lab test results, medical procedures and drugs. This presents a major problem as patients frequently need to visit various health facilities so for effective process mining, event logs representing activities of various systems must be considered. In healthcare, the data preparation task is very critical as healthcare data are very sensitive and therefore semantics of the data must be preserved [14]. Lack of standards for data definitions and reporting mechanisms in health data across various disciplines makes it very difficult to analyse the large spectrum of health profiles. Event logs from a variety of systems using various data definitions and formats must therefore be harmonized before they can be analysed by any process mining algorithm.

Identifying common pathways for patient flow in healthcare systems is complicated by the large variety of patient conditions, points of care and diagnoses.

Consider Table 1 which shows a portion of such an event log. The resulting process model is usually too large to provide meaningful information. Even after filtering to keep, for example, only the patient cases which are admitted to the radiology department, the model is still too large. By pre-processing event logs so that we exploit the hierarchical information structure in healthcare such as organizational structure of hospitals and clinics, or ontologies of healthcare terminologies, we can support various levels of abstraction and reduce the size of the process model. We need a mechanism to specify how to exploit ontological hierarchies to change abstraction levels.

Table 1. Portion of a healthcare event log (Sample data)

Id	Event time	Event name	Resource
1	2017-03-20 13:30	Surgical clinic	Kristi Salazar
1	2017-03-20 13:30	(N39_9) disorder of urinary system	Darla Ramirez
2	2017-03-07 14:00	Radiology department	Ricky Alvarado
2	2017-03-07 15:00	(N63) unspecified lump in breast	Deborah Tyler
2	2017-03-07 15:15	(N64_5) other symptoms in breast	Johanna Buchanan
3	2017-04-06 08:30	Division of mental health protection	Henrietta King
3	2017-04-06 08:30	(F321) depressive episode	Beatrice French

While analyzing common pathways for patients, different contexts are required to allow clinicians to focus on different groups of patients and to visualize their careflows. For instance, for patients with mental disorders, psychologists may be interested in patient visits to various service points while researchers may be interested in investigating the efficiency of new medications or procedures. The psychologists need to select a patient group based on diagnosis but display information about patient visits to different service points, while researchers require the health assessment related information. We need efficient tool support where one can filter the data and specify the context for data visualization. Existing process mining techniques may be used to visualize flow but event logs must be prepared in different ways to support a wider variety of queries. Existing process mining tools such as Fluxicon Disco [1] support filtering over event logs; however, since the events are not categorized, they do not support grouping of similar events from an abstraction level (e.g., disease group from ICD-10) to extract an abstract process model over another type of events (e.g., visit to health service points).

3   Model Based Pre-processing Step for Process Mining

In this section we propose a model-based slicing technique for handling the complexity of process mining in the healthcare domain. The proposed slicing technique is centered on the use of dimensional modeling and ontologies and it consists of pre-processing steps for process mining. The slicing technique includes filtering and grouping of activities where we use ontological perspectives to identify semantically related cases and provide a higher level of abstraction in the data, which at the same time gives meaningful information to healthcare professionals. Usually these professionals focus on a specific domain (their area of specialization) but often they are interested in also getting an abstract view of aspects of their patients' use of services from other disciplines. An interdisciplinary view of process models along with zoom-in features are essential to allow healthcare professionals to understand the flow of patients and/or their symptoms and diagnoses. We address this issue by incorporating dimensional models where we use ontologies along various dimensions. We allow healthcare professionals to specify on which area they wish to focus and for which area they want an abstract view. This requirement of mixing abstraction levels has not been addressed in the state-of-art process mining literature. In the following subsections we present a slicing technique for process mining by means of a graphical language based on ontologies and dimensional modeling.

3.1 Role of Ontologies in Process Mining

Ontologies can play two roles in process mining. First, they provide vocabularies to integrate data from multiple healthcare information systems. We propose using the SNOMED-CT and ICD-10 ontologies to group activities in event logs across disciplines enabling process mining over multiple data sources. We also propose using hospital- or regional health authority-specific ontologies to standardize information of an organizational or administrative nature. Second, ontologies provide suitable levels of abstraction for (i) specifying filters to select particular patient groups and for (ii) grouping information to capture and/or visualize the careflow process at a high (and more useful) level of abstraction.

3.2 Dimensional Modeling for Contextual Analysis of Careflow

The concept of dimensional modeling originated from data warehousing and business intelligence (DW/BI). The DW/BI systems emphasize collecting and processing raw data quickly and turning them into useful information while preserving the consistency of the data. Dimensional models package the data in a simple format so that information may be displayed in a manner easily understood by business users, and support efficient data analytic tools in terms of query performance. We present a new application area of dimensional modeling, showing that it can be used for specifying context-related requirements for process mining.

Figure 1 shows how a dimensional model can be used in a healthcare setting to capture process mining requirements. The purpose of this dimensional model is to provide a visualization allowing the user to investigate care flow from different contexts. Typically dimensional models are used to represent detailed atomic information captured by a business process. However, we propose to use

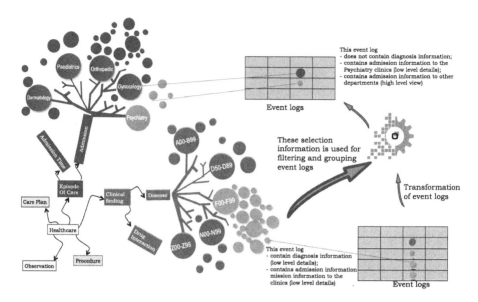

Fig. 1. Use of dimensional model for specifying process mining requirements (Color figure online)

ontological hierarchies to provide hierarchical representation of healthcare information along each dimension of a dimensional model for healthcare.

Suppose we have a dimensional model for Healthcare as indicated in Fig. 1 with the dimensions: Episode of Care, Clinical Finding, Procedure, Observation and Care Plan. Figure 1 shows a fragment of the ICD-10 ontology representing several diseases linked to the Clinical Finding dimension. We now show how dimensional modeling can be used to support analysis of healthcare processes, by supporting both filtering and selecting the level of abstraction (i.e., grouping) for visualizing the process mining output.

Suppose an analyst is interested in investigating the flow of patients with mental and behavioral disorders admitted to the various departments in a hospital. The analyst is interested in the movement of the patient in psychiatry clinics but the specifics of other clinics in not needed, only the information at the department level. We will assume that the department hierarchy of the hospital is used for the 'Episode of Care - Admission' dimension. We illustrate the situation in Fig. 1 to help visualize how the dimensional model and the hierarchical representation of data can be utilized to obtain the information. In Fig. 1, 'F00-F99' is the ICD-10 code for 'mental and behavioral disorder' diseases. Selecting 'F00–F99' for filtering means to filter based on the sub-diseases under 'F00–F99' (depicted as small orange circles in the figure), extracting event logs for patients with one of the sub-disease codes of 'F00–F99'. From these event logs we now extract events related to admission. An event log with patient's admission information contains information about the patient's visits to different clinics. We are interested in clinic information only for psychiatry but we need to display patient

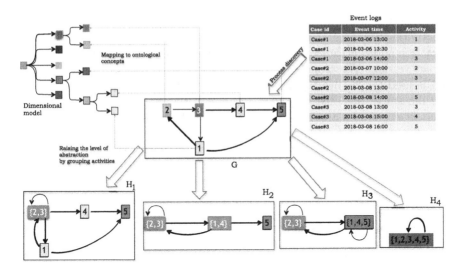

Fig. 2. A process model and its different abstractions

admission to other departments. We use the department hierarchical information (Ontology) to group the results displaying a higher level of abstraction for
departments (i.e., department names, e.g., Gynocology, Orthopedics, etc.) displaying only department name rather than clinic name for visits to clinics other
than psychiatry clinics.

4   Structural Property

There are several process mining tools which produce process models of various
kinds. For example, ProM [7], an open-source process mining tool, produces Petri
nets [12] as output to describe the process models extracted from event logs.
Disco by Fluxicon [1], a commercial process mining tool, produces attributed
graphs to present discovered process models. RapidProM [5] consists of state-
of-the-art process mining algorithms and produces process models with various
formalisms such as BPMN Models [13], Petri nets [12], colored Petri nets [8],
process trees [9], etc. Since these process models are (essentially) graph-based, we
illustrate the abstraction in graph-based process model and discuss a structural
property which is needed to ensure that abstract process model correctly reflects
the abstraction in the ontology.

Suppose we apply process mining technique over a set of traces T representing event logs of a system and obtain a directed graph G representing the
discovered process model (see Fig. 2). We refer to this graph G as the base process model. The use of a dimensional model and ontological hierarchies allows
us to group some of the nodes from the base process model. On the upper left
of Fig. 2 we see a dimensional model with five dimensions, two of which have
associated ontological hierarchies. The ontology-based slicing approach allows

us to group the activities according to the ontological hierarchies. While grouping activities based on the ontological hierarchies, one can choose the level of abstraction and this choice allows us to transform the original event logs into an abstract version. The transformed event log (which is now at a more abstract level) is used for discovering a more abstract process model. The remainder of Fig. 2 illustrates the effects of some groupings of activities on the base process model. The colours of the five tasks in G reflect the position the associated task in the dimensional model. These colours show that activities 2 and 3 belong to the ontological hierarchy associated to the top dimension. Using this higher level of abstraction we group activities 2 and 3, producing a single node representing the set of activities $\{2, 3\}$. See H_1 at the lower left hand side. It is possible to also group nodes based on their ontological hierarchy from other dimensions as shown in process models H_2, H_3 and H_4. (Two levels of the second ontological hierarchy are used in succession to get H_2 and H_3.) These groupings of activities provide even more compressed process models. It is desirable to obtain an abstract process model H such that there exists a graph homomorphism between the base process model G and H. The graph homomorphism ensures that the abstract process model reflects the abstraction in the ontology.

Theorem 1 (Correctness of abstraction). *Given a dimensional model and a set of traces T representing event logs, if the mapping of activities to the ontological concepts relates each element from its domain to a maximum of one leaf node of the dimensional model then combining the activities based on the dimensional model compresses the base process model G to a graph H such that there exists a graph homomorphism between G and H.*

Proof Hint: The theorem can be proved by showing an equivalence class relationship from the nodes and edges of the process model from G to the abstract process model H following the level of abstraction in the ontological models.

5   Conclusion

To analyze the vast amount of healthcare information, better visualization techniques are needed to get an abstract and transparent view of what processes have been executed. In this paper we propose a model based approach based on dimensional modelling and associated ontological hierarchies that will allow analysts to specify process mining requirements such as the context and abstraction level. The idea of using a combination of dimensional modeling with ontologies is novel in this paper. We envision a healthcare information system that provides access to information from various healthcare providers. We are currently developing a careflow analysis tool which offers a diagrammatic language for slicing event logs.

This diagrammatic representation of the dimensional model gives an easy-to-use interface allowing the user to collect process mining requirements. After the needed preprocessing, the tool uses an existing process mining tool called *Disco*

[1] to show the results of the process mining. The tool provides a visualization to aid healthcare workers in specifying their process mining requirements. In future an expert user group from the Helse Vest IKT will be involved in evaluating the tool.

References

1. Fluxicon Disco. https://fluxicon.com/disco/
2. Helse Vest IKT. https://helse-vest-ikt.no/seksjon-engelsk
3. SNOMED CT. www.snomed.org/snomed-ct
4. van der Aalst, W.M.P.: Process Mining: Discovery, Conformance and Enhancement of Business Processes. 1st edn. Springer Publishing Company Incorporated (2011)
5. van der Aalst, W.M.P., Bolt, A., van Zelst, S.J.: RapidProM: mine your processes and not just your data. CoRR abs/1703.03740 (2017). http://arxiv.org/abs/1703.03740
6. Bistarelli, S., Noia, T.D., Mongiello, M., Nocera, F.: PrOnto: an ontology driven business process mining tool. Procedia Comput. Sci. **112**, 306–315 (2017). https://doi.org/10.1016/j.procs.2017.08.002, http://www.sciencedirect.com/science/article/pii/S1877050917313418
7. van Dongen, B.F., de Medeiros, A.K.A., Verbeek, H.M.W., Weijters, A.J.M.M., van der Aalst, W.M.P.: The ProM framework: a new era in process mining tool support. In: Ciardo, G., Darondeau, P. (eds.) ICATPN 2005. LNCS, vol. 3536, pp. 444–454. Springer, Heidelberg (2005). https://doi.org/10.1007/11494744_25
8. Jensen, K., Kristensen, L.M.: Coloured Petri Nets: Modelling and Validation of Concurrent Systems, 1st edn. Springer Publishing Company, Incorporated (2009)
9. Leemans, S.J.J., Fahland, D., van der Aalst, W.M.P.: Scalable process discovery with guarantees. In: Gaaloul, K., Schmidt, R., Nurcan, S., Guerreiro, S., Ma, Q. (eds.) CAISE 2015. LNBIP, vol. 214, pp. 85–101. Springer, Cham (2015). https://doi.org/10.1007/978-3-319-19237-6_6
10. Mans, R.S., van der Aalst, W.M.P., Vanwersch, R.J.B., Moleman, A.J.: Process mining in healthcare: data challenges when answering frequently posed questions. In: Lenz, R., Miksch, S., Peleg, M., Reichert, M., Riaño, D., ten Teije, A. (eds.) KR4HC/ProHealth -2012. LNCS (LNAI), vol. 7738, pp. 140–153. Springer, Heidelberg (2013). https://doi.org/10.1007/978-3-642-36438-9_10
11. Alves de Medeiros, A.K., van der Aalst, W.M.P.: Process mining towards semantics. In: Dillon, T.S., Chang, E., Meersman, R., Sycara, K. (eds.) Advances in Web Semantics I. LNCS, vol. 4891, pp. 35–80. Springer, Heidelberg (2008). https://doi.org/10.1007/978-3-540-89784-2_3
12. Murata, T.: Petri nets: properties, analysis and applications. Proc. IEEE **77**(4), 541–580 (1989). https://doi.org/10.1109/5.24143
13. OMG: Business Process Model and Notation (BPMN) Version 2.0, January 2011. http://www.omg.org/spec/BPMN/2.0/
14. Pyle, D.: Data Preparation for Data Mining, 1st edn. Morgan Kaufmann Publishers Inc., San Francisco (1999)
15. Rojas, E., Munoz-Gama, J., Sepúlveda, M., Capurro, D.: Process mining in healthcare: a literature review. J. Biomed. Inf. **61**, 224–236 (2016). https://doi.org/10.1016/j.jbi.2016.04.007, http://www.sciencedirect.com/science/article/pii/S1532046416300296
16. WHO: International classification of diseases (version 10), icd-10, www.who.int/classifications/icd/en/

Validity Frame Driven Computational Design Synthesis for Complex Cyber-Physical Systems

Bert Van Acker$^{(\boxtimes)}$ ⓘD, Yon Vanommeslaeghe$^{(\boxtimes)}$ ⓘD, Paul De Meulenaere$^{(\boxtimes)}$ ⓘD, and Joachim Denil$^{(\boxtimes)}$ ⓘD

2020 Antwerp, Belgium Flanders Make – AnSyMo/CoSys Core Lab,
University of Antwerp, Antwerp, Belgium
{Bert.VanAcker,Yon.Vanommeslaeghe,
Paul.Demeulenaere,Joachim.Denil}@uantwerpen.be
http://www.uantwerpen.be

Abstract. The increasing complexity and performance demands of cyber-physical systems (CPS) force the engineers to switch from traditional, well understood single-core embedded platform to complex multi-core or even heterogeneous embedded platforms. The deployment of a control algorithm on such advanced embedded platforms can affect the control behavior even more than on a single-core embedded platform. It is therefore key to reason about this deployment early within the design process. We propose the use of the Validity Frame concept as enabling technique within the Computational Design Synthesis (CDS) process to automatically generate design alternatives and to prune nonsensical alternatives, narrowing the design space and thus increasing efficiency. For each valid control algorithm alternative, the control behavior under deployment is examined using a custom simulator enabled by modeling the embedded platform and the application deployment explicitly. We demonstrate our approach in the context of a complex cyber-physical system: an advanced safety-critical control system for brushless DC motors.

Keywords: Validity Frame · Cyber-physical systems · Computational Design Synthesis · Hybrid simulation · Control embedded co-design · Domain-specific languages

1 Introduction

In the development of software-intensive systems, for example in the avionics and automotive domains, engineers need to cope with highly complex devices composed of different interacting and deeply intertwined components citech7Lee08. The development of these cyber-physical systems (CPS) is becoming increasingly complex, caused not only by the synergistic interaction between software and physical elements [6], but also by the vast demand for improved performance [4]. This pushes the boundaries of the available resources of the implementation platform, causing a shift from the traditional, well-understood single-core

ⓒ Springer Nature Switzerland AG 2020
Ö. Babur et al. (Eds.): ICSMM 2020, CCIS 1262, pp. 82–90, 2020.
https://doi.org/10.1007/978-3-030-58167-1_7

embedded platforms to multi-core or even heterogeneous[1] embedded platforms. Deployment of complex algorithms on these complex embedded platforms can be very challenging as a traditional, sequential design process becomes insufficient to ensure efficient deployment and integration due to the drastically expanded design space. In these situations, Computational Design Synthesis (CDS) can be used to find design alternatives, however this needs to be performed efficiently. By reasoning about the validity of the design alternatives, the design space can be narrowed by pruning invalid alternatives, thus increasing efficiency.

In this paper, we propose the use of the Validity Frame (VF) concept, which enables us to explicitly capture the validity range of the algorithm components, to increase the efficiency of the Computational Design Synthesis process. The VFs of the algorithm components are used to (i) automate the generation of control algorithm alternatives and (ii) to prune the nonsensical alternatives, thus narrowing the design space. A set of domain-specific languages is used to specify the deployment problem and is used as input for the CDS process.

Model-based design (MBD) helps to cope with the increasing complexity of cyber-physical systems. By building a model of the CPS and its environment, the system can be tested and simulated offline, enabling the verification of the system's functionality, assumptions about its interacting environment, and end-to-end behavior. The model-based verification of a CPS control algorithm is typically performed in different stages, namely *model-, software-, processor- and hardware-in-the-loop* (MiL, SiL, PiL and HiL). In such a process, the *functional and temporal behavior* of the system after deployment are generally verified at the later HiL stage, which is costly. By *front-loading* this verification to the earlier MiL or SiL stage, the design flexibility and verification efficiency increases. More specifically, the effort to explore and verify control architecture alternatives decreases by virtually deploying the control algorithm on a model of the embedded platform. As such, we focus on the verification of the *functional and temporal behavior* at the model level in this paper.

This paper is organized as follows: Sect. 2 shows the literature review. Section 3 discusses the basic concepts of the proposed framework. Section 4 shows the results of applying the framework to an academic safety-critical case study. Lastly, Sect. 5 summarizes the conclusions of the paper and defines future work.

2   Literature Review

In [8], they propose combining Contract-based Design (CBD) and Computational Design Synthesis (CDS) to automatically generate a range of design alternatives and automatically pruning nonsensical alternatives using the Assume/Guarantee (A/G) contracts. The use of A/G contracts is limited to pruning design alternatives at the system model level by means of interface consistency checking. We propose the use of the Validity Frame (VF) concept instead of the A/G contracts to further increase the performance of the CDS

---

[1] Embedded systems comprising multiple processing elements of fundamentally different types, e.g. embedded platform with a CPU and a FPGA.

process by extending the pruning mechanism e.g. taking the embedded deployment characteristics into account. The frames concept is not a novelty but has been around since the early 1980s when Zeigler [12] defined the original "experimental frames" idea. These experimental frames (EF) helped to document the meta-information necessary to execute the model itself. [10] formalized this EF concept and [9] showed the use within the model-based testing of simulation models. In [3], the authors observed that a model's frame depends on the activity that is performed and describes why different activities require different frames. They proposed the validity frame concept which defines the experimental context of a model in which that model gives predictable results. In [11], we made this Validity Frame concept tangible and showed a basic use case within the development of cyber-physical systems. This work extends the use of the Validity Frame concept by introducing it in the Verification and Validation process for narrowing the design space, by using the available VF meta-data of the system components, and by this, optimizing the V&V process.

3 Validity Frame Supported Computational Design Synthesis

This section introduces the integration of the Computational Design Synthesis and the Validity Frame concept to automatically explore design alternatives and prune nonsensical design alternatives. This limits the design space and by this the effort needed for further verification of the design alternatives. The proposed method consists of 3 main parts, which are discussed in detail in subsequent subsections.

3.1 Data Gathering

The first step is defining the input for the CDS process. As discussed before, we use an explicit model of (i) the application architecture, (ii) the embedded multi-core platform, and (iii) the mapping of the application architecture on the embedded platform. To allow modeling at the right level of abstraction, a domain-specific language is developed for each input model.

The first input for the CDS process is the *application architecture model* of the complex controller connected to its (controlling) environment. As the goal is to facilitate the design space exploration of possible application architectures comprising variants of the same component, we specify an **abstract application architecture**. An abstract application architecture comprises the *abstract application components*, with their corresponding VF, the *component interfaces* and identification of the *variables* passed between application components. The key feature of using VFs in this model is that the comprising application components can be adapted using component alternatives from the available model library. The usability of a component variant is assessed using the meta-data available within its corresponding VF.

The next input for the CDS process is the *platform architecture model*. The explicit modeling of an embedded platform can be very complex as it can be modeled on different abstraction levels, depending on the goal. This domain-specific language allows the engineer to model this platform architecture at the right level of abstraction, allowing to characterize the most essential influence factors of the multi-core embedded platform. The memory architecture is the most critical element which serves as input for the CDS process optimization.

The last input for the CDS process is the *task mapping model*, which is the glue between the application architecture and the platform architecture. It provides a way to (i) map the application elements onto one or more RTOS tasks, (ii) define the triggering mechanisms, e.g. time-triggered by providing the period, and (iii) specify a preferred processor core, if applicable, for each RTOS task.

3.2 CDS

With the *abstract application architecture*, the *platform architecture* and the *task mapping* defined, we can perform design space exploration of the possible integration variants. The DSE in the current implementation of the proposed methodology is focusing on the *application architecture variants*, introduced by changing component implementations within the application architecture.

Candidate Validation. A first step in the DSE process is **validation of application architecture candidates**. This is a necessary step to narrow the design space and by this, limiting the amount of conducted experiments, reducing the further verification effort. Validation of the application candidates comprises validity reasoning of (i) the interface between connected components and (ii) the estimated memory consumption of the combined components. This is enabled via the Validity Frame, containing all meta-information such as interface characteristics and memory consumption for each of the integrated components.

The memory usage estimation is a first method used to prune application architecture candidates based on their total memory footprint. If the estimated memory footprint is bigger than the total available memory on the embedded platform, derived from the explicit modeled embedded platform architecture, the application candidate is discarded.

For the validation of the interfaces between the components, we use the following meta-data available within the VF of each component, specifying the component interface:

- **Boundaries:** Definition of the *expected signal ranges*, for input ports and *guaranteed signal ranges*, for output ports of the component.
- **Unit:** Identification of the unit of measurement for in- and output ports of the component.
- **Datatype:** Identification of the datatype for in- and output ports of the component.

The validation of the unit and datatype of the interface signal is trivial, the validation of the matching boundaries not. Within the current version of the validation method, the boundaries are validated using the boundary validation scheme shown in Fig. 1.

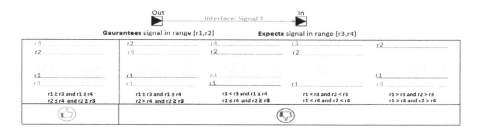

Fig. 1. Interface validation - boundary analysis

Using this boundary validation scheme, all interfaces between the application architecture candidate are validated. If one of the investigated interfaces is not matching, meaning that the guaranteed signal range is outside the expected signal range, the application candidate is discarded.

3.3   Simulator Generation

The next step in the proposed methodology is generating a simulator for each of the valid candidates to analyze both the *temporal and functional behavior* of these candidates. For the core of the simulator, we rely on a **DEVS simulator** to enable correct and generic simulations of the cross-domain simulations/evaluations. DEVS is a formalism for modelling discrete-event systems in a hierarchical and modular way, rooted in systems theory [5]. To enable heterogeneity within the simulation models, we propose the use of the proven **Functional Mock-up Interface (FMI) standard** [1]. This enables to *co-simulate* different models with their own solver in a co-simulation environment. This way, all components of the complex control system and its environment can be modeled on their correct level(s) of abstraction, using the most appropriate formalism(s) [7]. The conceptual overview of the simulator architecture is shown in Fig. 2.

As shown in Fig. 2, the explicit model of (i) the application architecture, (ii) the embedded multi-core platform, and (iii) the mapping of the application architecture on the embedded platform are used to either calibrate configurable DEVS models or to generate (partial) custom DEVS models, FMI simulation models, and/or DEVS-FMI interfaces. This custom DEVS simulation allows the execution of the application model as it would run on the embedded platform, allowing the verification of the temporal and functional behavior.

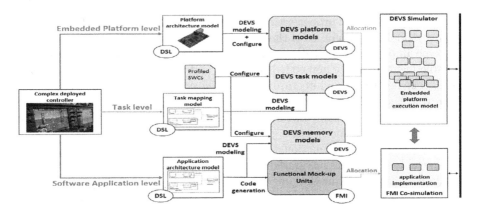

Fig. 2. Conceptual overview cross-domain DEVS simulator

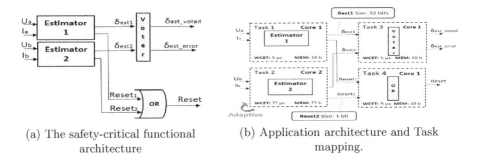

(a) The safety-critical functional
architecture

(b) Application architecture and Task
mapping.

Fig. 3. Safety-critical load-angle controller

4 Case Study

The proposed methodology is demonstrated on an advanced safety-critical control system for brushless DC motors [2].

4.1 Description

Based on the algorithm proposed by De Viaene et al. [2], the control algorithm controls the load angle, in a closed-loop, by varying the current amplitude. This load-angle controller consists of two parts, namely (i)a **monitoring** part that contains an estimator which estimated the actual load angle of the motor (δ_{est}) from measured phase voltages and currents (u and i respectively) and (ii) a **controlling** part that controls the load angle to follow the setpoint ($\delta_{setpoint}$) by changing the current setpoint of the motor driver ($I_{setpoint}$).

The monitoring part also contains a watchdog, monitoring the estimated load angle. This watchdog will overrule and reset the controller if the load angle becomes too large. For proper estimation of the actual load angle of the motor (δ_{est}), a model-of-the-physics of the controlled brushless DC motor is used. This has some important implications on the necessary computational power and available memory of the embedded platform, and the achievable control performance. The functional architecture of the BLDC controller is shown in Fig. 3 (a). To prevent the stall of the motor under all circumstances, some safety mechanisms are added to the controller architecture such as redundant monitoring and corresponding voting mechanism.

Within the proposed functional architecture, 2 estimator components, shown in yellow in Fig. 3 (a), are integrated. By measuring the phase voltage and current of different phases within the different estimators, respectively U_a, I_a and U_b, I_b, the integrity of the estimated load angle together with the availability of the reset signal can be increased.

This safety-architecture introduces overhead on the used embedded platform resources, such as computation time and memory consumption. A possible reduction technique is not using the same models-of-the-physics in both estimators. By using different models-of-the-physics, at different abstraction levels, important deployment metrics, such as Worst-Case Execution Time (WCET) and memory consumption, can be altered to enable deployment on constrained embedded platforms.

4.2   Design Space Exploration

To perform the CDS process as defined within Sect. 3, we need to explicitly model the application architecture, the task mapping, and the embedded platform. In Fig. 3 (b), the partial application architecture together with partial task mapping is shown. It shows that 4 application components, shown as black rectangles, are defined. For simplification of the case study, only one application component, Estimator 2, is variable/adaptive, indicated with the green arrow. The variables used for inter-component communication are shown as rounded rectangles. The task mapping is shown by means of a task, indicated with a dashed line, comprising the component or components it contains. The essential data is defined for each task, such as Worst-Case Execution Time (WCET) and Memory consumption (MEM).

The explicit model for the embedded platform does contain 2 ARM Cortex A9 processor cores with one DDR3 SDRAM shared memory and a dedicated scheduler for each processor core, with a priority-based scheduling mechanism. Note that this is modeled at a high abstraction level as in practice a memory architecture exists between the on-chip memory of each processor core and the shared memory. The timing of the read/write operation between these memory elements is very small and is therefore neglected.

Results. As mentioned before, we limited the design space by only considering one variable application element, namely Estimator 2. For Estimator 2, 5 different estimator models are available, ranging from computationally efficient

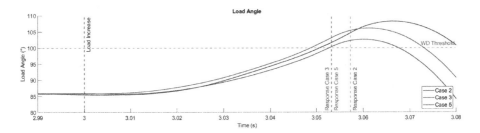

Fig. 4. Functional behavior comparison of valid candidates.

models with a big memory footprint to computationally inefficient models with a low memory footprint. This is caused by the different implementation details of the model-of-the-physics that can either be completely computed at run-time or implemented as some kind of lookup table. The validation step of the DSE process shows that only 3 variants are valid. Case 4 is invalid as there is an interface mismatch of the containing Estimator (upper-bound of the input range for I_b violated). The memory footprint of Case 1 is too big for the available memory on the embedded platform. In this case, Estimator 2 was implemented as a big look-up table, which is very memory inefficient. Cases 2, 3, and 5 are valid alternatives and for each case, a custom simulator is generated. The results of the functional behavior trace are shown in Fig. 4.

The results show the load angle of the motor (δ_{est}) and the watchdog (WD) activation for each of the cases. The performance of all cases is acceptable as the stall of the motor is prevented before the critical load angle is reached but the WD activation of case 2 kicks in slightly later, which is undesired. The behavior of case 3 and 5 is approximately equal. To select one over the other, extra performance criteria need to be assessed, e.g. energy efficiency. In this case, the proposed CDS process is proven to be very efficient as the evaluation of the control behavior performance under deployment using the custom simulator would take nearly 5 h to evaluate all design alternatives. By narrowing the design space, this is reduced to approximately 3 h, giving a 40% effort reduction.

5   Conclusions and Future Work

In this work, we presented a method of combining the Validity Frame concept with a Computational Design Synthesis (CDS) process. The Validity Frame concept is introduced as enabling technique to (i) explore design alternatives and (ii) enhanced the pruning mechanism by taking not only the validity of the application architecture into account but also the embedded deployment characteristics, such as memory footprint. Using explicit models of (i) the application architecture, (ii) the embedded platform architecture and (iii) the task mapping, a custom simulator for each valid design alternative can be generated, enabling the front-loading of the verification of the functional and temporal behavior of the deployed control algorithm. Using an academic safety-critical cyber-physical system, we demonstrated the proposed CDS process where the VF concept is used to explore the design space and prune the design alternatives.

In the future, we plan to extend the design space exploration algorithm to not only cope with variants in the application architecture, but also in the task mapping and/or the embedded platform architecture.

References

1. Blochwitz, T., et al.: Functional mockup interface 2.0: the standard for tool independent exchange of simulation models. In: Proceedings of the 9th International MODELICA Conference, 3–5 September 2012, Munich, Germany, pp. 173–184. No. 076, Linköping University Electronic Press (2012)
2. De Viaene, J., Verbelen, F., Derammelaere, S., Stockman, K.: Energy-efficient sensorless load angle control of a BLDC motor using sinusoidal currents. IET Electr. Power Appl. **12**(9), 1378–1389 (2018)
3. Denil, J., Klikovits, S., Mosterman, P.J., Vallecillo, A., Vangheluwe, H.: The experiment model and validity frame in m&s. In: Proceedings of the Symposium on Theory of Modeling & Simulation, pp. 1–12 (2017)
4. EMPHYSIS: Emphsis - embedded systems with physical models in the production code software, September 2017–August 2020 (2018). https://itea3.org/project/emphysis.html
5. Kim, T.G., Zeigler, B.P.: The devs formalism: hierarchical, modular systems specification in an object oriented framework. Technical report, Institute of Electrical and Electronics Engineers (IEEE) (1987)
6. Lee, E.A.: Cyber physical systems: design challenges. In: Smythe, R.N., Noble, A. (eds.) 2008 11th IEEE International Symposium on Object and Component-Oriented Real-Time Distributed Computing (ISORC), vol. 3, pp. 363–369. IEEE (2008). https://doi.org/10.1109/ISORC.2008.25. http://doi.ieeecomputersociety.org/10.1109/ISORC.2008.25
7. Mosterman, P.J., Vangheluwe, H.: Computer automated multi-paradigm modeling: an introduction. Simulation **80**(9), 433–450 (2004)
8. Ribeiro dos Santos, C.A., Hany Saleh, A., Schrijvers, T., Nicolai, M.: Condense: contract based design synthesis. In: 2019 ACM/IEEE 22nd International Conference on Model Driven Engineering Languages and Systems (MODELS), pp. 250–260 (2019)
9. Schmidt, A., Durak, U., Pawletta, T.: Model-based testing methodology using system entity structures for MATLAB/simulink models. Simulation **92**(8), 729–746 (2016). https://doi.org/10.1177/0037549716656791
10. Traore, M.K., Muzy, A.: Capturing the dual relationship between simulation models and their context. Simul. Model. Pract. Theory **14**(2), 126–142 (2006)
11. Van Acker, B., De Meulenaere, P., Denil, J., Durodie, Y., Van Bellinghen, A., Vanstechelman, K.: Valid (re-)use of models-of-the-physics in cyber-physical systems using validity frames. In: 2019 Spring Simulation Conference (SpringSim). pp. 1–12, April 2019. https://doi.org/10.23919/SpringSim.2019.8732858
12. Zeigler, B.P., Kim, T.G., Praehofer, H.: Theory of Modeling and Simulation. Academic Press, Cambridge (2000)

Industrial Plant Topology Models to Facilitate Automation Engineering

Heiko Koziolek[1]($\boxtimes$), Julius Rückert[1], and Andreas Berlet[2]

[1] ABB Corporate Research, Ladenburg, Germany
heiko.koziolek@de.abb.com
[2] Hochschule Pforzheim, Pforzheim, Germany

Abstract. Industrial plant topology models can potentially automate many automation engineering tasks that are today carried out manually. Information on plant topologies is today mostly available in informal CAD drawings, but not formal models that transformations could easily process. The upcoming DEXPI/ISO15926 standard may enable turning CAD drawings into such models, but was so far mainly used for data exchange. This paper proposes extensions to the CAYENNE method for control logic and process graphics generation to utilize DEXPI models and demonstrates the supported model transformation chain prototypically in two case studies involving industrial plants. The results indicate that the model expressiveness and mappings were adequate for the addressed use cases and the model processing could be executed in the range of minutes.

Keywords: Model-driven development · Model transformation · Industrial automation · Code generation · Graphics generation

1 Introduction

With the progressing digitalization, the use of models and related artifacts in the domain of industrial automation will increase significantly in the next few years [27]. Industrial automation enables complex production processes for chemicals, oil&gas, power, paper, steel, etc. Such production plants require careful planning of facilities, equipment, and devices, so that process engineers use CAD-tools to express their requirements and designs [11]. Industrial automation systems for such processes may include thousands of sensors (e.g., for temperature, level, flow, pressure) and actuators (e.g., valves, motors, pumps). Cost pressure requires engineers to find ways to make the engineering process more efficient.

Although process engineers already create lots of the required information using CAD-tools, they usually produce informal drawings (e.g., piping-and-instrumentation diagrams, P&ID) that are later subject to manual interpretation by automation engineers. While this approach offers flexibility, the involved

---

Electronic supplementary material The online version of this chapter (https://doi.org/10.1007/978-3-030-58167-1_8) contains supplementary material, which is available to authorized users.

© Springer Nature Switzerland AG 2020
O. Babur et al. (Eds.): ICSMM 2020, CCIS 1262, pp. 91–108, 2020.
https://doi.org/10.1007/978-3-030-58167-1_8

media discontinuities may lead to misinterpretations, create overhead for re-entering information into engineering tools, and often cause costly feedback communication loops between process engineers and automation engineers [2].

Industrial plant topology models are formal representations of the structure of a processing plant including the required automation equipment [29]. The scientific community has demonstrated a range of use cases for industrial topology models [2]. For example, model transformations can map industrial plant topology models to simulation libraries [3], which creates low-fidelity plant simulators for factory acceptance tests and plant operator training. Plant topology models can be queried to perform root cause analyses of anomalies during plant operation [29]. Almost all of these approaches utilized topology models in the CAEX (IEC 62424) XML format, which still lacks commercial tool support from CAD-tool vendors today[1]. The alternative DEXPI[2] XML standard based on ISO15926 is however in the process of being supported by all major CAD tool vendors (e.g., Autodesk, Hexagon, Siemens) and thus may become a key enabler for creating and exchanging industrial plant topology models.

In this paper, we introduce an extension to the CAYENNE method for topology engineering [16] to support DEXPI-based topology models. CAYENNE can already synthesize interlocking IEC 61131-3 control logic from topology models as well as process graphics and simulation models. The contributions of this paper are 1) a DEXPI importer enabling the CAYENNE use cases directly for topology models created with commercial CAD tools, 2) a Cause-and-Effect visualization of interlocking logic, 3) two case studies, where the entire model processing chain is demonstrated as a proof-of-concept, and 4) a survey on use cases for industrial plant topology models, as well as methods for obtaining them.

The two case studies illustrate the approach on a small example (minimal plant based on 1 P&ID) and a larger example (commercial plant based on 10 P&IDs). The cases studies showed that the mappings were sufficient to support the desired use cases. The performance in both cases was acceptable, since the model processing lasted only a few minutes. While principle feasibility has been shown in this paper with one of the first tool chains utilizing DEXPI plant topology models for automation engineering, more case studies and tool refinements are needed to transfer the concepts into a commercial tooling.

The remainder of this paper is structured as follows: Sect. 2 provides a definition of plant topology models and a survey of use cases. Section 3 describes the CAYENNE method and models in five simple steps. Section 4 reports the results of the two cases studies, before Sect. 5 characterizes future challenges. Section 6 concludes the paper.

---

[1] https://www.automationml.org/o.red.c/tools.html.

[2] https://dexpi.org.

2   Plant Topology Models

2.1   Definition

A plant topology model is a special object-oriented model that captures industrial plant equipment (e.g., tanks, mixers, centrifuges), process automation
instruments (e.g., sensor, actuators), and their dependencies (e.g., pipes, information connectors, electrical connections). Figure 4 shows the simplified abstract
syntax of such a model (not showing attributes or dependencies), while Fig. 1
shows a visualization (i.e., concrete syntax) of a sample topology model instance
as a P&ID. Figure 1 for example includes a tank (column shape labeled 'T4750'),
two pumps (circles labelled 'P4711' and 'P4712'), two heat exchangers (rectan-
gular shapes labelled 'H1007' and 'H1008'), as well as sensors (green circles),
valves (butterfly shapes), pipes (straight, directed lines) and information flows
(dashed lines).

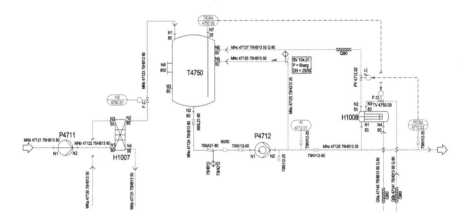

Fig. 1. DEXPI Reference Example as sample topology model (Source: https://bit.ly/
2UkWT89). (Color figure online)

Process engineers today draw P&IDs using CAD tools (e.g., AutoCAD) that
are usually used for other types of diagrams as well. Thus, the diagrams are
persisted as drawings of graphical shapes (e.g., lines, circles, rectangles, labels,
etc.), but not as object-oriented topology models carrying semantic information. As the shapes often show subtle differences between CAD tools or are even
custom-drawn for a specific plant, it is not trivial to map them to a generic
topology model for further processing. The AutoCAD DWG file format is the
de-facto standard for storing such files and supported by many drawing tools.
However, the drawings are usually exchanged as PDF files with included vector-
ized or rasterized versions of the drawing. In some cases, the drawings are only
exchanged as print-outs on paper. They are then subject to manual interpretation by automation engineers, who plan the plant automation.

Plant topology models are more formal models based on domain-specific concepts instead of generic drawing concepts. If P&IDs were available according an object-oriented topology model carrying semantic information, algorithms could easily process them to realize a number of use cases automating various plant engineering tasks that are today executed manually. It is however conceivable to alter CAD tools to export P&IDs as topology models instead of only drawings. Therefore process engineers and software developers are working on common topology model standards that could additionally enable model exchange between CAD tools of different vendors.

2.2 Use Cases and Related Work

Researchers and practitioners have proposed a number of use cases for plant topology models [2]. Figure 2 shows a use case diagram with the involved actors.

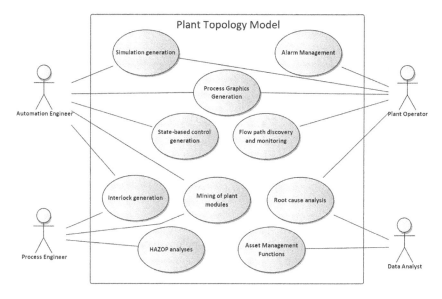

Fig. 2. Use cases for plant topology models: the models can be used both during engineering and operation of a plant by different actors.

We briefly describe these use cases in the following and reference respective literature. All of these use cases utilize the explicit dependencies between plant equipment and automation instruments encoded in topology models as 'pipes' or 'information flows'.

- **Interlock generation** [8, 16, 22, 23]: interlocking control logic makes two elements in a plant mutually dependent on each other (e.g., open a valve in case of a high pressure event). This logic is executed by automation controllers and

today often handcrafted by process engineers [15]. Many interlocks can however be derived by analyzing a plant topology model using domain-specific
rules.

- **Generation of state-based control** [5]: state-based control refers to
  sequentially specified control logic, often used for batch processes. The order
  of vessels and equipment encoded in a plant topology model can for example
  be used to automatically generate start-up or shutdown sequences.
- **Mining of plant modules** [12,14]: Modular automation engineering suggests to compose automation systems from higher-level building blocks (i.e.,
  modules, e.g., a mixing module or a temperation module), instead of individual sensors, actuators, and controllers. Monolithically designed plant specifications based on P&IDs can be automatically mined for such modular building blocks in order to enable reuse of engineering knowledge.
- **Root Cause analysis for plant disturbances** [1,4,25,29]: users can query
  plant topology models to identify root causes for plant anomalies. With a
  topology model the flow paths can be exploited to speed up data analytics.
- **HAZOP analyses** [9]: a hazard and operability study is a systematic exam-
  ination of a process in order to identify potential risks for equipment or
  humans. Using a rule-based approach involving a topology model, repetitive
  tasks in such a study can be automated.
- **Simulation generation** [2,3]: topology model elements can be mapped to
  object types in simulation frameworks (e.g. Modelica), to generate low-fidelity
  plant simulations to be used in factory acceptance tests.
- **Flow path discovery and monitoring** [10,17]: all possible flow paths in
  a plant area can be derived from a topology model. Flow path monitoring
  can then utilize these flow paths for early detection of leaks and unintended
  product mixtures.
- **Process graphics generation** [16,21,26]: human machine interfaces for
  process automation systems often provide operators schematic process visualizations based on P&IDs overlayed with current, live-updating sensor data.
  While automation engineers mostly handcraft such visualizations today, they
  can be generated automatically to a large extent from plant topology models.
- **Alarm Management** [19]: cascades of alarm messages in an industrial plant
  may overload human operators. Therefore plant topology models have been
  used to limit the effects of 'alarm floods' using a set of rules derived from the
  alarm history of a plant.
- **Asset Management Functions** [20]: in order to conduct predictive and
  preventive maintenance of automation equipment, the method of 'overlapping
  field device monitoring' has been proposed to detect deteriorating automation
  equipment early. The information required for this method, e.g., overlapping
  flow and pressure sensors on the same vessel, can be derived from a plant
  topology model.

Most of these use cases have so far been implemented only prototypically
in academia and research labs and not become part of commercial products.
The lack of readily available topology models in today's engineering practices

has created a hurdle for the implementation of these use cases that must be overcome in order to make them commercially viable. Additional use cases for plant topology models may be developed in future research.

2.3   Concrete Topology Models

Several meta-models to capture plant topologies have been developed. Having an industry-wide standard supported by CAD tool vendors and automation suppliers could significantly aid implementing the use cases sketched earlier.

CAEX: The Computer Aided Engineering eXchange (CAEX) format is in development for more than 15 years and became the IEC 62424 standard, of which the latest revision was released in 2018. It is embedded as an integral part of AutomationML (IEC 62714) [7]. CAEX is an XML-format defined by automation providers and customers as the least common denominator between different engineering tool file formats. It includes abstract concepts, such as InstanceHierarchy, InternalElement, InternalLink, RoleClass, SystemUnitClass, which can be augmented with additional semantics using role class libraries. IEC 62424:2018 provides definitions of process equipment (PCE) requests as a role class library, which can be used to assign concrete P&ID semantics (e.g., flow sensor, motor) to generic CAEX elements. More details for modelling PCE requests have be collected by the NAMUR container [24] developed by GMA 6.16. In 2018, a CAEX-based data exchange for System control Diagrams (IEC PAS 63131) was implemented for Siemens Comos P&ID to derive logic information from a P&ID-like representation [6].

DEXPI: The Data Exchange in the Process Industry (DEXPI) working group of DECHEMA (German platform for chemical engineering) is creating a common P&ID exchange XML format for more than eight years. While the DEXPI model was originally not intended for the use cases sketched in the previous subsection, it can nevertheless be considered as a generic plant topology model. The DEXPI information model is based on Proteus Schema 4.0.1 and shall cover graphics, topology, and attributes. The current DEXPI Specification Version 1.2 contains more than 160 classes referring to concrete elements, such as a rotary pump, check valve, or signal generating function. Major P&ID CAD-tool vendors including Autodesk, Aveva, Bentley Systems, Intergraph, and Siemens are developing DEXPI importers and exporters, which are frequently tested for interoperability in DEXPI hackathons. Large chemical companies including BASF, Bayer, Covestro, Equinor, Evonik, and Merck are actively involved in the DEXPI development.

Researchers have also used specialized topology models often heavily optimized for certain use cases. For example, Bauer and Thornhill [4] used simple adjacency matrices to express topological and timing dependencies between automation equipment. OntoCape [18] is an ontology for chemical process engineering that captures topological information. Gruener and Epple [10] encoded P&ID information into the graph database Neo4J and executed Cypher graph queries for flow path discovery. Arroyo et al. [2] defined a simplified topology model as a separate semantic for CAEX serialization. This was later enhanced by Koziolek et al. [16] for interlock generation and is also used in this paper for process graphics generation.

Topology models could be connected to other models to enable more use cases [28].

2.4   Obtaining Topology Models

Creating topology models is not explicitly foreseen in classical engineering processes, which largely rely on comparably informal drawings, besides tabular and prose textual specifications. However, different methods for obtaining topology models already exist:

- **Export from CAD tool:** while dedicated software to create topology models is conceivable, it seems more efficient to simply equip existing CAD tools with capabilities to create topology models from drawing data and keep existing processes intact. For example, SmartPlant PID already provides a DEXPI exporter, while AutoCAD Plant 3D, Aveva PID, and COMOS PID are currently being extended by their vendors with DEXPI importers and exporters. COMOS PID can additionally serialize system component diagrams (SCD) to CAEX [6]. Using such exporters may require adhering to certain conventions and only using pre-defined shapes for which a mapping to the topology model is specified. Therefore, designers who classically produced drawings within limited constraints may need additional training or validation tools to create valid topology models.
- **Extract with Image Recognition:** for existing, operational plants, the initial P&ID specifications may only be available on paper or as an electronical drawing lacking semantic clearness. Researchers have proposed to perform optical symbol recognition on rasterized bitmaps of these diagrams to reverse engineer topology models [2,14]. The company Bilfinger offers a commercial service called PIDGRAPH[3] to turn bitmap-based P&IDs into DEXPI topology models. There is limited empirical data available how well such an image recognition procedure works, especially considering cluttered and nonstandard legacy P&IDs often seen in real-world projects. The baseline for such approaches is creating the topology models manually from scratch by simply redrawing them in a CAD tool equipped with a topology model exporter.
- **Infer from Automation System:** in case an automation system is already available for an operational industrial plant, simple topology models can for example be derived from operator process graphics [13], which usually provide a coarse-grained representation of the plant topology. Other elements of the automation system, e.g., the control logic or device configurations, could additionally be used as information sources for a topology model.

In most cases, the method to choose is dictated by the project context, e.g., if a greenfield or brownfield scenario needs to be addressed or what kind of artifacts

---

[3] https://digitalnext-bilfinger.com/solutions/pidgraph.

are already available. The CAYENNE method described in the following relies on extracting topology models from a CAD tool.

3   CAYENNE Method and Models

The CAYENNE method [16] is centered around a specific topology model and supports the use cases of interlock generation and process graphics generation. It consists of five steps and includes multiple models and model transformations, as explained in the following.

Step 1: Create P&ID. In step 1, a process engineer uses a CAD tool to draw a P&ID, which captures the plant structure and the requirements for automation (e.g., sensors, actuators, controllers). This step is not special for the CAYENNE method, and can be considered as a prerequisite for the later model processing. Figure 3 shows our running example modeled with AutoCAD Plant 3D 2020. Other CAD tools could be used as well.

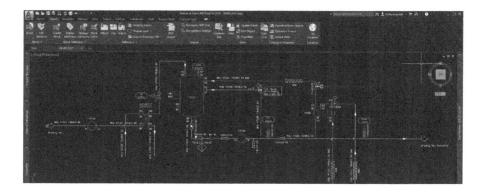

Fig. 3. DEXPI reference example in AutoCAD Plant 3D

Step 2: Export P&ID to DEXPI Format. The process engineer exports the P&ID drawing from the proprietary drawing format of the CAD tool into an object-oriented topology model format. Typically, a pre-defined mapping exists from the CAD tool vendor, so that this step runs completely automated. Some tools allow a customization of the mapping, for example the AutoCAD Mapping Editor. The process engineer must ensure that custom drawings are correctly mapped to the DEXPI topology model, e.g., by defining according shapes and adding them in the mapping customization.

Step 3: Map DEXPI Model to CAYENNE Topology Model. CAYENNE features a custom-built topology model, intentionally streamlined for certain use cases (Fig. 4). This model focuses on the domain concepts and strips away much of the drawing-related information in a DEXPI topology model, thereby lowering complexity for the implementation of model processing tools. In CAYENNE this model is implemented as a C#-object model that can be serialized to CAEX. These CAEX XML files can be used by other engineering tools providing respective importers in order to utilize topological information.

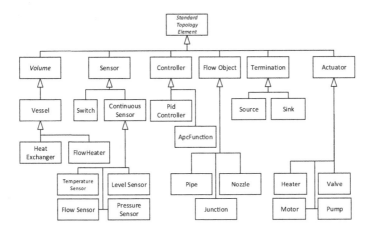

Fig. 4. CAYENNE metamodel of plant topologies for simulation, code generation, and process graphics generation [16] (simplified view)

In order to map DEXPI topology models to CAYENNE topology models, the CAYENNE DEXPI importer allows users to link individual DEXPI classes to CAYENNE topology classes. As there are 1-to-n and m-to-1 mappings needed for certain classes, the DEXPI importer provides special mechanisms. For example, for a 'sensor' there is only one class in DEXPI (ProcessInstrumentationFunction), and the type of sensor is an attribute of this class. The CAYENNE topology model instead has a dedicated class for each sensor type (e.g., flow sensor, pressure sensor). In this case the importer reads out the attribute of ProcessInstrumentationFunction and adds each type of sensor as a separate entry into the mapping table, so that the user can map it to the respective CAYENNE topology class (Fig. 5).

Step 4: Rule-Based Interlock Generation. CAYENNE includes a rule engine that can apply domain-specific rules on imported topology models in order to generate interlocking control logic. An interlock links two topology elements together to implement a plant saftey mechanism. Hundreds to thousands of interlocks are required for an industrial plant. Consider the following simple example for the DEXPI Reference Example, formulated in the custom syntax of the CAYENNE rule engine:

```
1  Vessel.AlarmTemperatureHigh
2  -> Vessel/Pipe/*/HeatExchanger
3  => HeatExchanger.Stop
```

DEXPI Classes	CAYENNE Classes
Equipment (GeneralServicePump)	Pump
Equipment (Tank)	Vessel
Nozzle (FlangedNozzle)	Nozzle
Equipment (Chamber)	Vessel
Equipment (HeatExchanger)	HeatExchanger
CenterLine	Pipe
PipingComponent (GateValve)	Valve
PipingComponent (BallValve)	Valve
PipingComponent (VolumetricFlowMetering)	FlowSensor
PipingComponent (PipeTee)	Junction
ProcessInstrumentationFunction(LAH)	LevelSensor
ProcessInstrumentationFunction(LAL)	LevelSensor
...	

DEXPI Class	DEXPI Attribute	CAYENNE Class	CAYENNE Attribute
Equipment	TagNameAssignmentClass	Vessel	_TagName
Equipment\Tank	NominalCapacity	Vessel	n/a
Equipment\Tank	CylinderLength	Vessel	n/a
Equipment\Chamber	n/a	Vessel	_AtmosphericTypeOpen
Equipment\Chamber	n/a	Vessel	_LevelStart
Equipment\Chamber	Height	Vessel	_Height
Equipment\Chamber	InsideDiameter	Vessel	_Diameter
Equipment\Chamber	Width	Vessel	n/a
Equipment\Chamber	LowerLimitDesignPressure	Vessel	n/a
Equipment\Chamber	UpperLimitDesignPressure	Vessel	n/a
Equipment\Chamber	ChamberFunctionAssingment	Vessel	n/a
Equipment\Chamber	ChamberFunctionSpecializatio	Vessel	n/a
...	...	...	...

Fig. 5. Exemplary model mapping between DEXPI and CAYENNE topology model: class mapping (left-hand side) and attribute mapping for one class (tank, right-hand side)

The rule engine interprets this rule as follows: it first (line 1) identifies all vessels in the topology model, and filters them for vessels with a connected temperature sensor and a specified alarm level. Then (line 2) it traverses the topology model starting from the vessel and searches for a pipe on an outlet. Afterwards the wildcard operator ("*") directs to rule engine to follow the material flow and search for a heat exchanger. Once such a heat exchanger is found, the alarm signal of the temperature sensor is linked to the stop signal of the heat exchanger to prevent overheating in the vessel. For the DEXPI reference example (Fig. 1), the rule above would be instantiated for temperature sensor TICSA4750.03 (max temperature 100°) and heat exchanger H1008, which is connected to vessel T4750.

The CAYENNE code generator can either directly synthesize IEC 61131-3 control logic for this interlock (as in [16]), or create an interactive Cause-and-Effect (C&E) Matrix that lists causing elements (e.g., temperature sensor TICSA4750.03) in lines and effecting elements (e.g., heat exchanger H1008) in columns. The cell where the causing and effecting elements cross is marked with a cross if an interlock is generated. This representation of interlocks is often used by process engineers, because it is streamlined and allows quick manual reviews. The CAYENNE C&E matrix generation was newly created in the context of this paper. Generated control logic can be imported into a control engineering tool and later be deployed to an automation controller. More than 90 interlocking rules have been defined for the CAYENNE rule engine so far [16]. Some of them are generic and can be applied in almost any plant, others are more domain-specific and describe certain patterns of specific production processes.

Step 5: Mapping to Process Graphics. Additionally, the CAYENNE process graphics generator can map topology models to industrial process graphics used as human machine interface for plant operators. Normally, these graphics are crafted by automation engineers by interpreting P&IDs. The CAYENNE generator partially automates this process by mapping topology model elements to corresponding process graphics shapes, while preserving their graphical positions and thus the rough layout from the P&ID. The output of this step is a generated process graphic, that an automation engineer can enhance and complete in a HMI engineering tool. This procedure could be improved in the future to let the engineer (de-)select certain topology elements not desired in the process graphics, and by implementing domain-specific layouting algorithms. An example for a generated process graphic will be shown in the next section.

4   Case Studies

We report on two case studies to evaluate the CAYENNE method and models. Koziolek et al. [16] executed four additional case studies focusing on other aspects.

4.1   Case 1: FESTO MPS PA Compact-Workstation

The goal of the first case study was to test the basic concepts of the CAYENNE method including the newly developed DEXPI importer for the CAYENNE topology model. We selected the FESTO Modular Production Station Process Automation Compact-Workstation as test case. It is a minimal production plant developed for training courses and universities. This case includes two tanks, four types of sensors (level, flow, pressure, temperature), a centrifugal pump, a PLC, and a controllable ball valve besides several manual valves.

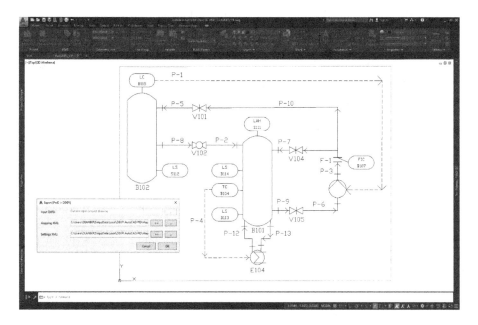

Fig. 6. P&I Diagram of the FESTO MPS PA Compact-Workstation modeled with AutoCAD Plant 3D. The user can configure the DEXPI exporter to map the AutoCAD shapes to specific DEXPI elements.

Referring to **Step 1** of the CAYENNE method sketched in the previous section, we drew a P&ID of the system in AutoCAD Plant 3D 2020 (Fig. 6) using ISO shapes. The structure of this P&ID was derived from the user manuals of the FESTO MPS PA. In **Step 2**, we exported the drawing into a DEXPI XML file according to the Proteus schema version 4.0.1 using a pre-release version of the AutoCAD DEXPI Exporter, kindly provided by Autodesk. We only required a few minor additions on top of a pre-specified AutoCAD-to-DEXPI mapping, e.g., adding a heat exchanger for the FESTO MPS PA case. The resulting DEXPI XML file's size was 350 KByte and it spanned 6600 lines. The file contains a significant amount of drawing-related information, since the intention of the DEXPI standard is to allow exchanging P&IDs between different tools while preserving the graphical representation. Our resulting file contained four DEXPI 'equipments' (2 tanks, 1 heat exchanger, 1 pump) and 11 DEXPI 'piping network segments'.

In **Step 3**, we mapped the DEXPI model to the CAYENNE Topology Model, by importing the DEXPI XML file with the CAYENNE DEXPI importer. The case required to map 15 DEXPI classes to corresponding Topology Model classes. The importer implicitly maps class attributes if possible. The resulting Topology Model can be serialized to a CAEX XML file, which was 215 KByte large in this case, already roughly indicating the amount of information stripped away from the original DEXPI file. It contained 128 CAEX 'InternalElements' and 60 CAEX 'InternalLinks'.

Using this topology model we generated interlocking control logic in **Step 4** according to the method described by Koziolek et al. [16]. This required applying several generic interlocking rules by traversing the topology model. Table 1 exemplary shows three applied interlocking rules, how they were instantiated by the CAYENNE rule engine for this case, and what IEC 61131-3 Structured Text was generated as control logic. A control engineer can feed this code in to a control engineering tool and extend and enhance it with additionally required logic. Here, as a example, the third rule in Table 1 requires stopping a heat exchanger when the temperature in a vessel gets too high and raises an alarm. The rule engine instantiated this rule for vessel B101 and temperature sensor B104. In this case the traversal was simple and only required to navigate from B101 via pipe P-12 to the heat-exchanger E104. The generated Structured Text links the concrete heat exchanger stop signal with the alarm signal of the temperature sensor.

Finally, in **Step 5** we generated process graphics. Figure 7 shows the output of the CAYENNE process graphics generator, in the format for ABB's 800xA System. Vessel, pump, and heat exchanger have been mapped to the corresponding visual shapes in the system's engineering library. The generator preserved their coordinates and sizes from the original topology model, by mapping the topology model's coordinate system to the process graphic's coordinate system. For pipes, a whole chain of coordinates needs to be transferred to preserve the original layout. Analog indicators and valves are mapped to the corresponding function blocks of the system's engineering library, which then enables access

Table 1. Rule-based interlock generation for the FESTO MPS PA Compact-Workstation: the CAYENNE rule engine instantiates generic interlocking rules for the equipment of the case study and generates IEC 61131-3 Structured Text to implement the corresponding interlock.

Interlocking Rule	Case Study Interlocking Rule Instantiation	Generated 61131-3 Structured Text
Pipe.AlarmFlowLow -> Pipe\Pump => Pump.Stop	Pipe(P-3).FlowSensor(B107) -> Pipe(P-3)\Pump(P101) => Pump(P101).Stop	B107.ALARM_FLOW_Low := B107.limit < 10; P101.Stop := B107.ALARM_FLOW_LOW;
Vessel.AlarmLevelHigh -> Vessel\Pipe\Valve => Valve.Close	Vessel(B102).LevelSensor(B115) -> Vessel(B102)\Pipe(P-5)\Valve(V101) => Valve(V101).Close	B115.ALARM_LEVEL_HIGH := B115.limit > 90; V101.Close := B115.ALARM_LEVEL_HIGH;
	Vessel(B101).LevelSensor(B114) -> Vessel(B101)\Pipe(P-7)\Valve(V104) => Valve(V104).Close	B114.ALARM_LEVEL_HIGH := B114.limit > 90; V104.Close := B114.ALARM_LEVEL_HIGH;
	Vessel(B101).LevelSensor(B114) -> Vessel(B101)\Pipe(P-2)\Valve(V102) => Valve(V102).Close	B114.ALARM_LEVEL_HIGH := B114.limit > 90; V102.Close := B114.ALARM_LEVEL_HIGH;
Vessel.AlarmTemperatureHigh -> Vessel/Pipe/HeatExchanger => HeatExchanger.Stop	Vessel(B101).TemperatureSensor(B104) -> Vessel(B101)\Pipe(P-12)\HeatExchanger(E104) => HeatExchanger(E104).Stop	B104.ALARM_TEMPERATURE_HIGH := B104.limit > 70; E104.Stop := B104.ALARM_TEMPERATURE_HIGH;

to faceplates and to display live updating values. An HMI engineer can import this generated process graphic into a display engineering tool, which may save significant engineering time compared to starting from scratch.

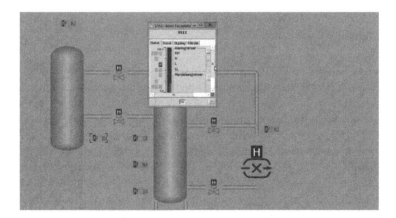

Fig. 7. Interactive process graphic generated from topology model for the FESTO MPS PA Compact-Workstation: the layout of the original P&ID was preserved by mapping the shape coordinates accordingly. A plant operator can interact with the system via the process graphic.

4.2   Case 2: Commercial Chemical Plant

For the second case, we studied a larger plant specification, to achieve a higher coverage of topology model elements, to test the correct linking of multiple P&IDs (using off-page references), and to check the performance and scalability of our model processing importers and rule engines. We selected a segment of a chemical plant from South America, which included approximately 1000 IO signals.

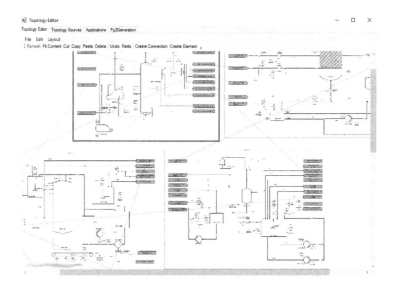

Fig. 8. Screenshot CAYENNE topology editor: excerpt of the chemical plant topology model imported from Microsoft Visio

In **Step 1** we got 10 P&IDs for this plant segment, which were drawn using Microsoft Visio P&ID stencils and included 18 different vessels and 9 pumps besides numerous valves connected via a complex piping network (more than 220 connectors including pipes and information flows). As MS Visio does not provide a DEXPI exporter, we omitted **Step 2** and directly used the CAYENNE Visio Importer in **Step 3**. Figure 8 shows an excerpt of the topology model spanning multiple connected P&IDs in the CAYENNE topology editor. The import required mapping 47 different Visio Types to corresponding CAYENNE Topology Model elements. The resulting importer topology model contained 1731 CAEX 'Internal Elements' and 830 CAEX 'Internal Links' and had a total file size of 2.5 MBytes. The import took below 1 min for the entire model.

After the validity of the model was assured manually through visual inspection via the Topology editor, we generated control logic in **Step 4**. More than 25 interlocking rules applied for this plant segment and the rule engine generated more than 100 interlocks. Table 2 shows an excerpt of the generated interlocking logic, visualized as a C&E matrix for brevity. Existing code generator can process such matrices and generate corresponding IEC 61131-3 code.

Due to topology's complexity that results in elaborated model traversals, the application of specific rules took several minutes. For some interlocks, the rule engine had to traverse multiple P&IDs via off-page references, therefore validating the correct implementation of this functionality. The overall performance of

Table 2. Sample Cause-and-Effect Matrix with generated interlocks using rules for the chemical plant. The entire matrix includes more than 100 generated interlocks. These tables can be used for generating control logic code.

the control logic generation was deemed satisfactory. However, even larger models may warrant more performance optimizations of the tool chain, e.g., mapping the topology models to efficient graph data structures, pre-processing the models to store links of indirectly connected elements, or by further caching traversal data. For this case we do not show process graphics generation (**Step 5**).

5   Future Challenges

This paper has demonstrated how to automate specific automation engineering tasks based on plant topology models. There are a number of open future challenges:

- **Standardized topology models:** although the DEXPI XML specification has been released, it is still not fully defined and requires further refinements. It is complex with more than 160 classes, hindering rapid implementation. It is optimized for the use case of data exchange between CAD tools aiming at a faithful graphical redrawing of P&ID shapes between different vendors. Additional use case-specific abstractions as in the CAYENNE method may be needed.
- **Improved tool support:** process engineers need additional support to create topology models, e.g., guidelines on how to use CAD tools to created valid DEXPI models or validators and test routines to analyze created drawings. This rather practical challenge needs to be addressed by tool vendors.
- **Mining repositories of topology models:** Having many topology models in standardized formats would enable mining useful patterns and best practices from them. A large number of models (e.g., based on thousands of P&IDs) could even make the use of machine learning techniques on such models viable. However, while such an approach may be theoretically interesting, in practice it is limited by the amount of data that can be realistically assembled in one repository due to data protection and intellectual property concerns.

- **Linking topology models with other models:** there are lots of opportunities to combine topology models with other models (e.g., building architecture models, runtime models, kinematics models, statistical models). This could enable a new range of use cases. Models could also be combined with unstructured data, e.g., video feeds, audio logs, free text, etc. to provide analytics software the required context for predictive maintenance or plant optimization.
- **Enhancing existing use cases:** each of the use cases sketched in Sect. 2 includes its own challenges and offers vast potential for conceptual contributions. Interlock generation needs domain-specific interlocking rules. The limits for deriving state-based control from topology models are unclear. Plant modules can be mined in principle, but this has been shown only on small examples so far. Root cause analysis of plant anomalies needs to be supported by efficient query mechanisms. Process graphics generation could benefit from smart element selection and auto-layouting.
- **Empirical studies on reverse engineering topology models:** obtaining topology models from P&ID images has been demonstrated in the lab so far, but it remains unproven whether it would be a cost-efficient measure in case of realistic, large-scale plants with cluttered diagrams as input. More experiences in this direction could improve commercial viability.

6   Conclusions

This paper described how industrial plant topology models could automate several engineering tasks. Specifically, it introduced an extension to the CAYENNE method for control logic and process graphics generation that allows utilizing DEXPI/ISO15926 topology models as input. Generated control logic can be visualized as a C&E matrix supporting existing work processes of process engineers and allowing quick manual reviews. Two case studies demonstrated the concepts prototypically in two different settings.

Practitioners get evidence that the small overhead for creating topology models via CAD-tools may be justified. They can focus on maturing existing standards, implementing them in their modeling tools, and instructing process engineers how to correctly use topology models. Researchers can derive a state-of-the-art review on topology models from this paper and investigate fruitful conceptual contributions for the sketched use cases further. CAYENNE shows that custom topology models can support tool development, which could be explored further in the future.

As future work, we plan to carry out additional case studies to evaluate and refine the CAYENNE approach. The DEXPI importer can be tested with different CAD tools as input providers. We also aim at working out further concepts for utilizing topology models for root cause analysis in anomaly situations during plant runtime.

References

1. Arroyo, E., Fay, A., Chioua, M., Hoernicke, M.: Integrating plant and process information as a basis for automated plant diagnosis tasks. In: Proceedings of the 2014 IEEE Emerging Technology and Factory Automation (ETFA), pp. 1–8. IEEE (2014)
2. Arroyo, E., Hoernicke, M., Rodríguez, P., Fay, A.: Automatic derivation of qualitative plant simulation models from legacy piping and instrumentation diagrams. Comput. Chem. Eng. **92**, 112–132 (2016)
3. Barth, M., Fay, A.: Automated generation of simulation models for control code tests. Control Eng. Pract. **21**(2), 218–230 (2013)
4. Bauer, M., Thornhill, N.F.: A practical method for identifying the propagation path of plant-wide disturbances. J. Process Control **18**(7–8), 707–719 (2008)
5. Bloch, H., et al.: State-based control of process services within modular process plants. Procedia CIRP **72**, 1088–1093 (2018)
6. Drath, R., Ingebrigtsen, I.: Digitalization of the IEC PAS 63131 Standard with AutomationML. In: 2018 IEEE 23rd International Conference on Emerging Technologies and Factory Automation (ETFA), vol. 1, pp. 901–909, September 2018. https://doi.org/10.1109/ETFA.2018.8502458
7. Drath, R.: Datenaustausch in der Anlagenplanung mit AutomationML: Integration von CAEX, PLCopen XML und COLLADA. Springer, Heidelberg (2009)
8. Drath, R., Fay, A., Schmidberger, T.: Computer-aided design and implementation of interlock control code. In: IEEE Conference on Computer Aided Control System Design, pp. 2653–2658. IEEE (2006)
9. Fay, A., Schmidberger, T., Scherf, T.: Knowledge-based support of HAZOP studies using a CAEX plant model. Inside Funct. Saf. **2009**(2), 5–15 (2009)
10. Grüner, S., Weber, P., Epple, U.: Rule-based engineering using declarative graph database queries. In: 2014 12th IEEE International Conference on Industrial Informatics (INDIN), pp. 274–279. IEEE (2014)
11. Gutermuth, G.: Engineering. In: Collaborative Process Automation Systems, pp. 156–182. ISA (2010)
12. Hahn, A., Hensel, S., Hoernicke, M., Urbas, L.: Concept for the detection of virtual functional modules in existing plant topologies. In: 2016 IEEE 14th International Conference on Industrial Informatics (INDIN), pp. 820–825. IEEE (2016)
13. Hoernicke, M., Fay, A., Barth, M.: Virtual plants for brown-field projects. In: 2015 IEEE 20th Conference on Emerging Technologies & Factory Automation (ETFA), pp. 1–8. IEEE (2015)
14. Koltun, G., Kolter, M., Vogel-Heuser, B.: Automated generation of modular PLC control software from P&ID diagrams in process industry. In: 2018 IEEE International Systems Engineering Symposium (ISSE), pp. 1–8. IEEE (2018)
15. Koziolek, H., Burger, A., Platenius-Mohr, M., Jetley, R.: A classification framework for automated control code generation in industrial automation. J. Syst. Softw. (JSS) (2020, To appear)
16. Koziolek, H., et al.: Rule-based code generation in industrial automation: four large-scale case studies applying the CAYENNE method. In: Proceedings of 42nd International Conference on Software Engineering (ICSE 2020). Software Engineering in Practice TRack (SEIP) (2020)
17. Krausser, T., Quirós, G., Epple, U.: An IEC-61131-based rule system for integrated automation engineering: concept and case study. In: 2011 9th IEEE International Conference on Industrial Informatics, pp. 539–544. IEEE (2011)

18. Morbach, J., Yang, A., Marquardt, W.: Ontocape-a large-scale ontology for chemical process engineering. Eng. Appl. Artif. Intell. **20**(2), 147–161 (2007)
19. Schleburg, M., Christiansen, L., Thornhill, N.F., Fay, A.: A combined analysis of plant connectivity and alarm logs to reduce the number of alerts in an automation system. J. Process Control **23**(6), 839–851 (2013)
20. Schmidberger, T., Horch, A., Fay, A., Drath, R., Breitenecker, F., Troch, I.: Rule based engineering of asset management system functionality. In: 5th Vienna Symposium on Mathematical Modelling, vol. 8 (2006)
21. Schmitz, S., Epple, U.: Automated engineering of human machine interfaces. In: VDI/VDE Gesellschaft Mess-und Automatisierungstechnik, pp. 127–138 (2007)
22. Steinegger, M., Melik-Merkumians, M., Schitter, G.: Ontology-based framework for the generation of interlock code with redundancy elimination. In: Proceedings of 22nd IEEE International Conference on Emerging Technologies and Factory Automation (ETFA), pp. 1–5. IEEE (2017)
23. Steinegger, M., Zoitl, A.: Automated code generation for programmable logic controllers based on knowledge acquisition from engineering artifacts: concept and case study. In: Proceedings of 2012 IEEE 17th International Conference on Emerging Technologies & Factory Automation (ETFA 2012), pp. 1–8. IEEE (2012)
24. Tauchnitz, T.: Schnittstellen für das integrierte engineering. ATP Mag. **56**(01–02), 30–36 (2014)
25. Thambirajah, J., Benabbas, L., Bauer, M., Thornhill, N.F.: Cause-and-effect analysis in chemical processes utilizing xml, plant connectivity and quantitative process history. Comput. Chem. Eng. **33**(2), 503–512 (2009)
26. Urbas, L., Doherr, F.: autoHMI: a model driven software engineering approach for HMIS in process industries. In: 2011 IEEE International Conference on Computer Science and Automation Engineering, vol. 3, pp. 627–631. IEEE (2011)
27. Vogel-Heuser, B., Fay, A., Schaefer, I., Tichy, M.: Evolution of software in automated production systems: challenges and research directions. J. Syst. Softw. **110**, 54–84 (2015)
28. Wiedau, M., von Wedel, L., Temmen, H., Welke, R., Papakonstantinou, N.: Enpro data integration: extending DEXPI towards the asset lifecycle. Chem. Ing. Tech. **91**(3), 240–255 (2019)
29. Yim, S.Y., Ananthakumar, H.G., Benabbas, L., Horch, A., Drath, R., Thornhill, N.F.: Using process topology in plant-wide control loop performance assessment. Comput. Chem. Eng. **31**(2), 86–99 (2006)

Methods, Techniques and Tools

On the Replicability of Experimental Tool Evaluations in Model-Based Development

Lessons Learnt from a Systematic Literature Review Focusing on MATLAB/Simulink

Alexander Boll$^{(\boxtimes)}$ and Timo Kehrer$^{(\boxtimes)}$

Department of Computer Science,
Humboldt-Universität zu Berlin, Berlin, Germany
`{boll,kehrer}@informatik.hu-berlin.de`

Abstract. Research on novel tools for model-based development differs from a mere engineering task by providing some form of evidence that a tool is effective. This is typically achieved by experimental evaluations. Following principles of good scientific practice, both the tool and the models used in the experiments should be made available along with a paper. We investigate to which degree these basic prerequisites for the replicability of experimental results are met by recent research reporting on novel methods, techniques, or algorithms supporting model-based development using MATLAB/Simulink. Our results from a systematic literature review are rather unsatisfactory. In a nutshell, we found that only 31% of the tools and 22% of the models used as experimental subjects are accessible. Given that both artifacts are needed for a replication study, only 9% of the tool evaluations presented in the examined papers can be classified to be replicable in principle. Given that tools are still being listed among the major obstacles of a more widespread adoption of model-based principles in practice, we see this as an alarming signal. While we are convinced that this can only be achieved as a community effort, this paper is meant to serve as starting point for discussion, based on the lessons learnt from our study.

Keywords: Model-based development · Tools · MATLAB/Simulink · Experimental evaluation · FAIR principles · Replicability

1 Introduction

Model-based development [6,46] is a much appraised and promising methodology to tackle the complexity of modern software-intensive systems, notably for embedded systems in various domains such as transportation, telecommunications, or industrial automation [30]. It promotes the use of models in all stages of

---

This work has been supported by the German Ministry of Research and Education (BMBF) under grant 01IS18091B in terms of the research project *SimuComp*.

O. Babur et al. (Eds.): ICSMM 2020, CCIS 1262, pp. 111–130, 2020.
https://doi.org/10.1007/978-3-030-58167-1_9

development as a central means for abstraction and starting point for automation, e.g., for the sake of simulation, analysis or software production, with the ultimate goal of increasing productivity and quality.

Consequently, model-based development strongly depends on good tool support to fully realize its manifold promises [13]. Research on model-based development often reports on novel methods and techniques for model management and processing which are typically embodied in a tool. In addition to theoretical and conceptual foundations, some form of evidence is required concerning the effectiveness of these tools, which typically demands an experimental evaluation [40]. In turn, to ensure scientific progress in general, experimental results should be transparent and replicable. Therefore, both the tool and the experimental subject data, essentially the models used in the experiments, should be made available following the so-called FAIR principles—Findability, Accessibility, Interoperability, and Reusability [28,48].

In this paper, we investigate to which degree these principles of good scientific practice are actually adopted by current research on tools for model-based development of embedded systems. We focus on tools for MATLAB/Simulink, which has emerged as a de-facto standard for automatic control and digital signal processing. In particular, we strive to answer the following research questions:

RQ1: Are the experimental results of evaluating tools supporting model-based development with MATLAB/Simulink replicable in principle?

RQ2: From where do researchers acquire MATLAB/Simulink models for the sake of experimentation?

We conduct a systematic literature review in order to compile a list of relevant papers from which we extract and synthesize the data to answer these research questions. Starting from an initial set of 942 papers that matched our search queries on the digital libraries of IEEE, ACM, ScienceDirect and dblp, we identified 65 papers which report on the development and evaluation of a tool supporting MATLAB/Simulink, and for which we did an in-depth investigation. Details of our research methodology, including the search process, paper selection and data extraction, are presented in Sect. 2.

In a nutshell, we found that models used as experimental subjects and prototypical implementations of the presented tools, both of which are essential for replicating experimental results, are accessible for only a minor fraction (namely 22% and 31%) of the investigated papers (RQ1). The models come from a variety of sources, e.g., from other research papers, industry partners of the paper's authors, open source projects, or examples provided along with MATLAB/Simulink or any of its toolboxes. Interestingly, the smallest fraction of models (only 3%) is obtained from open source projects, and the largest one (about 18%) is provided by industrial partners (RQ2). While we think that, in general, the usage of industrial models strengthens the validity of experimental results, such models are often not publicly available due to confidentiality agreements. Our findings are confirmed by other research papers which we investigated during our study. Our detailed results are presented in detail in Sect. 3.

While we do not claim our results to represent a complete image of how researchers adopt the FAIR principles of good scientific practice in our field of interest (see Sect. 4 for a discussion of major threats to validity), we see them as an alarming signal. Given that tools are still being listed among the major obstacles of a more widespread adoption of model-based principles in practice [47], we need to overcome this "replicability problem" in order to make scientific progress. We are strongly convinced that this can only be achieved as a community effort. The discussion in Sect. 5 is meant to serve as a starting point for this, primarily based on the lessons learnt from our study. Finally, we review related work in Sect. 6, and Sect. 7 concludes the paper.

2 Research Methodology

We conduct a systematic literature review in order to compile a list of relevant papers from which we extract the data to answer our research questions RQ1 and RQ2. Our research methodology is based on the basic principles described by Kitchenham [24]. Details of our search process and research paper selection are described in Sect. 2.1. Section 2.2 is dedicated to our data extraction policy, structured along a refinement of our overall research questions RQ1 and RQ2, respectively.

2.1 Search Process and Research Paper Selection

Scope. We focus on research papers in the context of model-based development that report on the development of novel methods, techniques or algorithms for managing or processing MATLAB/Simulink models. Ultimately, we require that these contributions are prototypically implemented within a tool whose effectiveness has been evaluated in some form of experimental validation. Tools we consider to fall into our scope are supporting typical tasks in model-based development, such as code generation [38] or model transformation [26], clone detection [43], test generation [31] and priorization [32], model checking [33] and validation [36], model slicing [15] and fault detection [23]. On the contrary, we ignore model-based solutions using MATLAB/Simulink for solving a specific problem in a particular domain, such as solar panel array positioning [35], motor control [34], or wind turbine design [14].

Databases and Search Strings. As illustrated in Fig. 2, we used the digital libraries of *ACM*,[1] *IEEE*,[2] *ScienceDirect*,[3] and *dblp*[4] to obtain an initial selection of research papers for our study. These platforms are highly relevant in the field of model-based development and were used in systematic literature reviews on

---

[1] https://dl.acm.org.

[2] https://ieeexplore.ieee.org/Xplore/home.jsp.

[3] https://www.sciencedirect.com.

[4] https://dblp.uni-trier.de.

IEEE: ("Abstract":Simulink OR "Abstract":Stateflow) AND ("Abstract":model) AND ("Abstract":evaluat* OR "Abstract":experiment* OR "Abstract":"case study") AND ("Abstract":tool OR "Abstract":program OR "Abstract":algorithm)

ACM: [[Abstract: simulink] OR [Abstract: stateflow]] AND [[Abstract: evaluat*] OR [Abstract: experiment*] OR [Abstract: "case study"]] AND [[Abstract: tool] OR [Abstract: program] OR [Abstract: algorithm]] AND [Abstract: model]

ScienceDirect: (Simulink OR Stateflow) AND (evaluation OR evaluate OR experiment OR "case study") AND (tool OR program OR algorithm)

dblp: (Simulink | Stateflow) (model (tool | program | algorithm | method))

Fig. 1. Digital libraries and corresponding search strings used to obtain an initial selection of research papers.

model-based development like [37] or [12]. By using these four different digital libraries, we are confident to capture a good snapshot of relevant papers.

According to the scope of our study, we developed the search strings shown in Fig. 1. We use IEEE's and ACM's search feature to select publications based on keywords in their abstracts. Some of the keywords are abbreviated using the wildcard symbol ($\star$). Since the wildcard symbol is not supported by the query engine of ScienceDirect [16], we slightly adapted these search strings for querying ScienceDirect. The same applies to dblp [16], where we also included the keyword "method" to obtain more results. To compile a contemporary and timely representation of research papers, we filtered all papers by publication date and keep those that were published between January 1st, 2015 and February 24th, 2020. With these settings, we found 625 papers on IEEE, 88 on ACM, 214 on ScienceDirect[5] and 15 on dblp.

Using the bibliography reference manager JabRef,[6] these 942 papers were first screened for clones. Then, we sorted the remaining entries alphabetically and deleted all duplicates sharing the same title. As illustrated in Fig. 2, 912 papers remained after the elimination of duplicates.

Inclusion and Exclusion Criteria. From this point onwards, the study was performed by two researchers, referred to R1 and R2 in the remainder of this paper (cf. Fig. 2).

Of the 912 papers (all written in English), R1 and R2 read title and abstract to see whether they fall into our scope. Both researchers had to agree on a paper being in scope in order to include it. R1 and R2 classified 92 papers to be in scope, with an inter-rater reliability, measured in terms of Cohen's kappa

---

[5] ScienceDirect presented an initial selection of 217 papers on their web interface, out of which 214 could be downloaded.

[6] https://www.jabref.org.

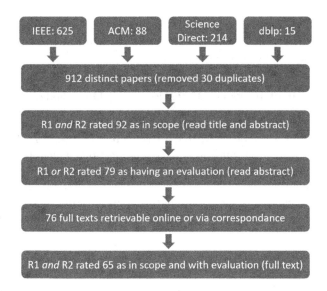

Fig. 2. Overview of the search process and research paper selection. Numbers of included research papers are shown for each step. After the initial query results obtained from the digital libraries of *ACM*, *IEEE*, *ScienceDirect* and *dblp*, the study has been performed by two researchers, referred to as R1 and R2.

coefficient [11,24], at 0.86. To foster a consistent handling, R1 and R2 classified the first 20 papers together in a joint session, and reviewed differences after 200 papers again.

Next, R1 and R2 read the abstracts and checked whether a paper mentions some form of evaluation of a presented tool. Because such hints may be only briefly mentioned in the abstract, we included papers where either R1 and R2 gave a positive vote. As a result of this step, the researchers identified 79 papers to be in scope *and* with some kind of evaluation.

We then excluded all papers for which we could not obtain the full text. Our university's subscription and the social networking site ResearchGate[7] could provide us with 45 full text papers. In addition, we found 5 papers on personal pages and obtained 28 papers in personal correspondence. We did not manage to get the full text of 3 papers in one way or the other. In sum, 76 papers remained after this step.

Finally, we read the full text to find out whether there was indeed an evaluation, as indicated in the abstract, and whether MATLAB/Simulink models were used in that evaluation. We excluded 10 full papers without such an evaluation and one short paper which we considered to be too unclear about their evaluation. For this last step R1 and R2 resolved all differences in classification: concerning papers were read a second time, to decide together about their inclusion or exclusion. We did this so that R1 and R2 could work with one consistent

---

[7] https://www.researchgate.net.

set for the data extraction. After all inclusion and exclusion steps, R1 and R2 collected 65 papers which were to be analyzed in detail in order to extract the data for answering our research questions.

2.2 Refinement of Research Questions and Data Extraction

In order to answer our research questions, R1 and R2 extracted data from the full text of all the 65 papers selected in the previous step. To that end, we refined our overall research questions into sub-questions which are supposed to be answered in a straightforward manner, typically by a classification into "yes", "no", or "unsure". After the first 20 papers have been investigated by researchers R1 and R2, they compared their different answers in order to clarify potential misunderstandings in the phrasing of the questions and/or the interpretation of the papers' contents.

RQ1: Are the Experimental Results of Evaluating Tools Supporting Model-Based Development with MATLAB/Simulink Replicable in Principle?

Accessibility of the Models. We assume that the effectiveness of a tool supporting model-based development can only be evaluated using concrete models serving as experimental subjects. These subjects, in turn, are a necessary precondition for replicating experimental results. They should be accessible as a digital artifact for further inspection. In terms of MATLAB/Simulink, this means that a model should be provided as a *.mdl or *.slx file. Models that are only depicted in the paper may be incomplete, e.g., due to parameters that are not shown in the main view of MATLAB/Simulink, sub-systems which are not shown in the paper, etc.

The aim of RQ1.1 is to assess if a paper comprises a hint on the accessibility of the models used for the sake of evaluation:

RQ1.1: Does the paper describe whether the models are accessible?

To answer this question for a given paper, we read the evaluation section of the paper, and also looked at footnotes, the bibliography as well as at the very start and end of the paper. In addition, we did a full text search for the keywords "download", "available", "http" and "www.". Please note that, for this question, we are only looking for a general statement on the accessibility of models. That is, if a paper states that the models used for evaluation cannot be provided due to, e.g., confidentiality agreements, we nonetheless answer the question with "yes".

On the contrary, a positive answer to RQ1.2 not only requires some statement about accessibility, but it requires that the models indeed *are* accessible:

RQ1.2: Are all models accessible?

The accessibility of models can only be checked if the paper includes a general statements on this. Thus, we did not inspect those papers for which RQ1.1 has been answered by "no" or "unsure". For all other papers, a positive answer to RQ1.2 requires that each of the models used in the paper's evaluation falls into one of the following categories:

– There is a non-broken hyperlink to an online resource where the MAT-LAB/Simulink model file can be obtained from.
– There is a known model suite or benchmark comprising the model, such as the example models provided by MATLAB/Simulink. In this case, the concrete model name and version of the files or suite must also be mentioned.
– The model is taken from another, referenced research paper. In this case, we assume it to be accessible without checking the original paper.

Accessibility of the Tool. Next to the models, the actual tool being presented in the research paper typically serves as the second input to replicate the experimental results. In some cases, however, we expect that the benefits of a tool can be shown "theoretically", i.e., without any need for actually executing the tool. To that end, before dealing with accessibility issues, we assess this general need in RQ1.3:

RQ1.3: Is the tool needed for the evaluation?

We read the evaluation section to understand whether there is the need to execute the tool in order to emulate the paper's evaluation. For those papers for which RQ1.3 is answered by "yes", we continue with RQ1.4 and RQ1.5.

Similar to our investigation of the accessibility of models, we first assess if a paper comprises a hint on the accessibility of the presented tool:

RQ1.4: Does the paper describe whether the tool is accessible?

In contrast to the accessibility of models, which we assume to be described mostly in the evaluation section, we expect that statements on the accessibility of a tool being presented in a given research paper may be spread across the entire paper. This means that the information could be "hidden" anywhere in the paper, without us being able to find it in a screening process. To decrease oversights, we did full text searches, for the key words "download", "available", "http" and "www.". If a tool was named in the paper, we also did full text searches for its name.

The actual check for accessibility is addressed by RQ1.5:

RQ1.5: Is the tool accessible?

A tool was deemed accessible if a non-broken link to some download option was provided. If third-party tools are being required, we expected some reference on where they can be obtained. On the contrary, we considered MATLAB/Simulink or any of its toolboxes as pre-installed and thus accessible by default.

RQ2: From Where Do Researchers Acquire MATLAB/Simulink Models for the Sake of Experimentation?

Next to the accessibility of models, we are interested in where the researchers acquire MATLAB/Simulink models for the sake of experimentation. In order to learn more about the context of a model or to get an updated version, it may be useful to contact the model creator, which motivates RQ2.1:

RQ2.1: Are all model creators mentioned in the paper?

By the term "creator" we not necessarily mean an individual person. Instead, we consider model creation on a more abstract level, which means that a model creator could also be a company which is named in a paper or any other referenced research paper. If creators of all models were named, we answered RQ2.1 with "yes".

Next to the model creator, RQ2.2 dives more deeply into investigating a model's origin:

RQ2.2: From where are the models obtained?

RQ2.2 is the only research question which cannot be answered by our usual "yes/no/unsure scheme". Possible answers were "researchers designed model themselves"*, "generator algorithm", "mutator algorithm", "industry partner"*, "open source", "other research paper"*, "MATLAB/Simulink-standard example"*, "multiple" and "unknown". The categories marked with a * were also used in [12]. As opposed to us, they also used the category "none", which we did not have to consider, due to our previous exclusion steps. The category "multiple" was used whenever two or more of these domains were used in one paper. Note that even if RQ2.1 was answered with "no", we may still be able to answer this question. For example, if the model was acquired from a company which is not named in the paper (e.g. due to a non-disclosure agreement), we may still be able to classify it as from an industry partner.

3   Results

In this section, we synthesize the results of our study. All paper references found, raw data extracted and calculations of results synthesized can be found in the replication package of this paper [5]. The package includes all the MATLAB/Simulink models we found during our study.

3.1   Are the Experimental Results of Evaluating Tools Supporting Model-Based Development with MATLAB/Simulink Replicable in Principle? (RQ1)

In this section, we first summarize the results for the research questions RQ1.1 through RQ1.5 (see Fig. 3 for an overview), before we draw our conclusions for answering the overall research question RQ1.

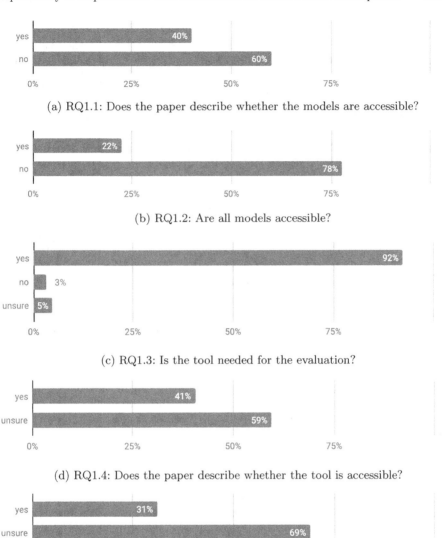

(a) RQ1.1: Does the paper describe whether the models are accessible?

(b) RQ1.2: Are all models accessible?

(c) RQ1.3: Is the tool needed for the evaluation?

(d) RQ1.4: Does the paper describe whether the tool is accessible?

(e) RQ1.5: Is the tool accessible?

Fig. 3. Overview of the results for research questions RQ1.1 through RQ1.5. Percentage values are representing the average of the answers of researchers R1 and R2.

RQ1.1: *Does the paper describe whether the models are accessible?* On average, 26 (R1: 25, R2: 27) of the 65 papers for which we did a detailed analysis include a hint on whether the models used as experimental subjects are accessible (see Fig. 3a). For this question, researchers R1 and R2 achieve an inter-rater reliability of 0.62, measured in terms of Cohen's kappa coefficient.

RQ1.2: *Are all models accessible?* As for the actual accessibility, on average, 14.5 (R1: 13, R2: 16) of the papers including descriptions on the availability of models indeed gave access to all models (see Fig. 3b). The results have been achieved with an inter-rater reliability of 0.78. One paper includes a broken link [50], and we were not able to find the claimed web resources of 4 papers.

RQ1.3: *Is the tool needed for the evaluation?* Of all the 65 papers, on average, 60 (R1: 62, R2: 58) require their developed tool to be executed for the sake of evaluation. While the tool evaluations for 2 of the papers clearly do not rely on an actual execution of the tool (R1: 2, R2: 2), we were unsure in some of the cases (R1: 1, R2: 5), see Fig. 3c. Cohen's kappa is at 0.58 for this question. As for RQ1.4 and RQ1.5, we analyze the 58 papers for which both R1 and R2 gave a positive answer to this question.

RQ1.4: *Does the paper describe whether the tool is accessible?* We initially answered this question with average values of 23.5 (R1: 26, R2: 21), 11.5 (R1: 19, R2: 4) and 23 (R1: 13, R2: 33) regarding the possible answers of "yes", "no" and "unsure", respectively. This reflects a rather poor inter-rater reliability of 0.38. However, our observation was that it is almost impossible to be sure that there is *no* description of a tool's accessibility, since it could be "hidden" in multiple places. We thus revised our answers and merged the "no" and "unsure" categories to become "unsure". With the merged categories, 34.5 (R1: 32, R2: 37) of the papers were listed as "unsure" (see Fig. 3d), and a kappa of 0.61.

RQ1.5: *Is the tool accessible?* Similarly to RQ1.4, we initially ended up in a poor inter-rater reliability of 0.42 for classifying the accessibility of 18 (R1: 19, R2: 17), 17 (R1 26, R2 8) and 23 (R1 13, R2 33) as "yes", "no" and "unsure", respectively. Again, we revised the answers, merging the categories "no" and "unsure", as in RQ1.4. Finally, we got average values of 18 (R1: 19, R2: 17) "yes" and 40 (R1: 39, R2: 41) "unsure" (see Fig. 3e), with a kappa of 0.68.

Aggregation of the Results. To answer RQ1, we combine RQ1.2 and the revised answers of RQ1.5. For those papers where there was no tool needed (RQ1.3), RQ1.5 was classified as "yes". The formula we used is "If RQ1.2 = 'no' then 'no' else RQ1.5". This way, on average, 6 (R1: 5, R2: 7) papers have been classified as replicable, 50.5 (R1: 52, R2: 49) as not replicable, and 8.5 (R1: 8, R2: 9) for which we were unsure (see Fig. 4), with Cohen's kappa of 0.67. In sum, 8 papers were classified to be replicable by at least one of the researchers.

However, we have to stress here that being replicable *in principle* does not imply that the results of the paper are in fact replicable. In fact, the accessibility of models and tools used in the evaluation is only a necessary but not a sufficient condition for replicability. We did not try to install or run the tools according to the experimental setups described in the papers.

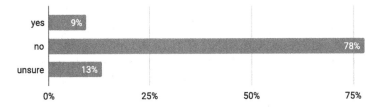

Fig. 4. RQ 1: Are studies of model-based development replicable in principle?

RQ 1: Are studies of model-based development replicable in principle?
We found 9% of the examined papers to be replicable in principle. For 78%, either the tool or the models used as experimental subjects were not accessible, and were not able to determine the principle replicability of 13% as we were unsure about the accessibility of tools.

3.2 From Where Do Researchers Acquire MATLAB/Simulink Models for the Sake of Experimentation? (RQ2)

RQ 2.1 Are all model creators mentioned in the paper? As can be seen in Fig. 5, Of the 65 papers investigated in detail, on average, 44 (R1: 43, R2: 45) papers mention the creators of all models. On the contrary, no such information could be found for an average of 20.5 (R1 22, R2 19) papers. Finally, there was one paper for which R2 was not sure, leading to an average value of 0.5 (R1: 0, R2: 1) for this category. In sum, this question was answered with an inter-rater reliability of 0.79.

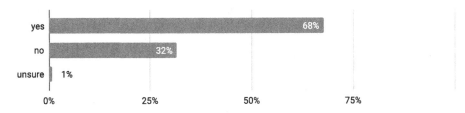

Fig. 5. RQ 2.1: Are all model creators mentioned in the paper?

RQ 2.2 From where are the models obtained? As shown in Fig. 6, there is some variety for the model's origins. Only 3% used open source models, 8% used models included in MATLAB/Simulink or one of its toolboxes, 12% cited other papers, 13% built their own models, and 18% obtained models from industry partners. A quarter of all papers used models coming from two or more different sources. For 19% of the papers, we could not figure out where the models come from. This mostly coincides with those papers where we answered "no" in RQ2.1. For some papers, we were able to classify RQ2.2, even though we answered RQ2.1 with "no". E.g. we classified the origin of a model of [18] as "industry partner" based on the statement "a real-world electrical engine control system of a hybrid car", even though no specific information about this partner was given. RQ2.2 was answered with Cohen's kappa of 0.68.

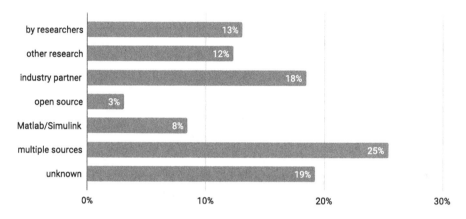

Fig. 6. RQ 2.2: From where are the models obtained?

An interesting yet partially expected perspective arises from combining RQ2.2 and RQ1.2. None of the models obtained from an "industry partner" are accessible. Three papers which we classified as "multiple" in RQ2.2 did provide industrial models though: [33] provides models from a "major aerospace and defense company" (name not revealed due to a non-disclosure agreement), while [1] and [2] use an open source model of electro-mechanical braking provided by Bosch in [44]. Finally, [3] and [27] use models for an advanced driver assistance system by Daimler [4], that can be inspected on the project website.[8]

> **RQ 2: From where do researchers acquire MATLAB/Simulink models for the sake of experimentation?**
> A wide variety of sources is used. 25% used multiple sources, another 25% used models of their own or from other researchers, 18% used models by an industry partner. 8% used models of MATLAB/Simulink or a toolbox and only 3% used open source models. We could not determine 19% of the models' origins.

---

[8] https://www.se-rwth.de/materials/cncviewscasestudy.

4   Threats to Validity

There are several reasons why the results of this study may not be representative, the major threats to validity as well as our countermeasures to mitigate these threats are discussed in the remainder of this section.

Our initial paper selection is based on selected databases and search strings. The initial query result may not include all the papers being relevant w.r.t. our scope. We tried to remedy this threat by using four different yet well-known digital libraries, which is sufficient according to [25] and [41] and using wild-carded and broad keywords in the search string.

For the first two inclusion/exclusion steps, we only considered titles and abstracts of the papers. If papers do not describe their topic and evaluation here, they could have been missed.

It turned out to be more difficult than originally expected to find out whether a paper provides a replication package or not. One reason for this is that just scanning the full text of a paper for occurrences of MATLAB/Simulink or the name of the tool is not very useful here since there are dozens of matches scattered all over the paper. In fact, almost every sentence could "hide" a valuable piece of information. We tried to remedy this problem by searching the *.pdf files for the key words mentioned in Sect. 2.2. We also merged our answers of "no" and "unsure" for RQ1.4 and RQ1.5 in reflection of this problem.

More generally, the data collection process was done by two researchers, each of which may have overlooked important information or misinterpreted a concrete research question. We tried to mitigate these issues through intermediate discussions. Furthermore, we calculated Cohen's kappa coefficient to better estimate the reliability of our extracted data and synthesized results.

Our methodology section does not present a separate quality assessment which is typical in systematic literature review studies [42]. Thus, our results could be different if only a subset of high quality papers, e.g. those published in the most prestigious publication outlets, would be considered. Nonetheless, a rudimentary quality assessment (paper's language, experimental evaluation instead of "blatant assertion" [40]) was done in our inclusion/exclusion process.

In this study, we focused on the accessibility of models and tools for replicating findings. Another critical part of replicating results, is the concrete experimentation setup. We did not analyze this aspect, here. Thus the number of studies deemed replicable may even be overestimated.

5   Discussion

Limited Accessibility of Both Models and Tools. Although generally accepted, the FAIR guiding principles of good scientific practice are hardly adopted by current research on tools for model-based development with MATLAB/Simulink. From the 65 papers which have been selected for an in-depth investigation in our systematic literature review, we found that only 22% of the models and 31% of the tools required for replicating experimental results are accessible. Thus, future research that builds on published results, such as larger user or field studies, studies comparing their results with established results, etc., are hardly possible, which ultimately limits scientific progress in general.

Open Source Mindset Rarely Adopted. One general problem is that the open source mindset seems to be rarely adopted in the context of model-based development. Only 3% of the papers considered by our study obtained all of their models from open source projects. On the contrary, 18% of the studied papers obtain the models used as experimental subjects from industry partners, the accessibility of these models is severely limited by confidentiality agreements.

Selected Remarks from Other Papers. These quantitative findings are also confirmed by several authors of the papers we investigated during out study. We noticed a number of remarks w.r.t. the availability of MATLAB/Simulink models for evaluation purposes. Statements like "To the best of our knowledge, there are no open benchmarks based on real implementation models. We have been provided with two implementation models developed by industry. However, the details of these models cannot be open." [45]; "Crucial to our main study, we planned to work on real industrial data (this is an obstacle for most studies due to proprietary intellectual property concerns)." [3]; "[...] most public domain Stateflows are small examples created for the purpose of training and are not representative of the models developed in industry." [19]; or "Such benchmarking suites are currently unavailable [...] and do not adequately relate to real world models of interest in industrial applications." [36] discuss the problem of obtaining real-world yet freely accessible models from industry. Other statements such as "[...] as most of Simulink models [...] either lack open resources or contain a small-scale of blocks." [20] or "[...] no study of existing Simulink models is available [...]." [7,8] discuss the lack of accessible MATLAB/Simulink models in general.

Reflection of Our Own Eexperience. In addition, the findings reflect our own experience when developing several research prototypes supporting model management tasks, e.g., in terms of the SiDiff/SiLift project [21,22]. Likewise, we made similar observations in the SimuComp project. Companies want to save the intellectual property and do not want their (unobfuscated) models to be published.

As opposed to the lack of availability of models, we do not have any reasonable explanation for the limited accessibility of tools. Most of the tools presented in research papers are not meant to be integrated into productive development environments directly, but they merely serve as experimental research prototypes which should not be affected by confidentiality agreements or license restrictions.

Suggestions Based on the Lessons Learnt from Our Study. While the aforementioned problems are largely a matter of fact and can not be changed in a short-term perspective, we believe that researchers could do a much better job in sharing their experimental subjects. Interestingly, 12% of the studies obtain their experimental subjects from other papers, and 13% of the papers state that such models have been created by the authors themselves. Making these models accessible is largely a matter of providing adequate descriptions.

However, such descriptions are not always easy to find within the research papers which we considered in our study. Often, we could not find online resources for models or software and had to rate them as "unsure" or "no" in RQ1.2 and RQ1.4. It should be made clear where to find replication packages. In some cases a link to the project's website was provided, but we couldn't find the models there. To prevent this, we suggest direct links downloadable files or very prominent links on the website. The web resource's language should match the paper's language: e.g., the project site of [49] is in German. Four papers referenced pages that did not exist anymore, e.g., a private Dropbox[9] account. These issues can be easily addressed by a more thorough archiving of a paper's replication package.

We also suggest to name or cite creators of the models, so they can be contacted for a current version or context data of the model. In this respect, the results of our study are rather promising. After all, model creators have been mentioned in 68% of the studied papers, even if the models themselves were not accessible for a considerable amount of these cases.

Towards Larger Collections of MATLAB/Simulink Models. Our study not only reveals the severity of the problem, it may also be considered as a source for getting information about publicly available models and tools. We provide all digital artifacts that were produced in this work (.bibtex files of all papers found, exported spread sheets and retrieved models or paper references) online for download at [5]. Altogether we downloaded 517 MATLAB/Simulink models. We also found 32 referenced papers where models were drawn from. These models could be used by other researchers in their evaluation. Further initiatives of providing a corpus of publicly available models, including a recent collection of MATLAB/Simulink models, will be discussed in the next section.

6   Related Work

The only related secondary study we are aware of has been conducted by Elberzhager et al. [12] in 2013. They conducted a systematic mapping study in which they analyzed papers about quality assurance of MATLAB/Simulink models. This is a sub-scope of our inclusion criteria, see Sect. 2.1. One research question of them was "How are the approaches evaluated?". They reviewed where the models in an evaluation come from and categorized them into "industry example", "Matlab example", "own example", "literature example" and "none". We include more categories, see Sect. 2.2, apart from "none". All papers that would fall in their "none"-category were excluded by us beforehand. Compared to their findings, we categorized 2 papers using open source models, one with a generator algorithm and 16 with multiple domains. Furthermore we found 11 papers,

---

[9] https://www.dropbox.com.

where the domain was not specified at all. They also commented on our RQ1: "In addition, examples from industry are sometimes only described, but not shown in detail for reasons of confidentiality."

The lack of publicly available MATLAB/Simulink models inspired the SLforge project to build the only large-scale collection of public MATLAB/Simulink models [8,10] known to us. To date, however, this corpus has been only used by the same researchers in order to evaluate different strategies for testing the MATLAB/Simulink tool environment itself (see, e.g., [9]). Another interesting approach was used by [39]. They used Google BigQuery[10] to find a sample of the largest available MATLAB/Simulink models on GitHub.

In a different context focusing on UML models only, Hebig et al. [17] have systematically mined GitHub projects to answer the question when UML models, if used, are created and updated throughout the lifecycle of a project. A similar yet even more restricted study on the usage of UML models developed in Enterprise Architect has been conducted by Langer et al. [29].

7   Conclusion and Future Work

In this paper, we investigated to which degree the principles of good scientific practice are adopted by current research on tools for model-based development, focusing on tools supporting MATLAB/Simulink. To that end, we conducted a systematic literature review and analyzed a set of 65 relevant papers on how they deal with the accessibility of experimental replication packages.

We found that only 31% of the tools and 22% of the models used as experimental subjects are accessible. Given that both artifacts are needed for a replication study, only 9% of the tool evaluations presented in the examined papers can be classified to be replicable in principle. Moreover, only a minor fraction of the models is obtained from open source projects. Altogether, we see this as an alarming signal w.r.t. making scientific progress on better tool support for model-based development processes centered around MATLAB/Simulink. While both tool and models are essential prerequisites for replication and reproducibility studies, the latter may also serve as experimental subjects for evaluating other tools. In this regard, our study may serve as a source for getting information about publicly available models. Other researchers in this field have even started to curate a much larger corpus of MATLAB/Simulink models. However, besides some basic metrics, such as the number of blocks and connections comprised by these models, little is known about the methods and processes being adopted in the development of these models.

One potential data source which, to the best of our knowledge, has not yet been investigated in detail with a particular focus on MATLAB/Simulink and which we want to consider in our future work are open development platforms such as GitHub. They may not only host further models which are not yet included in any of the existing model collections, but also provide plenty of

---

[10] https://cloud.google.com/bigquery.

meta-data which can be exploited for a much more detailed characterization of the extracted models and projects.

References

1. Arrieta, A., Wang, S., Arruabarrena, A., Markiegi, U., Sagardui, G., Etxeberria, L.: Multi-objective black-box test case selection for cost-effectively testing simulation models. In: Proceedings of the Genetic and Evolutionary Computation Conference GECCO 2018, pp. 1411–1418. Association for Computing Machinery, New York (2018)
2. Arrieta, A., Wang, S., Markiegi, U., Arruabarrena, A., Etxeberria, L., Sagardui, G.: Pareto efficient multi-objective black-box test case selection for simulation-based testing. Inf. Softw. Technol. **114**, 137–154 (2019)
3. Bertram, V., Maoz, S., Ringert, J.O., Rumpe, B., von Wenckstern, M.: Component and connector views in practice: an experience report. In: Proceedings of the ACM/IEEE 20th International Conference on Model Driven Engineering Languages and Systems MODELS 2017, pp. 167–177. IEEE Press (2017)
4. Bertram, V., Maoz, S., Ringert, J.O., Rumpe, B., von Wenckstern, M.: Component and connector views in practice: an experience report. In: 2017 ACM/IEEE 20th International Conference on Model Driven Engineering Languages and Systems (MODELS), pp. 167–177. IEEE (2017)
5. Boll, A., Kehrer, T.: The download link of all digital artifacts of this paper. https://doi.org/10.6084/m9.figshare.13019183.v1
6. Brambilla, M., Cabot, J., Wimmer, M.: Model-driven software engineering in practice. Synth. Lect. Softw. Eng. **3**(1), 1–207 (2017)
7. Chowdhury, S.A.: Understanding and improving cyber-physical system models and development tools. In: 2018 IEEE/ACM 40th International Conference on Software Engineering: Companion (ICSE-Companion), pp. 452–453, May 2018
8. Chowdhury, S.A., Mohian, S., Mehra, S., Gawsane, S., Johnson, T.T., Csallner, C.: Automatically finding bugs in a commercial cyber-physical system development tool chain with SLforge. In: 2018 IEEE/ACM 40th International Conference on Software Engineering (ICSE), pp. 981–992, May 2018
9. Chowdhury, S.A., Shrestha, S.L., Johnson, T.T., Csallner, C.: SLEMI: Equivalence Modulo Input (EMI) based mutation of CPS models for finding compiler bugs in Simulink. In: Proceedings of 42nd ACM/IEEE International Conference on Software Engineering (ICSE). ACM (2020, To appear)
10. Chowdhury, S.A., Varghese, L.S., Mohian, S., Johnson, T.T., Csallner, C.: A curated corpus of simulink models for model-based empirical studies. In: 2018 IEEE/ACM 4th International Workshop on Software Engineering for Smart Cyber-Physical Systems (SEsCPS), pp. 45–48. IEEE (2018)
11. Cohen, J.: A coefficient of agreement for nominal scales. Educ. Psychol. Measur. **20**(1), 37–46 (1960)
12. Elberzhager, F., Rosbach, A., Bauer, T.: Analysis and testing of Matlab simulink models: a systematic mapping study. In: Proceedings of the 2013 International Workshop on Joining AcadeMiA and Industry Contributions to Testing Automation JAMAICA 2013, pp. 29–34. Association for Computing Machinery, New York (2013)

13. France, R., Rumpe, B.: Model-driven development of complex software: a research roadmap. In: Future of Software Engineering (FOSE 2007), pp. 37–54. IEEE (2007)
14. Gallego-Calderon, J., Natarajan, A.: Assessment of wind turbine drive-train fatigue loads under torsional excitation. Eng. Struct. **103**, 189–202 (2015)
15. Gerlitz, T., Kowalewski, S.: Flow sensitive slicing for MATLAB/Simulink models. In: 2016 13th Working IEEE/IFIP Conference on Software Architecture (WICSA), pp. 81–90, April 2016
16. Gusenbauer, M., Haddaway, N.R.: Which academic search systems are suitable for systematic reviews or meta-analyses? Evaluating retrieval qualities of Google Scholar, PubMed and 26 other resources. Res. Synth. Methods **11**, 181–217 (2019)
17. Hebig, R., Quang, T.H., Chaudron, M.R., Robles, G., Fernandez, M.A.: The quest for open source projects that use UML: mining GitHub. In: Proceedings of the ACM/IEEE 19th International Conference on Model Driven Engineering Languages and Systems, pp. 173–183 (2016)
18. Holling, D., Hofbauer, A., Pretschner, A., Gemmar, M.: Profiting from unit tests for integration testing. In: 2016 IEEE International Conference on Software Testing, Verification and Validation (ICST), pp. 353–363, April 2016
19. Hussain, A., Sher, H.A., Murtaza, A.F., Al-Haddad, K.: Improved restricted control set model predictive control (iRCS-MPC) based maximum power point tracking of photovoltaic module. IEEE Access **7**, 149422–149432 (2019)
20. Jiang, Z., Wu, X., Dong, Z., Mu, M.: Optimal test case generation for Simulink models using slicing. In: 2017 IEEE International Conference on Software Quality, Reliability and Security Companion (QRS-C), pp. 363–369, July 2017
21. Kehrer, T., Kelter, U., Ohrndorf, M., Sollbach, T.: Understanding model evolution through semantically lifting model differences with SiLift. In: 28th IEEE International Conference on Software Maintenance (ICSM), pp. 638–641. IEEE (2012)
22. Kehrer, T., Kelter, U., Pietsch, P., Schmidt, M.: Adaptability of model comparison tools. In: Proceedings of the 27th IEEE/ACM International Conference on Automated Software Engineering, pp. 306–309. IEEE (2012)
23. Khelifi, A., Ben Lakhal, N.M., Gharsallaoui, H., Nasri, O.: Artificial neural network-based fault detection. In: 2018 5th International Conference on Control, Decision and Information Technologies (CoDIT), pp. 1017–1022, April 2018
24. Kitchenham, B., Charters, S.: Guidelines for performing systematic literature reviews in software engineering (2007)
25. Kitchenham, B., et al.: Systematic literature reviews in software engineering-a tertiary study. Inf. Softw. Technol. **52**(8), 792–805 (2010)
26. Kuroki, Y., Yoo, M., Yokoyama, T.: A Simulink to UML model transformation tool for embedded control software development. In: IEEE International Conference on Industrial Technology, ICIT 2016, Taipei, Taiwan, 14–17 March 2016, pp. 700–706. IEEE (2016)
27. Kusmenko, E., Shumeiko, I., Rumpe, B., von Wenckstern, M.: Fast simulation preorder algorithm. In: Proceedings of the 6th International Conference on Model-Driven Engineering and Software Development MODELSWARD 2018, pp. 256–267. SCITEPRESS - Science and Technology Publications, Lda, Setubal, PRT (2018)
28. Lamprecht, A.L., et al.: Towards fair principles for research software. Data Sci. **1–23** (2019, Preprint)
29. Langer, P., Mayerhofer, T., Wimmer, M., Kappel, G.: On the usage of UML: initial results of analyzing open UML models. In: Modellierung 2014 (2014)
30. Liggesmeyer, P., Trapp, M.: Trends in embedded software engineering. IEEE Softw. **26**(3), 19–25 (2009)

31. Matinnejad, R., Nejati, S., Briand, L.C., Bruckmann, T.: Automated test suite generation for time-continuous Simulink models. In: 2016 IEEE/ACM 38th International Conference on Software Engineering (ICSE), pp. 595–606, May 2016
32. Matinnejad, R., Nejati, S., Briand, L.C., Bruckmann, T.: Test generation and test prioritization for Simulink models with dynamic behavior. IEEE Trans. Softw. Eng. **45**(9), 919–944 (2019)
33. Nejati, S., Gaaloul, K., Menghi, C., Briand, L.C., Foster, S., Wolfe, D.: Evaluating model testing and model checking for finding requirements violations in Simulink models. In: Proceedings of the 2019 27th ACM Joint Meeting on European Software Engineering Conference and Symposium on the Foundations of Software Engineering ESEC/FSE 2019, pp. 1015–1025. Association for Computing Machinery, New York (2019)
34. Norouzi, P., Kıvanç, Ö.C., Üstün, Ö.: High performance position control of double sided air core linear brushless DC motor. In: 2017 10th International Conference on Electrical and Electronics Engineering (ELECO), pp. 233–238, November 2017
35. Oussalem, O., Kourchi, M., Rachdy, A., Ajaamoum, M., Idadoub, H., Jenkal, S.: A low cost controller of PV system based on Arduino board and INC algorithm. Mater. Today: Proc. **24**, 104–109 (2019)
36. Rao, A.C., Raouf, A., Dhadyalla, G., Pasupuleti, V.: Mutation testing based evaluation of formal verification tools. In: 2017 International Conference on Dependable Systems and Their Applications (DSA), pp. 1–7, October 2017
37. Rashid, M., Anwar, M.W., Khan, A.M.: Toward the tools selection in model based system engineering for embedded systems-a systematic literature review. J. Syst. Softw. **106**, 150–163 (2015)
38. Rebaya, A., Gasmi, K., Hasnaoui, S.: A Simulink-based rapid prototyping workflow for optimizing software/hardware programming. In: 2018 26th International Conference on Software, Telecommunications and Computer Networks (SoftCOM), pp. 1–6. IEEE (2018)
39. Sanchez, B., Zolotas, A., Rodriguez, H.H., Kolovos, D., Paige, R.: On-the-fly translation and execution of OCL-like queries on simulink models. In: 2019 ACM/IEEE 22nd International Conference on Model Driven Engineering Languages and Systems (MODELS), pp. 205–215. IEEE (2019)
40. Shaw, M.: What makes good research in software engineering? Int. J. Softw. Tools Technol. Trans. **4**(1), 1–7 (2002)
41. Silva, R., Neiva, F.: Systematic literature review in computer science - a practical guide, November 2016
42. Stapić, Z., López, E.G., Cabot, A.G., de Marcos Ortega, L., Strahonja, V.: Performing systematic literature review in software engineering. In: CECIIS 2012–23rd International Conference (2012)
43. Stephan, M., Cordy, J.R.: Identifying instances of model design patterns and antipatterns using model clone detection. In: Proceedings of the Seventh International Workshop on Modeling in Software Engineering MiSE 2015, pp. 48–53. IEEE Press (2015)
44. Strathmann, T., Oehlerking, J.: Verifying properties of an electro-mechanical braking system. In: 2nd Workshop on Applied Verification of Continuous and Hybrid Systems (ARCH 2015), April 2015
45. Tomita, T., Ishii, D., Murakami, T., Takeuchi, S., Aoki, T.: A scalable Monte-Carlo test-case generation tool for large and complex simulink models. In: 2019 IEEE/ACM 11th International Workshop on Modelling in Software Engineering (MiSE). pp. 39–46, May 2019

46. Völter, M., Stahl, T., Bettin, J., Haase, A., Helsen, S.: Model-Driven Software Development: Technology, Engineering, Management. Wiley, Hoboken (2013)

47. Whittle, J., Hutchinson, J., Rouncefield, M., Burden, H., Heldal, R.: Industrial adoption of model-driven engineering: are the tools really the problem? In: Moreira, A., Schätz, B., Gray, J., Vallecillo, A., Clarke, P. (eds.) MODELS 2013. LNCS, vol. 8107, pp. 1–17. Springer, Heidelberg (2013). https://doi.org/10.1007/978-3-642-41533-3_1

48. Wilkinson, M.D., et al.: The fair guiding principles for scientific data management and stewardship. Sci. Data 3, 1–9 (2016)

49. Wille, D., Babur, Ö., Cleophas, L., Seidl, C., van den Brand, M., Schaefer, I.: Improving custom-tailored variability mining using outlier and cluster detection. Sci. Comput. Program. 163, 62–84 (2018)

50. Yang, Y., Jiang, Y., Gu, M., Sun, J.: Verifying Simulink Stateflow model: Timed automata approach. In: Proceedings of the 31st IEEE/ACM International Conference on Automated Software Engineering ASE 2016, pp. 852–857. Association for Computing Machinery, New York (2016)

Exploring Validity Frames in Practice

Simon Van Mierlo$^{(\boxtimes)}$ (ID), Bentley James Oakes(ID), Bert Van Acker(ID),
Raheleh Eslampanah(ID), Joachim Denil(ID), and Hans Vangheluwe(ID)

University of Antwerp - Flanders Make vzw, Antwerp, Belgium
{simon.vanmierlo,bentley.oakes,bert.vanacker,
raheleh.eslampanah,joachim.denil,hans.vangheluwe}@uantwerpen.be

Abstract. Model-Based Systems Engineering (MBSE) provides work-flows, methods, techniques and tools for optimal simulation-based design and realization of complex Software-Intensive, Cyber-Physical Systems. One of the key benefits of this approach is that the behavior of the realized system can be reasoned about and predicted *in-silico*, before any prototype has been developed. Design models are increasingly used after the system has been realized as well. For example, a (design) digital twin can be used for runtime monitoring to detect and diagnose discrepancies between the simulated and realized system. Inconsistencies may arise, however, because models were used at design time that are not valid within the operating context of the realized system. It is often left to the domain expert to ensure that the models used are valid with respect to their realized counterpart. Due to system complexity and automated Design-Space Exploration (DSE), it is increasingly difficult for a human to reason about model validity. We propose validity frames as an explicit model of the contexts in which a model is a valid representation of a system to rule out invalid designs at design time. We explain the essential and conceptual, yet practical, structure of validity frames and a process for building them using an electrical resistor in the optimal design of a high-pass filter as a running example. We indicate how validity frames can be used in a DSE process, as well as for runtime monitoring.

Keywords: Validity frames · Design-Space Exploration · Digital twin

1 Introduction

The systems we build today are characterized by an ever-increasing complexity. In recent decades, we have moved from systems that are largely restricted to one domain (mechanical, electrical, software) to large, integrated systems that combine components from many different domains, each with their own formalisms, techniques and tools. This has lead to a plethora of applications, typically called Software-Intensive Systems, and more recently Cyber-Physical Systems. Model-Based Systems Engineering (MBSE) provides workflows, methods, techniques and tools for optimal simulation-based design and realization of

© Springer Nature Switzerland AG 2020
O. Babur et al. (Eds.): ICSMM 2020, CCIS 1262, pp. 131–148, 2020.
https://doi.org/10.1007/978-3-030-58167-1_10

such systems [17]. Typically, domain experts create designs in specialized modeling and simulation languages and their accompanying tools. Such designs are an abstraction of the realized systems. For a specific purpose, they allow for the *in-silico* analysis of a limited set of properties of the system-to-be-built. This leads to a tremendous increase in productivity and other side-effects, such as improved communication between different domain experts, traceability to the final design, easier response to changing requirements, etc. [1].

Looking forward, the *digital twin* is seen as an enabler for advanced runtime monitoring [2,26], fault detection, and (automatic) recovery or reconfiguration [15]. A (design) digital twin, which is a (tracking) simulation of the design model, is run in real-time alongside the realized system and is provided with the same inputs as the realized system. When the results observed in the running system do not correspond to what is predicted by the digital twin, a *discrepancy* occurs, which might be due to a fault in the realized system (due to wear and tear, for example), an error made in the design model, or in simulation solver parameter settings. This might lead to further actions, such as fault localization, recovery of the system, and even a reconfiguration or redesign of the system. In this paper, design models are assumed to be used in some form to create a *design digital twin* that is used as a (advanced) runtime monitor as discussed above.

The search for an optimal design is not only performed manually, but is increasingly automated by providing a Design-Space Exploration (DSE) solver with a number of components, a set of design constraints, and a set of system properties that need to be satisfied and/or that have to be optimized. Exploiting vast computational power currently available, DSE allows exploring many more design candidates than before, possibly leading to original new designs [5].

The problem in any design endeavor, which is magnified when DSE is automated, is to come up with a design that is *valid*, *i.e.*, properties of interest obtained from the realized system are equivalent to those obtained from simulations. In DSE, some domain constraints are already encoded and provided to the solver in order to not come up with designs that can not be realized. However, often overlooked is the *validity* of the used models with respect to their realized counterparts, in their intended operational context. If such validity can not be guaranteed, simulation results and hence DSE results *cannot be trusted*!

Validity frames, first introduced by Zeigler [27], explicitly encode the conditions under which a model is a valid abstraction of the realized system. In the decades after its introduction, other researchers have extended the original definition and have attempted to apply these frames to certain applications in different domains. However, a practical guide for creating and using validity frames with a concrete example is currently missing from the state-of-the-art. In this paper, we introduce the concept of validity frames using a practical example, and show how frames can enhance the (automatic) DSE for a multi-component system.

Structure. Section 2 introduces the notion of validity frames with a running example: an electrical resistor whose behavior is specified using four different models. Section 3 demonstrates the use of validity frames on the design of a multi-component system: a (passive) high-pass filter (HPF). Section 4 discusses related work. Section 5 concludes the paper and provides pointers for future work.

2 Validity Frames

This section presents an overview of our vision on validity frames. In particular, the precise objective of checking the validity of the model will be detailed. Then, we will present the essential components of validity frames and their relations, using an electrical resistor as an example.

2.1 Example Component

An electrical resistor is a common element in many electrical circuits. Many different types of resistors exist; their material, geometry, connection points, insulating material, etc. can vary depending on the intended application. All resistors share a common property though in their reduction of current flow, typically by dissipating the energy as heat.

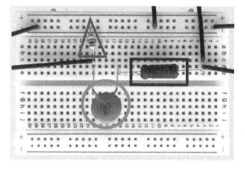

Fig. 1. A realized design of a high-pass filter: a circuit consisting of a resistor, capacitor, and inductor. (Explained further as a running example in Sect. 3.)

Figure 1 shows an example electrical circuit consisting of a resistor, a capacitor, and an inductor, marked by a triangle, circle, and square respectively. They are connected through wires, and when the circuit is connected to a voltage source, the effect that the elements have on the electrical signal (governed by the appropriate physical laws) can be observed by measuring the electrical signal at certain points in the circuit using "probe wires". Typically, such circuits are designed by domain experts (*i.e.*, electrical engineers) who have deep knowledge of these physical effects and can take into account the amount of current that will flow through the complete circuit (induced by the voltage source that is connected to the circuit). This may cause other physical effects to occur: the elements might heat up, their behavior might change if the frequency of the voltage signal is high, or magnetic fields might be induced, which causes (potentially unwanted) behavior changes in the components, or interactions between elements that are placed close together.

When modeling electrical networks, *models* of the electrical elements are used. In Fig. 2, four models for the resistor are shown. All of these models have the same interface, a set of physical ports, highlighted in the figures in yellow: a positive electrical connection P and a negative electrical connection

N (which, when connected, generate appropriate equations based on Kirchoff's laws), and a thermal port T. As such, they can be used interchangeably, but their behavior (both internal to the component and visible to the environment) will be different. We consider two influencing factors in this work: the frequency of the electrical signal (connected through the electrical interface of the resistor) and the temperature of the environment. The effects of these influencing factors can either be low or high on the behavior of the component. In Fig. 2, we have classified whether the model takes into account the high effects or not.

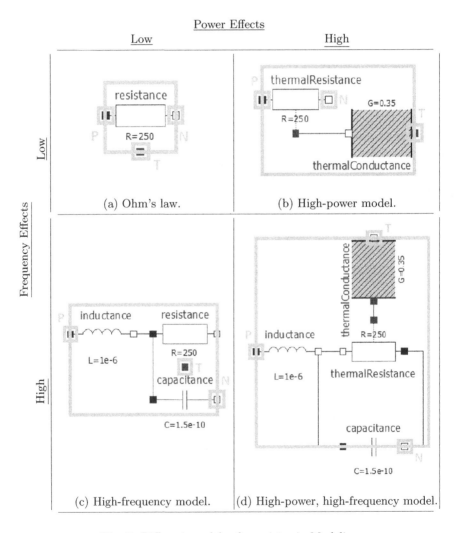

(a) Ohm's law.

(b) High-power model.

(c) High-frequency model.

(d) High-power, high-frequency model.

Fig. 2. Different models of a resistor in Modelica

Model (a), Ohm's law, models the resistor behavior as follows:

$$V = R_{nominal} * (1 + alpha * (T_{res} - T_{reference})) * I \qquad (1)$$

where $R_{nominal}$ is the nominal resistance value (equal to 250 in the model), $alpha$ is the temperature coefficient, $T_{reference}$ is the reference temperature of the resistor at which its resistance value is equal to the nominal resistance value, and T_{res} is the temperature of the resistor, in this case equal to the ambient temperature (coming into the red thermal port under the resistor in the figure). This effectively models a linear relation between the voltage V and the current I, where the gradient of the function depends on the ambient temperature.

Model (b) takes into account the fact that the resistor itself will heat up over time as a current flows through it. The behavior of the resistor is extended with the following equations:

$$LossPower = v * i \qquad (2)$$

$$\frac{dT_{res}}{dt} = \frac{-LossPower + v * i}{tc * K_d} \qquad (3)$$

where tc is the thermal time constant, a time unit that specifies how fast the resistor will heat up, and K_d is the dissipation factor, specifying how fast the heat of the resistor is dissipated into the environment.

Model (c) accounts for the fact that a resistor does not only resist the current flowing through it, but it also has slight capacitive and inductive properties. In this high-frequency model, such effects are modeled for AC applications. The electrical network now models the single (real-world) resistor component. The behavior of the inductor is governed by $\frac{di}{dt} = \frac{v}{L}$ where L is the inductance, and the behavior of the capacitor is governed by $\frac{dv}{dt} = \frac{i}{C}$ where C is the capacitance. Last, in model (d), both frequency and temperature effects are taken into account by combining the second and third models of the resistor.

We can run simulations using these models. Suppose we model an electrical network where a resistor is connected to a voltage source with a particular constant voltage V and a current sensor that senses the amount of current that is output by the resistor. This is illustrated in Fig. 3a, where we show a resistor model within an experimental context: it is connected to a voltage source, a current sensor, and a fixed ambient temperature. In Fig. 3, the results of the simulation are shown: the purple (constant) line is the result of using the simple model for the resistor, while the green (descending) line is the result of using the model of the resistor that takes into account heating effects. The linear model arrives at a value slightly below 0.39 for the current flowing through the resistor, while the model of the thermal resistor settles on a value slightly below 0.365.

2.2 Objective

Figure 4 displays the relationship between a *system* and its *model*, in an adaptation from the works of Zeigler [27]. Starting from a system to be realized, the

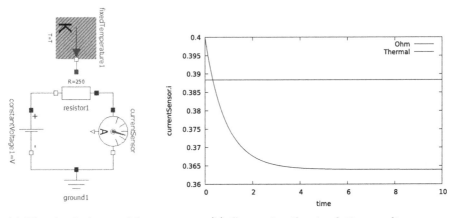

(a) The simulation model   (b) Comparing the simulation results.
for the resistor.

Fig. 3. A simulation and its results for two models of the resistor. (Color figure online)

context of the model and the *properties of interest* are defined. Then the model can be built or selected from a *model library* such as the Modelica library. If a model's *simulation results* reproduce the real-world system *experimental results* faithfully within an *experimental context* (and with a particular tolerance, since a perfect match will never be achievable), we say that the model is *valid* with respect to the real system. This validity condition is always in relation to the *properties of interest*; other properties that the system or model exhibits beyond these (as long as they do not influence the considered properties) are irrelevant with respect to the validity condition.

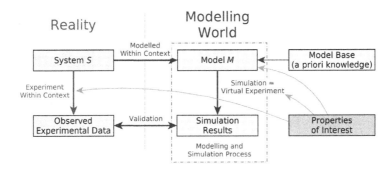

Fig. 4. The modelling relationship between the system and the model.

The objective of validity frames is to explicitly encode the *contexts* in which a *model* provides valid results for a specific set of *properties* with respect to a *real-world system*. Ultimately, this will enable the building of *frame-enabled model repositories*, where the repository contains (1) a set of models, (2) a set of validity frames, and (3) relations between models and validity frames, specifying which frames are *applicable* to which models, and vice versa, which models can be *accommodated* by which frames. This enables correct and efficient design of systems, in particular automated design-space exploration.

In the following subsections, we will provide additional details for these components of validity frames, applied to the electrical resistor.

2.3   Properties

Properties in the validity frame are those properties of the system-under-study that are relevant in the modeling activity, and which can be measured in some way, termed *value properties*. These properties therefore scope the considered context of the validity frame. They are at the core of the modeling activity and of validity frames. A property can be *evaluated* within an *experimental context*. The set of properties of interest gives rise to the abstraction relation between model and system: a model is only supposed to provide (correct) answers with respect to these properties, while other properties are abstracted away.

For the electrical resistor example, let us consider the constituent relation between the voltage V and the current I as the property of interest. In the most basic case, this relation is given by Ohms's law, *i.e.*, $I = \frac{V}{R}$, which constitutes a linear relation, since the resistance value R is supposed to be constant. Considering the models in Fig. 2, however, that relation will look different (and more difficult to solve analytically) as more effects are taken into account. We can compare the *fidelity* of a model with respect to a property when compared to the real system that the model represents. The evaluation of that fidelity (and, extended, of the range of validity of the model) can be performed by comparing the result of an experiment in the virtual world (on the model) with the result of a representative experiment in the real world (on the system), or by comparing the results of two experiments in the virtual world, one on the model, and the other on a higher-fidelity model (with a wider validity range).

2.4   Influencing Factors

Influencing factors are properties of the environment that are outside of the control of the model, but can potentially influence its behavior and/or the range of validity of the model with respect to a certain property. For example, in the resistor example from Sect. 2.1, the ambient temperature and the frequency and amplitude of the electrical signal are influencing factors. Therefore, certain frames may provide validity conditions using these influencing factors.

2.5 Experiments

The validation process relies on *experiments* to determine to what extent the provided model is valid to the real-world system. These experiments can be run in the real world (on the realized system) or in the virtual world (on a simulated model representing the system). An experiment places a model or a system in an *experimental context*. It also consists of an experimental setup, and the process to take the measurements; for details we refer to Denil *et al.* [8]. These experimental conditions must be precisely defined, such that the experiments can be accurately replicated. The results are used by the validation procedure to make the determination of validity for the provided model, including a measure of the model's fidelity with respect to the properties of the context.

In a basic form, these experiments may be input and output trajectories which the model is expected to match with some degree of tolerance. Additionally, the experiment needs to provide the influencing factors. For example, an experiment for the resistor may place a model of the resistor in an electrical network with an AC voltage source and a particular environment with fixed temperature (both influencing factors). It then can measure, as an output, the value property of interest, namely the constituent relation between (input) voltage and (output) current (as measured by a current sensor). Along with sufficient experimental conditions [13] (which includes, for example, the simulation platform which was used, the solver settings, etc.), and a tolerance, these experiments can determine the validity of the model with respect to the real system.

2.6 Validation Procedure

The *validation procedure* is an explicit activity stored within the validity frame to determine the fidelity of the provided model with respect to the real system, and to determine for each of the selected properties and the ranges in which the model is a valid abstraction of the system, considering the influencing factors. Along with performing the experiments, the validation procedure also has the responsibility of relating the output of each experiment stored in the validity frame to the model's results to determine the model's fidelity with respect to each property. That is, the validation procedure answers a) whether the model's behavior match (with some tolerance) the results of the experiments performed on the real-world system or high-fidelity model, and b) how well does the model perform with respect to each of the properties of the context captured by the validity frame. For this, a (validation) evaluation function needs to be defined.

A validation procedure for the resistor example could be as follows. Given a model of the resistor, it is placed in an electrical network with a variable (AC or DC) voltage source, an ambient temperature, and a current sensor. Then, a number of experiments are performed that excite the resistor with a number of different voltages, and the current flow is collected from the current sensor. The results of the real-world experiments would be compared to the model's results, and determine if the results were sufficiently close, within some tolerance. Finally, a robustness metric would determine how well the resistor model is valid with respect to temperature and frequency, based on the experimental results from the model and which properties are involved in each experiment.

2.7   Validity Conditions

Finally, *validation conditions* are synthesized from the experiments that were performed and they are stored as part of the relation between a model and its frame. These conditions are useful when using frames such as in a model catalog, where these relations can be exploited to choose the most appropriate model based on the context it will be used in, and which properties are of interest. An example validity condition could define a range for parameters, input values, or influencing factors; within these ranges, the condition specifies that the model is valid (considering the validation process used).

For the resistor example from Sect. 2.1, validity conditions could be extracted from the range of experiments performed on the model. If we have run a series of experiments for a particular ambient temperature (for example, 50 degrees Centigrade) with a varying voltage value for the voltage source, we know for each experiment whether the model provides a response that is close to its real-world counterpart value. From these responses, a validity condition will then state that the model is valid for voltages up to x volts, where x is the last voltage value for which the model provided a response within the tolerance range (at 50 degrees Centigrade).

2.8   Capturing Validity

To summarize, we capture the validity of the simplest model for the resistor, namely Ohm's law in Fig. 2a for one property, the constituent relation between voltage and current, and one influencing factor, ambient temperature. To do this, we take an experimental setup in the real world similar to Fig. 1, where we hook up a single resistor to a DC voltage source and put it in an environment where we can control the ambient temperature. We then probe the circuit to measure the current flowing through it, which will be the result of the resistor's physical properties as it dissipates energy as heat. We then note this value for different values of voltage input; these measurements, for an ambient temperature of 50 degrees Centigrade are plotted in Fig. 5 as red dots.

Taking these measurements, we can define a frame that specifies a validity condition that states that a model is valid with respect to these measured values if the simulated current value is equal to the measured value with a tolerance of 0.1 A. This allows us to put our model in an equivalent experimental setup (in the virtual world), such as can be seen in Fig. 3a and repeat the experiments by setting the ambient temperature to a fixed value (50 degrees Centigrades, in this case) and by sweeping over a voltage range (0–100) with a certain step size, and then collecting the value that is observed in the current sensor. When we plot these values, we get the green line in Fig. 5, a linear relation as specified by Ohm's law. For a particular range of voltages, the measured voltages almost follow this linear relation; after that other physical effects come into play. The

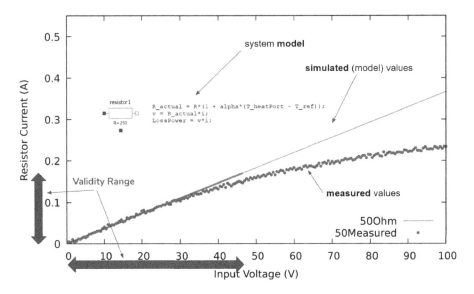

Fig. 5. Plot of validity range for Ohm's law at 50 degrees Centigrade. (Color figure online)

range of voltages in which the simple model is valid, in this particular ambient temperature, is [0 V, 48.1 V] with a tolerance of 0.001 A.

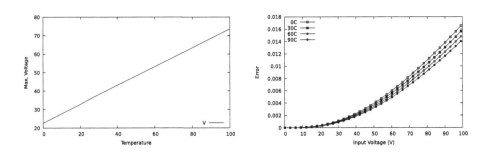

Fig. 6. Temperature dependence.   **Fig. 7.** Sensitivity.

This maximum voltage (for 50 degrees Centigrade, equal to 48.1 V) depends on the ambient temperature. If we repeat these experiments for different ambient temperatures, that maximum voltage value will change as well. These results can also be recorded in the relation between model and validity frame, and can be seen in Fig. 6. Furthermore, we can also store the sensitivity of the model (the error that is made in the simulation results with respect to the real system). This can be seen in Fig. 7. This information can help us to see what the increase in error is if we go outside of the validity range of the model; if it does not increase too much, it might mean there is some "stretch" on the validity range depending on the application and whether or not it is safety-critical.

3 Design-Space Exploration Using Validity Frames

In this section, we demonstrate the value of validity frames when used in the (automatic) domain-space exploration of a multi-component system. As a running example, we design a (passive) high-pass filter, which is implemented as an electrical network consisting of a number of electrical components, including a resistor. We demonstrate that performing the design-space exploration naively (without the use of validity frames) might result in a design that is invalid with respect to the behavior of the realized system, which means that the requirements are not satisfied. By using validity frames, we can avoid this costly error and ensure that the models of the components are used in a valid context; we focus on the resistor component.

3.1 Requirements

A (passive) high-pass filter is an electrical circuit that "lets through" electrical signals if their frequency is above a certain value. Signals below that cut-off frequency value are dampened (*i.e.*, only part of the magnitude of the signal passes). An ideal filter would dampen the signal completely if it is below the cut-off frequency (*i.e.*, the voltage would drop down to zero) and have a discontinuity at the cut-off frequency, letting through the

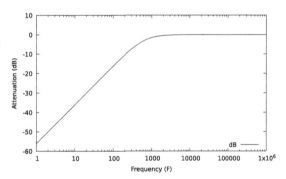

Fig. 8. Bode plot of the required behavior of the high-pass filter circuit.

whole signal. This is, however, physically not possible to achieve, and instead, the signal will gradually be let through as the frequency increases. In the example, we will design a simple high-pass filter, consisting of only passive electrical components, whose behavior will be far from ideal.

Typically, the (required) behavior of a high-pass filter is expressed as a Bode plot. It shows for increasing frequency values how much the input electrical signal is attenuated by the circuit. This attenuation is expressed in decibels (dB), which is the logarithm of the ratio of input and output voltage, as follows:

$$value_{dB} = 20 * log_{10}(\frac{V_{out}}{V_{in}}) \tag{4}$$

A dB value of zero means that the signal is not attenuated; a negative value means the signal is attenuated (where lower values mean the signal is attenuated more - with a logarithmic scale). The Bode plot expressing the requirement of our example is shown in Fig. 8:

– The cutoff frequency (where the dB value is −3) is approximately 460 Hz.
– After the cutoff frequency, the dB value should be zero.
– The slope of the curve before the cutoff frequency is not a strict requirement for the process.
– The high-pass filter needs to operate for an AC voltage source whose frequency can range between 0 Hz (DC voltage) and 1 MHz; the amplitude of the AC voltage source can range 0.1 V and 100 V.
– The circuit will be used in an environment of [20C, 50C] ambient temperature.

3.2   Initial Design

To design this system, we want to build an electrical circuit that, when connected to a voltage source for which we can vary the frequency, attenuates the signal as shown in Fig. 8. For this, we set up an experimental setups in the virtual and the real world from which we can deduce the dB values of the circuit. We assume that these setups lead to results we can trust, and any error in the measured values is a result from a fault in the system or model.

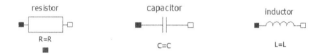

Fig. 9. Ideal physical models of electrical elements.

To create an initial design, we use a method closely related to what is described in [16]. We consider a library of component models, in this case consisting of a resistor, a capacitor, and an inductor. Their models are shown in Fig. 9. We further restrict any design with domain-specific rules, including the fact that there needs to be exactly one element of each type, the electrical elements need to be connected in a legal way, and their parameter values are filled in.

From this design-space exploration, an electrical circuit is generated, shown in Fig. 10, and its simulation result (as a Bode plot) is shown in Fig. 11 alongside the experimental results of the realized system. As can be seen, the simulation results predict a (near-)perfect match between the behavior of the circuit and the required behavior. As such, we can realize the circuit by placing the physical components on a bread board, similar to Fig. 1. However, when the experiment is run on this circuit, there is a significant discrepancy between these results. We can conclude that the virtual design does not result in a system that satisfies the required property; as such, the design model is invalid.

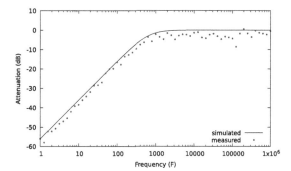

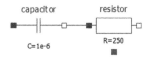

Fig. 10. The initial design of the high-pass filter circuit.

Fig. 11. The simulation results of the initial design and real-world experiment results.

3.3   The Resistor Frame

To deduce what has gone wrong during design-space exploration by focusing on one component of the electrical network, the resistor. We can ask whether, within the experimental context that the system is tested, the model we use is a valid abstraction of the resistor component.

We consider the validity range of the ideal physical model–a term introduced by Jan Broenink, see Chap. 2 of [6]–of the resistor for two influencing

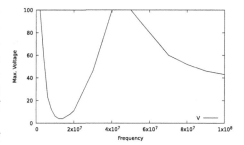

Fig. 12. Frequency dependence.

factors that are important for our application: ambient temperature (and power dissipation which may affect temperature) and frequency. The validity ranges (maximum voltage for which the model is valid) are plotted in Fig. 6 and Fig. 12. The validity range for the temperature influence is linear; the current running through the resistor has to be below $\frac{maxV}{R}$. For the frequency effects, the validity range decreases quickly up to 10 MHz, and as such is almost unusable in that range. The current running through the resistor in the circuit shown in Fig. 10 is higher than the value for which the model is valid; as such, the resistor model is used outside of its validity frame for the ambient temperature. Further, since the range of frequencies 0 Hz 1 MHz needs to be supported by the circuit, the model is also used outside of its validity frame for the frequency influencing factor.

3.4   Modified Design

To arrive at a modified design, we need to add further information to the design-space exploration process, considering the validity information of the resistor. When we do this, we have two options:

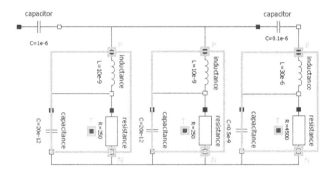

Fig. 13. The modified design of the high-pass filter circuit.

- We let the design-space exploration search for a design where the provided models have to stay within their validity range, which might mean we have to drop the constraint that states there should only be one "instance" of each component in the electrical network.
- We provide the design-space exploration with more detailed models of the component, considering the influencing factors. In Fig. 2, several models are shown that provide higher-fidelity results by considering the effects of power and frequency environments.

The advantage of the first option is efficiency; we keep the models simple and ensure that they are used within a range that they are valid. However, this might lead to more complex designs with more components. The advantage in the second option is that the component is modeled in more details, which means that it can be used in more contexts, since it has a wider validity range. However, simulation performance might be negatively affected.

In Fig. 13, the result of the design-space exploration, augmented with the extra constraints of the components staying within their validity range, is shown. The circuit is a second-order passive high pass filter with high fidelity resistor models. Fig. 14 shows the simulation results of the modified design, as well as the result of experimenting with the real system when it is realized. These results are similar which means that now the model faithfully represents the realized system.

Once we have a valid design, we can also use it as a *design digital twin*, as explained in Sect. 1. The information in the validity frames of the components can be used to deploy runtime monitors. These monitors continuously run the experiments that are defined in the frame, but feed it with the input data from the real system. For the resistor, this could mean that we monitor the input of the voltage source and probe the output electrical signal of the resistor. We can then check whether these values are within the validity range of the model that was used to design the system; otherwise the predictions made by the design model will no longer be valid. By continuously monitoring whether components do not go outside the range of the models that were used to represent them in the design, we can already raise a warning or error when that range is exceeded, effectively

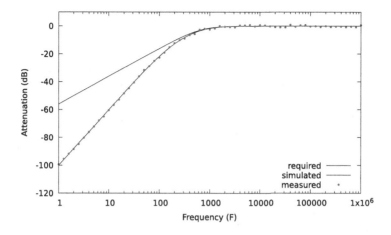

Fig. 14. The result of running the experiment on the realized high-pass filter circuit.

creating an efficient (but limited) digital twin. Using sensitivity information, as demonstrated in Fig. 7, a decision could be made whether the component is allowed to stay outside of its validity range for a while (because it is not very sensitive to its input), or whether the system should be brought to a failsafe mode as soon as possible.

4   Related Work

The notion of 'frames' in modeling and simulation is an old concept [28] where information about a model's context is formalized. For example, *experimental frames* are a "specification of the conditions under which the system is observed or experimented with" [27]. These experimental frames are composed of three components: a) a *generator* of input traces to the model, b) an *acceptor* which ensures that the experimental conditions are met, and c) a *transducer* to examine the output signals. Formal definition of these experimental frames allows for (semi-)automated creation [7,18], use in (semi-)automated trade-off analysis [12], and enabling frame-enabled hierarchical decomposition of the system [19].

The work of Traoré and Muzy generalize the experimental frames concept to instead define multiple frame utilizations [22]. An important aspect of their work is to relate a *system* and its *context*, a *model* and its *frame*, and a *simulator* and its *experimenter*. Here it is clear that the frame of a model represents the context of the original system which it captures. Further work by Foures *et al.* examines the generator, acceptor, and transducer components of the experimental frame to reason about how their inputs and output can be used to determine constraints on the model [10,11]. For example, the generator can be restricted in what events will be sent as input to the model, thereby structuring the context of the model.

Schmidt *et al.* approach our validity frame concept, as they define an experimental test framework for automatically evaluating fidelity of models with respect to complicated cyber-physical systems [21]. Their framework operates within the MATLAB/Simulink environment to implement test control and admissible model parameter configurations. The structure of modeling frames was addressed in work by Klikovits *et al.* [14], where a frame is structured as three components: a) a *modeling activity* with inputs, outputs, and a process, b) a *context* with objectives, assumptions, and constraints, and c) zero or more *sub-frames*. They emphasize the processes stored within frames, which can be used to (semi-)automatically perform the frame activity.

The work of Denil *et al.* specifically addresses validity frames, with an emphasis on capturing information to reproduce the results of experiments on the real system in the virtual world [8]. That work defines two uses for validity frames as *testing* the validity of the model against a real system, and on *calibrating* the model such that the model is valid. Recent work on validity frames by Van Acker *et al.* focuses on validity frames for models-of-the-physics in embedded domains [23]. These validity frames have two purposes: a) to assess the validity range of reduced-order models such as a neural net, and b) quantify the fidelity of these models versus the high-fidelity model. In that work, the validity frame is divided into (1) the *meta-data* about the model and its parameters, which includes information on the model solver and parameter datatype; (2) the *operational* part, which includes information about the equivalence ranges for parameters; and (3) the *process* part of the validity frame defines the validity and calibration processes as defined in [8].

5   Conclusion and Future Work

In this paper, we show how validity frames for individual components can be constructed based on the simulation results of their models and the experimental data obtained from real-world experiments. We demonstrate this by creating a validity frame for an electrical resistor, for two influencing factors: ambient temperature and frequency, and one property: the constituent relation between voltage and current. We use the frame information in an (automated) design-space exploration process and show that this information is crucial to arrive at valid design models and ultimately valid systems. We demonstrate this on the design of a (passive) high-pass filter, an example of a multi-component electrical circuit. We see several directions for future work. The validity frame concept can be investigated further in the optimization of the (design) digital twin, and its role explored in fault localization and (runtime) adaptivity. Further, we envision the creation of a model repository and framework which embraces the validity frame concept fully; it would not allow the creation and use of models without reasoning about its range of validity.

Acknowledgments. This work was partially funded by Flanders Make vzw, the strategic research centre for the Flemish manufacturing industry and by the University of Antwerp's Industrial Research Fund Strategic Basic Research (IOF-SBO).

References

1. Van der Auweraer, H., Anthonis, J., De Bruyne, S., Leuridan, J.: Virtual engineering at work: the challenges for designing mechatronic products. Eng. Comput. **29**(3), 389–408 (2013)
2. Bartocci, E., et al.: Specification-based monitoring of cyber-physical systems: a survey on theory, tools and applications. In: Bartocci, E., Falcone, Y. (eds.) Lectures on Runtime Verification. LNCS, vol. 10457, pp. 135–175. Springer, Cham (2018). https://doi.org/10.1007/978-3-319-75632-5_5
3. Benveniste, A., et al.: Contracts for system design. Found. Trends® Electron. Des. Autom. **12**(2–3), 124–400 (2018)
4. Breunese, A., Broenink, J.F., Top, J., Akkermans, J.: Libraries of reusable models: theory and application. Simulation **71**(1), 7–22 (1998)
5. Canedo, A., Richter, J.H.: Architectural design space exploration of cyber-physical systems using the functional modeling compiler. Procedia CIRP **21**, 46–51 (2014)
6. Challenger, M., Vanherpen, K., Denil, J., Vangheluwe, H.: FTG+PM: describing engineering processes in multi-paradigm modelling. Foundations of Multi-Paradigm Modelling for Cyber-Physical Systems, pp. 259–271. Springer, Cham (2020). https://doi.org/10.1007/978-3-030-43946-0_9
7. Daum, T., Sargent, R.G.: Experimental frames in a modern modeling and simulation system. IIE Trans. **33**(3), 181–192 (2001)
8. Denil, J., Klikovits, S., Mosterman, P.J., Vallecillo, A., Vangheluwe, H.: The experiment model and validity frame in M&S. In: Proceedings of the Symposium on Theory of Modeling & Simulation, pp. 1–12 (2017)
9. Ewald, R., Uhrmacher, A.M.: SESSL: a domain-specific language for simulation experiments. ACM Trans. Model. Comput. Simul. (TOMACS) **24**(2), 1–25 (2014)
10. Foures, D., Albert, V., Nketsa, A.: Formal compatibility of experimental frame concept and finite and deterministic DEVS model. In: International Conference on Modeling Optimization SIMulation (MOSIM 2012), pages-10, p. 94 (2012)
11. Foures, D., Albert, V., Nketsa, A.: Simulation validation using the compatibility between simulation model and experimental frame (2013)
12. Hu, J., Rozenblit, J.W.: Towards automatic generation of experimental frames in simulation-based system design. In: AI and Simulation Conference, pp. 1–6 (1988)
13. Ivie, P., Thain, D.: Reproducibility in scientific computing. ACM Comput. Surv. (CSUR) **51**(3), 1–36 (2018)
14. Klikovits, S., Denil, J., Muzy, A., Salay, R.: Modeling frames. In: CEUR Workshop Proceedings, pp. 315–320 (2017)
15. Madni, A.M., Madni, C.C., Lucero, S.D.: Leveraging digital twin technology in model-based systems engineering. Systems **7**(1), 7 (2019)
16. Meyers, B., Denil, J., Vanherpen, K., Vangheluwe, H.: Enabling design-space exploration for domain-specific modelling. In: Proceedings of the Model-driven Approaches for Simulation Engineering Symposium, p. 5. Society for Computer Simulation International (2018)
17. Ramos, A.L., Ferreira, J.V., Barceló, J.: Model-based systems engineering: an emerging approach for modern systems. IEEE Trans. Syst. Man Cybern. Part C (Appl. Rev.) **42**(1), 101–111 (2011)
18. Rozenblit, J.W.: Exp'a software tool for experimental frame specification in discrete event modelling and simulation. In: Proceedings of the Summer Computer Simulation Conference, pp. 967–971 (1984)

19. Rozenblit, J.W.: Experimental frame specification methodology for hierarchical simulation modeling. Int. J. Gen. Syst. **19**(3), 317–336 (1991)
20. dos Santos, C.A.R., Saleh, A.H., Schrijvers, T., Nicolai, M.: CONDEnSe: contract based design synthesis. In: 2019 ACM/IEEE 22nd International Conference on Model Driven Engineering Languages and Systems (MODELS), pp. 250–260. IEEE (2019)
21. Schmidt, A., Durak, U., Pawletta, T.: Model-based testing methodology using system entity structures for MATLAB/Simulink models. Simulation **92**(8), 729–746 (2016)
22. Traoré, M.K., Muzy, A.: Capturing the dual relationship between simulation models and their context. Simul. Model. Pract. Theor. **14**(2), 126–142 (2006)
23. Van Acker, B., De Meulenaere, P., Denil, J., Durodie, Y., Van Bellinghen, A., Vanstechelman, K.: Valid (re-)use of models-of-the-physics in cyber-physical systems using validity frames. In: 2019 Spring Simulation Conference (SpringSim), pp. 1–12, April 2019. https://doi.org/10.23919/SpringSim.2019.8732858
24. Van Acker, B., Denil, J., De Meulenaere, P., Aelvoet, B., Mahieu, D., Van Den Oudenhoven, J.: Generation of test strategies for model-based functional safety testing using an artifact-centric approach. In: Proceedings of MODELS 2018 Workshops co-located with ACM/IEEE 21st International Conference on Model Driven Engineering Languages and Systems (MODELS 2018) Copenhagen, Denmark, October, 14, 2018/Hebig, Regina [edit.], pp. 563–569 (2018)
25. Vangheluwe, H.: Multi-formalism modelling and simulation. D.Sc. dissertation, Faculty of Science, Ghent University (2000)
26. Weyns, D.: Software engineering of self-adaptive systems: an organised tour and future challenges. Chapter in Handbook of Software Engineering (2017)
27. Zeigler, B.P., Kim, T.G., Praehofer, H.: Theory of Modeling and Simulation. Academic Press, Cambridge (2000)
28. Zeigler, B.P.: Multifaceted Modelling and Discrete Event Simulation. Academic Press, London (1984)

Suitability of Optical Character Recognition (OCR) for Multi-domain Model Management

Weslley Torres[✉], Mark G. J. van den Brand[✉], and Alexander Serebrenik[✉]

Eindhoven University of Technology, Eindhoven, The Netherlands
{w.silva.torres,m.g.j.v.d.brand,a.serebrenik}@tue.nl

Abstract. The development of systems following model-driven engineering can include models from different domains. For example, to develop a mechatronic component one might need to combine expertise about mechanics, electronics, and software. Although these models belong to different domains, the changes in one model can affect other models causing inconsistencies in the entire system. There are, however, a limited amount of tools that support management of models from different domains. These models are created using different modeling notations and it is not plausible to use a multitude of parsers geared towards each and every modeling notation. Therefore, to ensure maintenance of multi-domain systems, we need a uniform approach that would be independent from the peculiarities of the notation. Meaning that such a uniform approach can only be based on something which is present in all those models, i.e., text, boxes, and lines. In this study we investigate the suitability of optical character recognition (OCR) as a basis for such a uniformed approach. We select graphical models from various domains that typically combine textual and graphical elements, and we focus on text-recognition without looking for additional shapes. We analyzed the performance of Google Cloud Vision and Microsoft Cognitive Services, two off-the-shelf OCR services. Google Cloud Vision performed better than Microsoft Cognitive Services being able to detect text of 70% of model elements. Errors made by Google Cloud Vision are due to absence of support for text common in engineering formulas, e.g., Greek letters, equations, and subscripts, as well as text typeset on multiple lines. We believe that once these shortcomings are addressed, OCR can become a crucial technology supporting multi-domain model management.

Keywords: Model management · Systems engineering · OCR

1 Introduction

Model-driven engineering (MDE) has been used in diverse engineering fields such as software engineering [31], robotics [46], and automotive [42]. The promised benefits of using this approach include increased development speed, earlier

© Springer Nature Switzerland AG 2020
O. Babur et al. (Eds.): ICSMM 2020, CCIS 1262, pp. 149–162, 2020.
https://doi.org/10.1007/978-3-030-58167-1_11

system analysis, and more manageable complexity [45]. However, managing interrelated models of different domains is challenging [33].

Since models from different domains use different modeling languages, to manage interrelated models of different domains one has to use a technology that can handle these models independently of the language used. Graphical models from various domains typically combine textual and graphical elements such as boxes, lines, and arrows. Such models can be designed using different tools, and usually these tools can export the model in a structured format such as XML, or as an image format such as PNG or JPEG [37]. The ideal setting for data extraction would be if all models were available in a structured default format. However, the situation becomes more complex when only the image of the model is available, either because the code that generates the model is lost, the model is only available in a paper instead of a digital format, or simply because the modeling tool does not export the model in the desired format.

Therefore, to ensure maintenance of multi-domain systems, we need a uniform approach that would be independent from the peculiarities of the notation. This also means that such a uniform approach can only be based on something which is present in all those models, i.e., text, boxes, and lines.

We believe that optical character recognition (OCR) can become a part of the uniformed approach. OCR is a collection of techniques aiming at recognizing text from handwritten or printed document and exporting the result as a machine-encoded text. Originally developed to support blind people [34], OCR is used nowadays for instance for automatic number plate recognition, and passport data recognition in airports [40].

Hence, in the current work we evaluate the precision of OCR on models from different domains focusing on text-recognition without looking for additional shapes. The aim is to answer the following research questions:

- **RQ1)** How accurate are off-the-shelf OCR services for extracting text from graphical models?
- **RQ2)** What are the common errors made by OCR services on models from different domains?

To answer RQ1 we apply Google Cloud Vision[1] and Microsoft Cognitive Services[2] to a collection of 43 models from different domains. We observe that Google Cloud Vision outperforms Microsoft Cognitive Services, being able to detect 70% of textual elements as opposed to 30% by Microsoft. To answer RQ2 we inspected errors made by Google Cloud Vision. We observed that in 100% of the cases, Google Cloud Vision was not capable of identifying Greek letters, subscripts, and text typeset in multiple lines. The lack of support for these elements represents the main challenge for adoption of OCR in multi-domain model management.

To encourage replication of our work the data we have collected and the source code we have used to perform the analysis has been made available on: bit.ly/ShareDataOCR.

---

[1] https://cloud.google.com/vision/.

[2] https://azure.microsoft.com/en-us/services/cognitive-services/.

The results presented in this work can be used to guide further research on OCR for multi-domain model management. For future work, we plan to combine different kind of image processing techniques to improve the results, for instance, being able to detect formulas, and semantic information by analyzing boxes, lines, and arrows.

2   Methodology

To answer RQ1 we apply Google Cloud Vision and Microsoft Cognitive Services to a collection of 43 models from different domains. To answer RQ2 we focus on the OCR service that has been shown to perform better on RQ1 and inspect the errors made by the service.

2.1   Models Selection

For reproducibility reasons, we arbitrarily select models from two UML open repositories[1,29], three control system engineering papers [30,36,47], and the example catalog of MatLab Simulink[3]. In total we analyzed 43 models as presented in Table 1. We only require the models to be graphical models, i.e., they must contain a mix of textual and graphical elements.

We select MatLab Simulink models because of its high adoption by the industry. These models are available on the official website as example catalog and they are used to describe control systems from different domains including automatic climate control, robot arm control, and fault-tolerant fuel control. We also include models from three scientific papers on control system engineering. The models from these papers are an intelligent control architecture of a small-Scale unmanned helicopter, an actuator control system, and a x-ray machine.

Among the UML models we focus on Class Diagram, Sequence Diagram, and Use Case Diagrams. These models are stored in two repositories: Git UML [1] and Models-db [29]. The former automatically generates diagrams from source code stored in git repositories. Models-db is automatically populated by crawlers identifying models from public GitHub repositories.

Table 1. List of models used to answer RQ1.

Source	Models	#Models
Ai et al. [30]	Figures 1, 4, 5	5
Kaliappan et al. [36]	Figures 1–3, 5, 7	5
Tovar-Arriaga et al. [47]	Figures 1, 5–8, 10, 15	7
UML	[12–28]	17
MatLab Simulink	[3–11]	9
Total		43

---

[3] https://www.mathworks.com/products/simulink.html.

2.2   Text Extraction

In order not to bias the evaluation towards a specific engineering domain, we opt for general-purpose OCR techniques.

Several OCR serves are available off the shelf, including Google Cloud Vision, Microsoft Cognitive Services, and Amazon AWS Rekognition[4]. For this work, we select the Google Cloud Vision and Microsoft Cognitive Services: these services have been shown to be effective in recognizing text from the photos of the pages of the Bible [44], and to outperform Amazon AWS on images of business names or movie names [2].

2.3   Measures for Accuracy

The validation consists of manually identifying the text from graphical models, and comparing the text extracted by OCR to the manually identified text. When deciding whether the OCR-extracted text matches the manually extracted one we do not distinguish between the letter case, i.e., *Velocity* is seen as the same as *veLoCitY*. We do distinguish between differently chunked texts, i.e., given the manually identified text *Velocity control* an OCR service extraction of *Velocity* and *Control* as two separate texts will be seen as wrong.

As common in information retrieval tasks we report precision, recall, and F-measure, i.e., the harmonic mean of precision and recall. In our context *precision* is the fraction of OCR-extracted texts that are also manually extracted compared to all OCR-extracted texts, and *recall* is the fraction of OCR-extracted texts that are also manually extracted compared to all manually extracted texts.

3   Results

3.1   R1: How Accurate Are Off-the-shelf OCR Services for Extracting Text from Graphical Models?

Overview. In overall, Google Cloud Vision correctly detected 854 out of 1,232 elements, while Microsoft Cognitive Services correctly detected 388 elements. This observation concurs with previous evaluations of these OCR services. Indeed, on the photos of the pages of the Bible Reis et al. [44] observed that Google Cloud Vision had a relative effectiveness of 86.5% as opposed to 77.4% of Microsoft Cognitive Services. On images of business names or movie names [2] Google Cloud Vision achieved 80% of both precision and recall as opposed to 65% of precision and 44% of recall of Microsoft Cognitive Services.

Hence, we hypothesize that also on our dataset Google Cloud Vision will outperform Microsoft Cognitive Services in terms of both precision and recall. Formally, we state the following hypotheses:

– H_0^p: The median difference between the *precision* for Google Cloud Vision and Microsoft Cognitive Services is zero.

---

[4] https://aws.amazon.com/rekognition/.

- H_a^p: The median difference between the *precision* for Google Cloud Vision and Microsoft Cognitive Services is greater than zero.
- H_0^r: The median difference between the *recall* for Google Cloud Vision and Microsoft Cognitive Services is zero.
- H_a^r: The median difference between the *recall* for Google Cloud Vision and Microsoft Cognitive Services is greater than zero.

To test these hypotheses we perform two paired Wilcoxon signed-rank tests, one for precision and another one for recall. The p-values obtained for precision and recall are 1.9×10^{-7} and 2.8×10^{-9}, respectively. Hence, we can reject H_0^p and H_0^r and state that Google Cloud Vision outperforms Microsoft Cognitive Services.

To illustrate this argument consider Fig. 1. It summarizes precision (y-axis) and recall (x-axis) organized by the type of models. Indeed, we can observe that while precision and recall obtained by Google Cloud Vision *mostly* exceed 0.5, precision and recall obtained by Microsoft Cognitive Services are *mostly* below 0.5. Moreover, the data for both Google Cloud Vision and Microsoft Cognitive Services suggests a linear relation between precision and recall: indeed, while the *number* of textual elements extracted by OCR tools is often close to the number of manually identified textual elements, the textual elements themselves are imprecise.

Finally, while Google Cloud Vision extracted *some* textual information from all models, Microsoft Cognitive Services failed on two models: Matlab Simulink model [6] and Figure 4.b from the paper by Ai et al. [30].

Performance on Models of Different Domains. While the previous discussion indicates that overall Google Cloud Vision outperforms Microsoft Cognitive Services, *a priori* this does not imply that this should also be the case for models of different domains. This is why we formulate the corresponding hypotheses separately for UML diagrams, Matlab Simulink models, and models from scientific papers. We test these hypotheses using paired Wilcoxon signed-rank tests, one for precision and another one for recall. However, since we perform multiple comparisons, we need to adjust the p-values to control for the false discovery rate. We use the method proposed by Benjamini and Hochberg [32].

The adjusted p-values are below the commonly used threshold of 0.05 for five of the six comparisons (three types of models × precision or recall). We conclude that Google Cloud Vision outperforms Microsoft Cognitive Services: for models of all domains in terms of recall; for UML diagrams and Matlab Simulink models in terms of precision as presented in Table 2.

Performance on Individual Models. Figure 2 shows that the F-measure for Google Cloud Vision is higher than for Microsoft Cognitive Services on 33 models, as opposed to five models where Microsoft Cognitive Services scores higher. For the remaining five models the F-measures are equal.

Inspecting Fig. 2 we also notice that for six models Microsoft Cognitive Services have precision equal to zero, i.e., either no textual elements have been

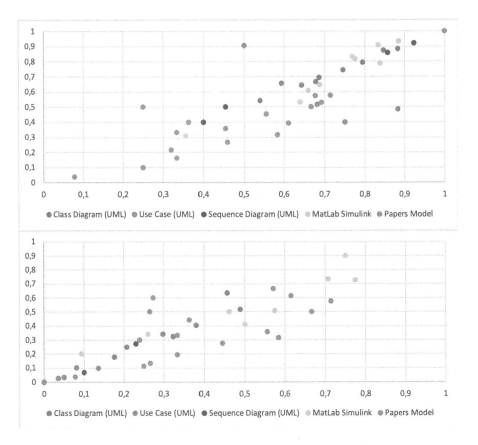

Fig. 1. Precision (y-axis) and recall (x-axis) obtained by Google Cloud Vision (top) and Microsoft Cognitive Services (bottom).

extracted (Matlab Simulink 4 and Paper model 3.3) or all textual elements extracted are wrong (UML Class Diagram 8, UML Use Case 4, UML Sequece Diagram 2 and 4). Unfortunately, we cannot precisely state the reasons why Microsoft Cognitive Services failed in process these models. Possible reasons could be related to the quality of the images, and size of font. However, these are unlikely to be the reasons for this fail, since all used images are in good quality and Google Cloud Vision managed to process the same images. In this study we did not look further in investing the reasons for the bad performance of Microsoft Cognitive Services.

Take away message

Google Cloud Vision was capable of detecting 70% of all elements, consistently outperforming Microsoft Cognitive Services.

Table 2. OCR service that presents statistically better results organized by the domain. The "-" means inconclusive result.

Models	Precision	Recall
UML	Google Cloud Vision	Google Cloud Vision
Matlab Simulink	Google Cloud Vision	Google Cloud Vision
Scientific papers	-	Google Cloud Vision

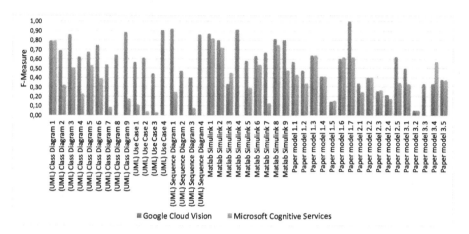

Fig. 2. F-Measure for all analyzed models

3.2   RQ2: What Are the Common Errors Made by OCR Services on Models from Different Domains?

Based on our answer to RQ1, one would prefer Google Cloud Vision as the OCR service to be integrated in a multi-domain model management solution. In this section we take a closer look at the errors made by Google Cloud Vision: addressing these errors is necessary in order to make OCR suited for multi-domain model management.

Table 3 summarizes the results of manual analysis of the errors made by Google Cloud Vision:

- The first category of errors is related to *non-alphanumerical characters* used in the models such as [, {, <, or _. These characters are sometimes confused with each other or missed by the OCR, e.g., the name of the element is '*file_version*' and OCR detects '*file version*', without the underscore.
- Engineering models can involve *mathematical formulas* such as equations, including subscripts and Greek letters.
- The next group of errors is related to *spacing* and relative positioning of the textual elements. For example, due to space limitations text can be positioned on multiple lines, making OCR to misinterpret as one textual element but as two separate elements, we call this error as *Multi-line Text*. When this

Table 3. Number of models affected by the identified problems. CD - Class Diagram, UC - User Case, SD - Sequence Diagram

Problem	Total	UML			MatLab	Paper
		CD	UC	SD		
Non-alphanumeric characters						
Brackets	1	0	0	0	1	0
Curly Brackets	2	0	0	2	0	0
Greater/Less Symbol	1	0	1	0	0	0
Parentheses	5	3	0	1	1	0
Slash	1	0	0	1	0	0
Underscore	8	7	0	0	1	0
Total	*18*	*10*	*1*	*4*	*3*	*0*
Mathematical formulas						
Equation	2	0	0	0	2	0
Subscript	2	0	0	0	0	2
Greek Letter	2	0	0	0	0	2
Total	*6*	*0*	*0*	*0*	*2*	*4*
Spacing						
Empty Space between Letters	15	6	4	3	1	1
Mix of Elements	8	4	0	0	3	1
Multi-line Text	28	4	3	0	7	14
Split Element	1	1	0	0	0	0
Total	*51*	*15*	*7*	*3*	*11*	*15*
Character confusion						
Character Confusion	8	1	2	0	3	2
Extra Char	11	4	2	0	2	3
Missing Char	14	5	1	0	3	5
Wrong Char	13	3	0	2	5	3
Total	*46*	*13*	*5*	*2*	*13*	*13*

misinterpretation happens in a textual element positioned in one single line, we call this error as *Split Element*. The difference between *Multi-line Text* and *Split Element* is that the latter occurs on textual element is written in one single line but have an empty space between the words, causing this misinterpretation. The opposite of the error *Split Element* is *Mix of Elements*. *Mix of Elements* occurs when OCR mixes the name of different elements due to their proximity.

– Finally, the last group of errors is related to single-character errors such as characters being wrongly added, removed, or recognized. An example of such error is *Character Confusion*. This error occurs when OCR is not capable

Table 4. Candidate Elements are the elements that contain characters that can cause a problem. Candidate Models are the models that have the candidate elements.

Problem	#Affected Models	#Candidate Models	#Affected Elements	#Candidate Elements
Non-alphanumeric characters				
Brackets	1	1	1	5
Curly Brackets	2	2	8	9
Greater/Less Symbol	1	12	4	60
Parentheses	5	5	11	137
Slash	1	11	1	39
Underscore	8	8	59	156
Mathematical formulas				
Equations	2	2	2	2
Subscript	2	2	15	15
Greek letters	2	2	2	2
Spacing				
Multi-line Text	27	27	130	130
Split Element	1	39	2	334

of identifying the letter due to the similarity to other letters. For instance, the name of the element is *'DeleteNodeById( )'*. However, OCR interprets the capital letter 'i' as the lowercase 'l', returning *'DeleteNodeByld( )'*. The difference between *Character Confusion* and *Wrong Char* is that the former occurs between similar characters, e.g., the letter 'o' and the number '0'. And *Wrong Char* occurs between any character.

Table 3 shows that errors present in the largest number of models are *Multi-line Text*, *Empty Space between Letters*, *Missing Char*, and *Wrong Char*. However, the number of models affected by the errors should be compared to the number of models that *can* be affected by those errors: while wrong characters might appear in any model, errors related to underscores can only be present if the models contain underscores.

Hence, Table 4 summarizes the number of models that can be affected (candidate models) and the models that are affected by errors. Similarly, it includes the number of elements that can be affected (candidate elements) and are affected by the errors.

Inspecting Table 4 we observe that the *Curly Brackets*, *Equations*, *Greek letters*, *Multi-line String*, *Parentheses*, *Subscript*, and *Underscore* occur in every single model that has the corresponding elements.

Even though *Parentheses*, and *Underscore* problems arise in 100% of the candidate models, Google Cloud Vision correctly identified 92% of textual elements that have parentheses and 60% of the textual elements that have underscores and this in sharp contrast with *Equations*, *Greek Letters*, *Multi-line String*, and *Subscript* that could not be recognized by Google Cloud Vision.

> **Take away message**
>
> The main OCR challenges are text that contains *Equations*, *Greek Letters*, *Multi-line String*, and *Subscript* due to the lower precision on correctly identify these elements.

4 Threats to Validity

As any empirical study our work is subject to threats to validity. Wohlin et al. [49] provide a list of possible threats that researchers can face during a scientific research. In this section, we describe the actions we took in order to increase the validity and decrease the threats.

Internal validity, concerns the unknown influences of independent variables can have on studies. In order to mitigate this concern, we have selected OCR services that have been evaluated by previous studies on different text recognition tasks. While the manual extraction of textual elements has been performed by one author only, the task is simple for an engineer and is unlikely to be affected by the subjectivity of their judgment.

External validity concerns the generalizability of the results and findings of the study. In order to mitigate this concern, we have diversified the collection of models analyzed to include models from different domains and different sources.

Construct validity concerns the issues related to the design of the experiment. In order to address this issue, we used metrics that were sufficiently defined in previous studies. Example of such metrics are precision, recall, and F-measure. We used these metrics to indicate which OCR service presents better performance.

Conclusion validity concerns about the relations between the conclusions that we draw and the analyzed data. In order to mitigate this concern, we paid special attention to use appropriate statistical techniques, and we described all decisions we made. Thus, this study can be replicated by other researchers, and we expect our results to be quite robust.

5 Discussion and Future Work

The results described in this paper can serve as a starting point for future research on the use of OCR for multi-domain model management, as well as for design of tools supporting multi-domain model management. We started by investigating accuracy of the off-the-shelf OCR services for extracting text from graphical models. Concurrent with the previous studies [2,44] Google Cloud Vision outperformed Microsoft Cognitive Services on both precision and recall. However, the precision and recall values of Google Cloud Vision were not as high as the ones presented in the previous studies [2]. We believe this is due to the difference between the analyzed items: graphical models vs. business names. As opposed to business names, graphical models often include mathematical elements such as Greek letters and subscripts, and non-alphanumeric characters. Moreover, extracting text from models that do not follow the same design rules, incurs additional challenges. Indeed, the precision and recall scores for models from scientific papers are much more spread out in Fig. 1, than for models from other data sources.

Next, we investigated the common errors produced by Google Cloud Vision. We identified 17 different types of errors organized by four categories: *non-alphanumeric characters, mathematical formulas, spacing*, and *character confusion*. Most common errors are related to Spacing and Character confusion; however, the main challenges seem to be related to the mathematical formulas—not a single Greek letter, subscript or equation appearing in the models could be correctly identified.

As future work, we intend to focus on the main challenges we identified in Sect. 3.2. Furthermore, we want to evaluate different OCR techniques on additional kinds of graphical models, including, for instance, models drawn on whiteboards and hand-written models. Simultaneously, we intend to combine OCR with image processing to analyze graphical elements such as boxes, lines, and arrows presented in the models.

6   Related Work

To the best of our knowledge, there are no studies on the use of off-the-shelf OCR services on models from different domains. However, OCR has been applied to domain-specific models. Img2UML [37,38] extracts UML Class Diagrams from images, identifying, e.g., class names, fields and methods. Img2UML uses Microsoft Office Document Imaging as the OCR technique for text recognition. While Img2UML is geared towards and evaluated on a specific domain, the techniques we have analyzed have been applied to models of multiple domains. Several studies have used OCR as part of a tool classifying images as UML diagrams: targeting class diagrams [35,41], sequence diagrams [43] and component diagrams [41].

Going beyond engineering models, Reis [44] compare Google Cloud Vision and Microsoft Cognitive Services in recognizing text from the photos of the pages of the Bible. Additional comparison studies have been published by Mello and Dueire Lins [39] and Vijayarani and Sakila [48].

7   Conclusion

We presented a study of suitability of the off-the-shelf OCR services in the context of multi-domain model management. We evaluated performance of two well-known services, Google Cloud Vision and Microsoft Cognitive Services, on a collection of 43 models from different domains: 17 UML diagrams, 9 MatLab Simulink models and 17 models from scientific papers from the control system engineering domain.

We observed that Google Cloud Vision overall outperforms Microsoft Cognitive Services both in terms of precision and in terms of recall. This observation is consistent both with the previous work [2, 44] and with a follow-up study investigating performance of the two OCR-services on models of different domains.

Focusing on Google Cloud Vision, we identified a list of 17 kinds of errors distributed over four categories: non-alphanumeric characters, mathematical formulas, spacing and character confusion. Among these errors, the most common are related to text written on multiple lines, wrong/missing characters, and an empty space between letters. It is also important that in presence of multi-line texts, Greek letters, subscripts, and equations because Google Cloud Vision failed every single time.

To conclude, we observe that even though Google Cloud Vision has some limitations, it produces satisfactory results. We believe that once the most problematic cases are solved, OCR can become a crucial technology to support multi-domain model management.

References

1. Git UML repository. https://www.gituml.com. Accessed 23 Jan 2020
2. Image text recognition APIs showdown. https://dataturks.com/blog/compare-image-text-recognition-apis.php. Accessed 08 Jan 2020
3. MATLAB Simulink model 1. https://nl.mathworks.com/help/simulink/slref/anti-windup-control-using-a-pid-controller.html. Accessed 24 Jan 2020
4. MATLAB Simulink model 2. https://nl.mathworks.com/help/simulink/slref/simulating-automatic-climate-control-systems.html. Accessed 24 Jan 2020
5. MATLAB Simulink model 3. https://nl.mathworks.com/help/simulink/slref/simulation-of-a-bouncing-ball.html. Accessed 24 Jan 2020
6. MATLAB Simulink model 4. https://bit.ly/simulinkModel4. Accessed 24 Jan 2020
7. MATLAB Simulink model 5. https://bit.ly/simulinkModel5. Accessed 24 Jan 2020
8. MATLAB Simulink model 6. https://bit.ly/simulinkModel6. Accessed 24 Jan 2020
9. MATLAB Simulink model 7. https://bit.ly/simulinkModel7. Accessed 24 Jan 2020
10. MATLAB Simulink model 8. https://nl.mathworks.com/help/simulink/slref/designing-a-guidance-system-in-matlab-and-simulink.html. Accessed 24 Jan 2020
11. MATLAB Simulink model 9. https://bit.ly/simulinkModel9. Accessed 24 Jan 2020
12. UML - class diagram 1. http://models-db.com/repository/70/classdiagram/238. Accessed 24 Jan 2020
13. UML - class diagram 2. https://www.gituml.com/viewz/5. Accessed 24 Jan 2020
14. UML - class diagram 3. https://www.gituml.com/viewz/87. Accessed 24 Jan 2020
15. UML - class diagram 4. https://www.gituml.com/viewz/26. Accessed 24 Jan 2020
16. UML - class diagram 5. https://www.gituml.com/viewz/27. Accessed 24 Jan 2020
17. UML - class diagram 6. https://www.gituml.com/viewz/20. Accessed 24 Jan 2020
18. UML - class diagram 7. http://models-db.com/repository/84/classdiagram/441. Accessed 24 Jan 2020
19. UML - class diagram 8. http://models-db.com/repository/84/classdiagram/449. Accessed 24 Jan 2020
20. UML - class diagram 9. http://models-db.com/repository/102/classdiagram/624. Accessed 24 Jan 2020

21. UML - sequence diagram 1. http://models-db.com/repository/108/classdiagram/781. Accessed 24 Jan 2020
22. UML - sequence diagram 2. http://models-db.com/repository/108/classdiagram/783. Accessed 24 Jan 2020
23. UML - sequence diagram 3. http://models-db.com/repository/108/classdiagram/808. Accessed 24 Jan 2020
24. UML - sequence diagram 4. http://models-db.com/repository/108/classdiagram/809. Accessed 24 Jan 2020
25. UML - use case diagram 1. http://models-db.com/repository/108/classdiagram/733. Accessed 24 Jan 2020
26. UML - use case diagram 2. http://models-db.com/repository/108/classdiagram/734. Accessed 24 Jan 2020
27. UML - use case diagram 3. http://models-db.com/repository/108/classdiagram/736. Accessed 24 Jan 2020
28. UML - use case diagram 4. http://models-db.com/repository/108/classdiagram/775. Accessed 24 Jan 2020
29. The UML repository. http://models-db.com. Accessed 23 Jan 2020
30. Ai, B., Sentis, L., Paine, N., Han, S., Mok, A., Fok, C.L.: Stability and performance analysis of time-delayed actuator control systems. J. Dyn. Syst. Measur. Control **138**(5), 051005-1–051005-20 (2016)
31. Atkinson, C.: Orthographic software modelling: a novel approach to view-based software engineering. In: Kühne, T., Selic, B., Gervais, M.-P., Terrier, F. (eds.) ECMFA 2010. LNCS, vol. 6138, p. 1. Springer, Heidelberg (2010). https://doi.org/10.1007/978-3-642-13595-8_1
32. Benjamini, Y., Hochberg, Y.: Controlling the false discovery rate: a practical and powerful approach to multiple testing. J. Roy. Stat. Soc. Ser. B (Methodol.) **57**(1), 289–300 (1995). https://doi.org/10.2307/2346101
33. Hebig, R., Giese, H., Stallmann, F., Seibel, A.: On the complex nature of MDE evolution. In: Moreira, A., Schätz, B., Gray, J., Vallecillo, A., Clarke, P. (eds.) MODELS 2013. LNCS, vol. 8107, pp. 436–453. Springer, Heidelberg (2013). https://doi.org/10.1007/978-3-642-41533-3_27
34. Herbert, H.: The history of OCR, optical character recognition. Recognition Technologies Users Association, Manchester Center, VT (1982)
35. Ho-Quang, T., Chaudron, M.R., Samúelsson, I., Hjaltason, J., Karasneh, B., Osman, H.: Automatic classification of UML class diagrams from images. In: 2014 21st Asia-Pacific Software Engineering Conference, vol. 1, pp. 399–406. IEEE (2014)
36. Kaliappan, V.K., Yong, H., Dugki, M., Choi, E., Budiyono, A.: Reconfigurable intelligent control architecture of a small-scale unmanned helicopter. J. Aerosp. Eng. **27**(4), 04014001 (2014)
37. Karasneh, B., Chaudron, M.R.: Extracting UML models from images. In: 2013 5th International Conference on Computer Science and Information Technology, pp. 169–178. IEEE (2013)
38. Karasneh, B., Chaudron, M.R.: Img2UML: a system for extracting UML models from images. In: 2013 39th Euromicro Conference on Software Engineering and Advanced Applications, pp. 134–137. IEEE (2013)
39. Melo, C.A.B., Dueire Lins, R.: A comparative study on OCR tools. In: Vision Interface (1999)
40. Modi, H., Parikh, M.: A review on optical character recognition techniques. Int. J. Comput. Appl. **160**(6), 20–24 (2017)

41. Moreno, V., Génova, G., Alejandres, M., Fraga, A.: Automatic classification of web images as UML diagrams. In: Proceedings of the 4th Spanish Conference on Information Retrieval, pp. 1–8 (2016)
42. Mustafiz, S., Denil, J., Lúcio, L., Vangheluwe, H.: The FTG+PM framework for multi-paradigm modelling: an automotive case study. In: Proceedings of the 6th International Workshop on Multi-paradigm Modeling, pp. 13–18 (2012)
43. Rashid, S.: Automatic classification of UML sequence diagrams from images (2019)
44. Reis, A., Paulino, D., Filipe, V., Barroso, J.: Using online artificial vision services to assist the blind - an assessment of Microsoft cognitive services and Google Cloud vision. In: Rocha, Á., Adeli, H., Reis, L.P., Costanzo, S. (eds.) WorldCIST'18 2018. AISC, vol. 746, pp. 174–184. Springer, Cham (2018). https://doi.org/10.1007/978-3-319-77712-2_17
45. Stahl, T., Voelter, M., Czarnecki, K.: Model-Driven Software Development: Technology, Engineering, Management. Wiley, Hoboken (2006)
46. Sun, Yu., Gray, J., Bulheller, K., von Baillou, N.: A model-driven approach to support engineering changes in industrial robotics software. In: France, R.B., Kazmeier, J., Breu, R., Atkinson, C. (eds.) MODELS 2012. LNCS, vol. 7590, pp. 368–382. Springer, Heidelberg (2012). https://doi.org/10.1007/978-3-642-33666-9_24
47. Tovar-Arriaga, S., Vargas, J.E., Ramos, J.M., Aceves, M.A., Gorrostieta, E., Kalender, W.A.: A fully sensorized cooperative robotic system for surgical interventions. Sensors 12(7), 9423–9447 (2012)
48. Vijayarani, S., Sakila, A.: Performance comparison of OCR tools. Int. J. UbiComp 6(3), 19–30 (2015)
49. Wohlin, C., Runeson, P., Höst, M., Ohlsson, M.C., Regnell, B., Wesslén, A.: Experimentation in Software Engineering. Springer, Heidelberg (2012). https://doi.org/10.1007/978-3-642-29044-2

Simplified View Generation in a Deep View-Based Modeling Environment

Arne Lange$^{(\boxtimes)}$, Colin Atkinson, and Christian Tunjic

Software Engineering Group, University of Mannheim, Mannheim, Germany
{lange,atkinson,tunjic}@informatik.uni-mannheim.de

Abstract. Projective modeling environments offer a more efficient and scalable way of supporting multiple views of large software systems than traditional, synthesis-based approaches to view-based development. However, the definition of the view projection transformations needed to create views, on demand, from the single underlying model and ensure that they remain synchronized is a complex and time-consuming process. In particular, to make views editable, the projection process involves the creation of "traces" to map view model elements to their sources in the single underlying model. While this is unavoidable for most view types, for a commonly occurring special case this level of complexity is not required. In this paper we therefore present a simpler approach, based on the OCL language, which simplifies the projection definitions for this kind of view. The approach is defined in the context of a deep, view-based modeling environment which combines support for views with multi-level modeling in order to seamlessly cover all phases of a system's life cycle.

Keywords: Multi-level modeling · View-based modeling · Deep OCL

1 Introduction

Although the use of "views" has a long history in software engineering, views are still supported in a rather ad-hoc and inconsistent manner in most methods and tools. For example, although the UML sublanguages clearly support distinct kinds of views of software systems (e.g. class/object views, state/transition views, object collaboration views etc.), in the MDA the term "view" is reserved for describing general abstraction levels (i.e. platform-independent and platform-specific views etc.) [5]. Similarly, the ISO 42010 standard for Systems and Software Engineering Architecture Description [3] reserves the term "view" to represent abstract perspectives of systems and refers to concrete views that actually portray information as "models". To address these issues, and provide more systematic and scalable approaches to view-based software engineering, there has been growing interest in so called "projective" modeling environments in which views are treated more uniformly and are generated (i.e. projected) on demand from a Single Underlying Model (SUM) [10,16,20,24]. This not only

© Springer Nature Switzerland AG 2020
O. Babur et al. (Eds.): ICSMM 2020, CCIS 1262, pp. 163–179, 2020.
https://doi.org/10.1007/978-3-030-58167-1_12

simplifies the conceptual notion of views, it also significantly reduces the number of inter-view correspondences that have to be maintained and thus the scalability of view-based approaches.

Although they have many advantages over synthetic approaches, most SUM-based approaches still focus almost exclusively on describing type-level information (e.g. classes, processes, interactions) since this is the most prevalent at design time. However, when the operation phase of a system's life cycle is taken into account, which underpins the trend towards continuous, phase-spanning software engineering, it is important to be able to portray instance-level information in the same way as type-level information, using the same view concepts [13]. Since multi-level modeling languages were developed specifically for this latter purpose (i.e. to support the seamless and uniform modeling of type and instance information across arbitrary numbers of classification levels), it makes sense to unify SUM-based modeling approaches with multi-level modeling approaches.

Currently, the only approach that does this is the deep, orthographic software modeling approach [22] which integrates the deep modeling variant of multi-level modeling [7] with the orthographic software modeling (OSM) variant of SUM-based modeling [19]. The resulting hybrid approach, deep OSM (DOSM) allows views showing information at multiple classification levels, or at any arbitrary classification level, (i.e. "deep views") to be projected on demand from a multi-level SUM using transformations defined in a multi-level aware dialect of ATL – deep ATL [9]. This extends the traditional features of ATL with capabilities to select between ontological and linguistic attributes and identify which ontological level model elements should be taken from and added to.

This technology can accommodate any kind of deep views, including editable and non-editable views. In the latter case, "traces" are created between elements appearing in the SUM and their "projections" in views so that the former can be updated according to the changes made to the latter. This is necessary when the abstraction level or the representation language changes since there is then rarely a one-to-one mapping of SUM model elements to view model elements. However, for one frequently occurring view type this approach is unnecessarily complex – "subsetting views" which simply shows a subset of the elements in the SUM without changing their form. For this kind of view, the general, deep ATL approach described in [11] is unnecessarily complex. In this paper we therefore present a "lightweight" mechanism for projecting subsetting views which avoids much of the complexity of the current approach but still allows views to be edited. This "lightweight" approach is based on an extension to deep OCL rather than on deep ATL. The deep OCL dialect caters for an arbitrary number of classification levels, which includes traditional two level modeling scenarios as a special case.

The rest of this paper is organized as follows. In the next section we provide an overview of the technologies which the approach is based on. In Sect. 3 we describe how view projection transformations are currently defined in the Doreen modeling environment using deep ATL. Section 4 follows with the main contribution of this paper, the presentation of the deep OCL variant for lightweight view projection filtering, and an illustration of how it can be used to describe projections in a simpler way. Section 5 then presents a more detailed example of the approach, before Sects. 6 and 7 conclude with related work and some closing remarks.

2   Foundations

This section describes the existing approaches and technologies that provide the foundation for our approach.

2.1   Projective, View-Based Modeling

The ISO 42010 standard for Systems and Software Engineering Architecture Description [3], mentioned previously, explicitly presents two fundamental approaches for supporting view-based modeling environments – synthetic and projective approaches. In the former, all information about the system is stored in the views themselves, while in the latter the views are projected, on demand, from a central source of data such as a SUM. Multiple users can therefore access, change and create model elements in different views simultaneously.

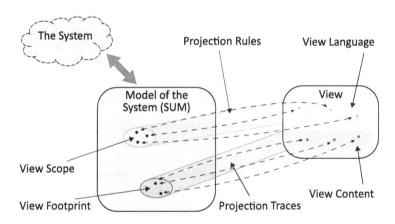

Fig. 1. SUM-based projective modeling [11]

Figure 1 shows the relationship between the SUM and views in the OSM [10] projective, view-based modeling approach in which the SUM is made as minimalistic and redundancy-free as possible. The deep view illustrated on the right-hand side is created, on demand, by projecting information from the SUM illustrated on the left-hand side, which represents the sole source of information about the system. The projection rules relate a subset of the types in the SUM (the View Scope) with the corresponding types representing a view type (the View Language), while the projection traces relate a subset of the instances of the types in the view scope, (the View Footprint) to instances of the view language (the View Content). The projection traces are used to update the model elements in the view footprint if and when the corresponding model elements in the view content are edited. The view language and the projection rules together define a "view type" in this approach [11].

2.2   Deep Modeling

Multi-level modeling, is a modeling paradigm that explicitly distinguishes between ontological and linguistic dimensions of classification. The ontological dimension that users work with is characterized by multiple ontological classification levels containing model elements known as 'clabjects'. The classification relationships in the ontological classification dimension represent those existing in the modeled domain. In general, clabjects have both an instance facet and a type facet, hence the name 'clabject' (CLAss and oBJECT) which reflects the fact that they can be instances of clabjects in the level above, and types for clabjects in the level below.

Some multi-level modeling languages, sometimes called deep modeling languages, use the notion of potency to govern the characterization properties of clabjects over multiple levels. Potency is a non-negative integer property of clabjects that indicates over how many levels a clabject can be instantiated. If the potency of a clabject is 0 it is either an abstract clabject or an individual (i.e. an instance that cannot be further instantiated). Clabjects with potencies greater than 0 can be instantiated at the level below to create clabjects with lower (but non-negative) potencies. Clabjects are also containers for Attributes and Methods and can be connected to each other as long as they reside at the same level. It is also possible to define inheritance relationships and other forms of associations such as aggregation and composition between clabjects of the same level.

Figure 2 shows a deep model with three ontological levels residing at the linguistic level L1. All model elements within the ontological levels are therefore linguistic instances of the (meta-)model at L2. The linguistic level L0 represents the real world instances. The top ontological level contains one clabject called *Organization Type* with a potency value of 2, which means this clabject can be instantiated over two more levels. The clabject University at the second level *O1* is simultaneously an instance of *Organization Type* and a type for the clabject *UniversityOfMannheim* at the third level *O2*. This paper focuses on the variant of deep modeling supported by the tool Melanee [4,14,15].

2.3   Deep Orthographic Software Modeling

The OSM approach was inspired by the ubiquitous "orthographic projection" metaphor widely used in the design of physical artifacts (e.g. in CAD systems) to build a tool to support the KobrA multi-view, software development method [6]. Two main ideas from orthographic projection form the foundation for our approach. The first is the idea of storing all information about the system under

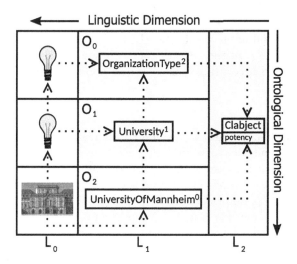

Fig. 2. Orthongonal classification architecture [22]

development in a SUM and arranging for all views of the systems to be projected on-demand from the SUM via bi-directional transformations (i.e. projective modeling). The second is the idea of organizing all views in terms of a multi-dimensional space of concerns, within which any specific view has a concrete set of coordinates. In contrast with normal CAD systems, where the main dimensions are the three physical dimensions of space, in the context of software modeling the dimensions can be such concerns as abstraction level (e.g. PIM, PSM etc.), information perspective (e.g. structural, behavioral etc.) or visibility (e.g black box versus white box). Since KobrA defines all these concerns, it was the focus of the original incarnations of the approach, however OSM is not restricted to KobrA.

The goal of deep Orthographic Software Modeling (DOSM) [22] is to integrate the benefits of deep (i.e. multi-level) modeling with OSM so that the SUM and views can cover any, or multiple, classification levels. Although the OSM approach is agnostic to the number of ontological classification levels, like most development approaches, the first incarnation was focused on traditional two-level modeling (like the KobrA method itself). However, this means that to cover "instance" level information where run-time information usually resides (e.g. running instances of business process, instances of domain classes etc.), significant accidental complexity arises. This in turn makes it difficult to extend the OSM approach to cover more phases than just the development phases (e.g. deployment and operation phases) and to support the continuous and seamless roll-out of new versions of a system in accordance with modern "devops" principles. DOSM addresses this problem by regarding the SUM as a deep model which can capture information across all relevant classification levels within a domain, and views as portrayals of the deep SUM which can show information at any arbitrary collection of adjacent classification levels (i.e. from one level within the SUM to all levels within the SUM).

This paper focuses on the DOSM approach supported by the Doreen tool [11] which is implemented using Melanee's deep modeling technology.

2.4   Deep ATL

In order to write effective view projection transformations in a deep, projective modeling environment such as DOSM, it is necessary to have a suitable transformation language that is aware of the two classification dimensions and multiple ontological classification levels in deep models. For this purpose Doreen uses the deep variant of ATL provided by Melanee which explicitly provides access to the two classification dimensions in an OCA modeling environment. This facilitates the definition of transformations that map multi-level models to traditional two-level models and vice versa or multi-level models to multi-level models [8]. To provide access to the linguistic properties, the operator '_l_' can be used, while the operator '_o_' provides access to ontological properties.

```
rule ComponentClass2Class {
    from s : PLM!O0.ComponentClass 1
    to t : UML!Class (
        name <- s._l_.name
    )
}
```

Transformation 2.1. Example transformation showing syntax extensions

Transformation 2.1 shows an example of the syntax extensions provided by deep ATL to make transformation rules multi-level aware. This shows how model elements from the second ontological level, *O1*, in Fig. 3 can be explicitly selected for transformation into the view. The source elements are *TravelBookingSys* and *AccountManager* which both are direct instances of *ComponentClass* from *O0*.

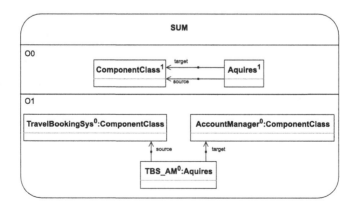

Fig. 3. ATL example from [8]

The rule *ComponentClass2Class* specifies that every direct instance of *ComponentClass* should be transformed into an instance of a Class. Moreover, the name of the newly created Class is the name of the *ComponentClass* instance, which is obtained from its linguistic property 'name'.

2.5 Deep OCL

Deep OCL [17] was developed to augment Melanee's multi-level models with OCL-like expressions by implementing a few syntactic and semantic enhancements to standard OCL [21]. The grammar for this dialect of OCL was implemented using ANTLR [2]. In order to refer to the linguistic dimension to call methods or access linguistic levels, clabjects, attributes or other elements it is possible to use a '#' symbol that indicates the switch to the linguistic dimension. This is similar to the '_1_' operator of deep ATL. The standard OCL classification operations, 'isInstanceOf()', 'oclIsTypeOf()', 'oclIsKindOf()' work in the usual way, so it is possible to write constraints spanning two levels of a multi-level model in the traditional way. However, deep OCL offers further operations, like 'isDeepInstanceOf()', 'isDeepDirectInstanceOf()', 'isDirectInstanceOf()', 'IsIndirectInstanceOf()' and 'isDeepIndirectInstanceOf()', to exploit deep classification hierarchies [14]. The 'isDeepInstanceOf()' is especially useful for checking the full classification hierarchy to establish whether a clabject is contained within it. With the deep OCL dialect it is also possible to have different definitions and execution contexts. For example, in our solution of the MULTI bicycle challenge [1,18] we defined constraints on the *O1* level but these constraint were executed on direct and indirect instances of the definition context on the levels below *O1*.

Standard OCL implementations are based on the UML meta-model and do not alter the model (i.e. a class diagram) in any shape or form. In other words, standard OCL expressions are declarative and are always evaluated on the instances of a model [23]. Since instances are regarded as part of a deep model, not external to it, deep OCL is not longer purely declarative dialect since it can alter the elements of a model in some ways, e.g. by calculating the value assigned to an attribute through a derive constraint.

3 View Projection Transformations

In this section we show how view projections are realized by deep ATL transformations in the Doreen tool. In Fig. 4, the view on the right-hand side is projected from the SUM. The yellow colored shape indicates the view scope which is projected to the view language by applying the projection rules. The blue colored shape indicates the view footprint of the projection traces which are created.

Transformation 3.1 shows the mandatory rules for transforming elements from the SUM, on the left-hand side of the Figure, to the view on the right-hand side. The rule *ProcessSum2ProcessView* transforms instances of 'Process' in the SUM, to instances of 'Process' in the view. The linguistic property *name* of the source instance is set to the respective property in the target instance.

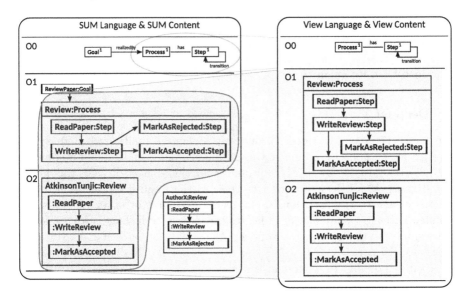

Fig. 4. Transformation example from [11] (Color figure online)

The transformation that creates 'Step' instances in the view works in the same way as the rule for processes. The third rule handles the connection called 'has'. Every instance of *Process* and *Step* in the SUM is transformed into corresponding instances in the view with corresponding connections between them. The last rule also transforms a connection from the SUM into a connection in the view. It creates connections that conform to *transition* in the SUM to connections in the view which connects 'Step' instances to one another.

```
rule ProcessSum2ProcessView {
    from s : SUM!O0.Process 1..2 (thisModule.isSubject(s)
                           or thisModule.neededProcess(s))
    to t : VIEW!O0.Process 1..2 (_l_.name <- s._l_.name)
}

rule StepSum2StepView {
    from s : SUM!O0.Step 1..2 (thisModule.neededStep(s))
    to t : VIEW!O0.Step 1..2 (_l_.name <- s._l_.name)
}
rule HasSum2HasView {
    from s : SUM!O0.has 1..2 (thisModule.neededHas(s))
    to t : VIEW!O0.has 1..2 (_l_.name <- s._l_.name,
        _o_.process <- s._o_.process, _o_.step <- s._o_.step)
}

rule TransitionSum2TransitionView {
    from s : SUM!O0.transition 1..2 (thisModule.neededTransition(s))
    to t : VIEW!O0.transition 1..2 (_l_.name <- s._l_.name,
        _o_.source <- s._o_.source, _o_.target <- s._o_.target)
}
```

Transformation 3.1. Deep ATL SUM to view transformation

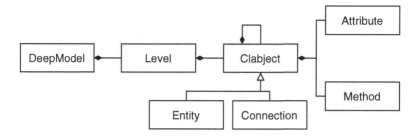

Fig. 5. Simplified Pan-Level Model (PLM) as defined in [15]

Although the transformation rules are defined at the most abstract level in the SUM their effects are at the *O1* and *O2* levels as indicated by the interval specified in the source and target patterns ('1..2').

4   View Projection Filters

In this section we present the modifications we made to deep OCL to support simpler specifications of view projections when a view merely portrays a subset of the model elements in the SUM. Figure 5 shows a simplified version of the PLM that serves as the foundation of the linguistic meta-model for the Melanee deep modeling tool upon which our implementation is based. In particular, it shows the way the main model elements can be nested within one another – *DeepModels* contain *Levels*, which in turn contain *Clabjects* which can be either *Entities* or *Connections*. As well as containing the usual *Attributes* and *Methods*, clabjects can also contain other clabjects. This containment structure is not only a natural way of organizing model elements, it also provides a natural foundation for writing deep constraints and element selections.

4.1   Filter Expressions

The new functionality in the deep OCL dialect is based on filters which are introduced by the keyword "filter". In this section we show how such "filter expressions" are defined and used. The keyword indicates that the result of this new kind of expression is a collection rather than a Boolean value as with normal OCL constraints. As usual, the expression is attached to a context which can be any instance of the linguistic meta-model (i.e. a deep model, level, or clabject). View expressions with the same name belong to exactly one view. They open a namespace, and every filter under that namespace will be executed when this view is called up. The syntax of filter expressions is shown in Fig. 6. A filter expression has to have a name, because all the expressions with a given name collectively define a view. The *specificationCS* grammar rule can be any OCL expression with any return type.

   The filter expression in our deep OCL dialect returns collections (i.e. Sets or Bags) and can be defined on every element of the linguistic meta-model.

Due to the hierarchical structure of Melanee's linguistic model as shown in Fig. 5, the largest level of granularity at which a filter expression can be defined is *DeepModel*. The next level of granularity is *Level*, and so on. It is important to name the filter expressions uniformly if they belong to the same view for two reasons. First, it indicates that they all contribute to the same view and second, it defines a namespace which indicates what expressions have to be evaluated to construct a certain view. The expressions have an execution order which follows the containment hierarchy described in the linguistic meta-model. Views are therefore defined by a collection of small, element-related expressions rather than by one complicated transformation rule or one complicated filter expression applied to the outer most element of the view.

The algorithm that searches for filtering expressions when a view is generated will search from the outer-most model element in the hierarchy, e.g. *DeepModel*, to the lowest elements, e.g. *Attribute* and *Method*, to locate filter expressions with the same name. When a filter is selected by the user the algorithm searches for all the filter expressions with that name and executes them from the top of the containment hierarchy to the bottom. If at any stage in the process an element has no associated filtering expression, everything contained by that element is included automatically.

Fig. 6. Syntax railroad diagram for the grammar rule 'filterCS'

4.2   View Definition Example

This section shows how the view created by the view projection transformation shown in Sect. 3, and illustrated in Fig. 4, can be defined using the aforementioned filter expressions rather than the deep ATL Transformation 3.1. These filter expressions select (i.e. "filter out") the model elements in the SUM that need to be portrayed and made available for editing in the view. Whereas in the deep OSM approach, the view language specification is always part of a deep view, in our case the filtered views do not conform to a specific view type but rather to the whole SUM. The first level, *O0*, is therefore not shown in our example.

```
context DeepModel
filter  ProcessView:  Level -> reject (l|l.#getLevelIndex ()# = 0)
```
OCL Expression 4.1. OCL filter for level *O1* and *O2*

The first filter Expression 4.1 shows a reflective query from the context of the *DeepModel* for *Level*, which returns every level that is contained within the deep model. This collection of levels is then processed by the reject expression which results in all the levels having a level index greater than 0.

```
context  O0  (1_2)
filter  ProcessView:  Clabject  ->  reject(c|c.isDeepInstanceOf(Goal))
```

OCL Expression 4.2. OCL view expression filtering out instances of Goal

The level specification in the Expression 4.2 indicates that this expression is executed at levels *O1* and *O2* although the definition context is level *O0* which is not part of the view. The expression filters out clabjects that are instances or deep instances of *Goal*.

```
context  O2
filter  ProcessView:  Clabject  ->  select(c|c.#getName()# = '
    AtkinsonTunjic')
```

OCL Expression 4.3. OCL view expression to just show the relevant process

Expression 4.3 shows the final filter expression in this example. In the view we only want to include the Process instance with the name *AtkinsonTunjic* from the SUM content. From the level *O2*, which is the definition and execution context, every clabject is filtered out that is not named *AtkinsonTunjic*. A further view constraint is not necessary because the contained clabjects in the process instances are displayed without any restrictions. If no filter expression is used in the context of a containment relationship, regardless of the dimension of this containment (i.e. linguistic vs. ontological), the containing elements are displayed without restrictions.

5   Bicycle Challenge Example

In this section we show a more complex example of the use of the filter expressions based on our solution [18] to the bicycle challenge of the MULTI 2018 workshop [1]. The challenge asked the multi-level community to model a bicycle store which offers different bicycle configurations in different categories. It was designed to showcase the characteristics of the different multi-level modeling approaches.

A simplified version of our solution, which consists of four ontological levels, is shown in Fig. 7. All of the view expressions presented below are based on the model in this figure. We show two example views, one called *SoldBikes* shows all sold bicycles but without their parts, and the other *modelSalesInformation* shows the sales information for all models in terms of the *averageActualSalesPrice*, *revenue* and *bestseller* attributes.

The goal of the first filter expression for the *SoldBikes* view is to filter out any part attached to the sold bicycle. The view should only contain information about the customer and the sold bike.

```
context  DeepModel
filter  soldBikes:  Level  ->  select(l|l.#getLevelIndex()# = 3)
```

OCL Expression 5.1. OCL filter for displaying only the last level

Expression 5.1 only filters elements from the lowest level in our model which has the index 3. The first part reflectively selects elements that are instances of

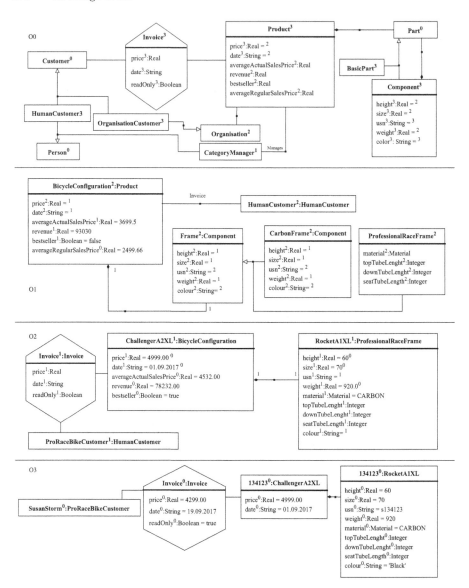

Fig. 7. Simplified version of the solution to the bicycle challenge

the linguistic type *Level*. In the select expression we check for the trait *levelIndex* from the linguistic dimension. To indicate this context switch from the ontological to the linguistic dimension, we use the '#' symbol. In this level, all the sold bikes are displayed with their respective features and parts. Hence, another filter expression is needed at this level to only show the sold bicycles, the customers and the connection that connects them.

```
context O3
filter soldBikes: Clabject -> select(c|c.isDeepInstanceOf(Invoice) or
    c.isDeepInstanceOf(BicycleConfiguration) or c.isDeepInstanceOf(
    Customer))
```

OCL Expression 5.2. Selecting clabjects by their deep type

The second filtering expression checks that clabjects are of a particular type. In this case, only clabjects that are offspring of the clabjects *Invoice*, *BicycleConfiguration* and *Customer* are selected. As in the first constraint, we query for all elements that have the linguistic type *Clabject* reflectively and then execute the select statement. Since *Clabject* is the abstract superclass of *Entities* and *Connections* in the linguistic meta-model, we do not need to distinguish them explicitly and can query for just *Clabjects*.

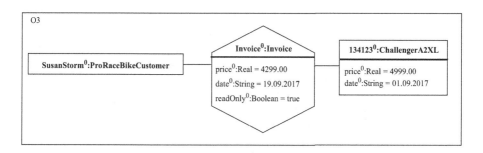

Fig. 8. 'soldBikes' view

In Fig. 8, the results of the first two filter expressions are shown. The first expression only filters out the first three levels so that only the last level is displayed. The second expression filters out every clabject that is not an offspring of the indicated types.

The second view example filters out attributes from clabjects. Instances of *BicycleConfiguration*, in this case indirect instances, have the following attributes *price*, *date*, *averageActualSalesPrice*, *revenue* and *bestseller*. These instances reside on level *O2* so as in our first example we have to filter out the other levels.

```
context DeepModel
filter modelSalesInformation: Level -> select(l|l.#getLevelIndex()# =
    2)
```

OCL Expression 5.3. Filtering out every level but level *O2*

Also, as in the first example, the goal is to only populate the level with clabjects that are typed by a clabject residing one level above. Expression 5.4 populates level *O2* solely with clabjects that are deep instances of *BicycleConfiguration*.

```
context O2
filter modelSalesInformation: Clabject -> select(c.isDeepInstanceOf(
    BicycleConfiguration))
```

OCL Expression 5.4. Selecting only deep instances of 'BicycleConfiguration'

In Expression 5.5 , the context is the clabject *BicycleConfiguration* but the level specification narrows down the execution context of this constraint. Although it is defined one level above the desired execution or filtering context, it is executed on level *O2* due to the level specification that is shown inside the parenthesis.

```
context  BicycleConfiguration(2_2)
filter   modelSalesInformation:  self.revenue
filter   modelSalesInformation:  self.bestseller
filter   modelSalesInformation:  self.averageActualSalesPrice
```

OCL Expression 5.5. Selecting attributes for the clabjects to show in this view

It is possible to define multiple filtering expressions on clabjects to select the attributes or methods that have to be shown in the view. These expressions are less complex than the previous filtering examples and are therefore less likely to be inconsistent.

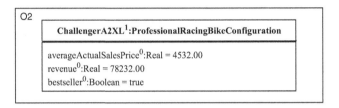

Fig. 9. 'modelSalesInformation' view

Figure 9 shows the result of the third filtering example. All the expressions under the namespace *sellingModelInformations* define this view which only shows the derived attributes of deep indirect instances of *BicycleConfiguration*.

6 Discussion

A comparison of the transformation rules in Sect. 3 and the filter expressions in Sect. 4 reveals that the latter requires far fewer statements than the former to create the same view as shown in Fig. 4. The deep ATL-based Transformation 3.1 needs 15 lines of code while the deep OCL-based filter Expressions from 4.1 to 4.3 required only 6 lines of code. Also, there is no need to keep the model elements synchronized in this approach, because it only filters model elements and displays them in the chosen graphical notation [14]. The Bicycle Challenge examples show how we use these filter expressions in more detail and variety. As shown in expression 5.5, it is possible to define more than one filter expression for any context. When users make changes to the views they are not working on a copy of the SUM but rather on the SUM itself.

The downside of the filter-based approach is that ontologically-typed model elements cannot be added to a view unless the ontological types are available in the view at the level above. However, this can easily be addressed. If the intention is to allow users to generate new model elements, the projection filters must ensure that the necessary types and levels are also included in the deep view. Otherwise, it is only possible to define derived attributes in a clabject that could serve the same purpose as created attributes from a transformation. This would add information that is by default available to the whole SUM. We claim that in the special case of views that represent a subset of the model elements in the SUM, the filter-based approach is significantly more straightforward than the fully-fledged transformation approach.

7   Related Work

Vitruvius (VIew-cenTRic engineering Using a VIrtual Underlying Single model) [16] is a tool that offers flexible, dynamically-created views that are also projected from a SUM. It keeps views consistent with the SUM via bi-directional transformations that are model-to-model or model-to-text transformations. In contrast to the deep OSM approach, Vitruvius does not use an essential (i.e. redundancy free) SUM but rather a combination of (meta-)models that might contain internal redundancies. This kind of SUM is called a virtual SUM (VSUM) [12]. It is a modular approach to SUM construction which simplifies the reuse of models. To maintain the consistency of meta-models, the Vitruvius approach uses mappings between the meta-models in order to react to changes in one of the views. Vitruvius also allows users to create view types (i.e. view specifications) in a flexible manner. It is possible to create view types that show information from different meta-models. Views can therefore display information from the SUM that not only conforms to one meta-model but rather a combination of meta-models. One of the advantages is support for "rapid definition" [12] which allows quick changes to the textual definition of flexible views. The emerging view types and transformations co-evolves automatically. In order to keep the views and VSUM updated Vitruvius needs two languages, one to define bi-directional transformations between the views and parts of the VSUM and one to manage consistency within the meta-models in the VSUM given that they are not redundancy free.

Moconsemi (MOdel CONSistency Ensured by Metamodel Integration) [20] also reuses existing meta-models but transforms them into one essential SUM like the OSM appraoch. In that way, the Moconsemi approach removes all redundant information from the SUM. This avoids the need to keep the elements of the SUM consistent using consistency preservation rules [19].

8   Conclusion

Given the expected increase in the size and complexity of software in coming years, there is a growing need to support the efficient creation and editing of projection-based views of systems. Moreover, this capability is required over all phases of a system's lifecycle, not just the development phase, which in turn requires technology that is agnostic to (i.e. works uniformly and seamlessly over) multiple ontological (i.e. domain) classification levels. The deep OSM technology developed by Tunjic et al. [22], satisfies all these requirements and supports a transformation-based projection approach that accommodates arbitrary changes to the abstraction level, granularity and language through which content from the SUM is portrayed.

However, this approach is unnecessarily complex for a commonly occurring kind of view type, "subsetting" views, which only portray a subset of the content in the SUM without changes in abstraction, granularity or representation language. In a sense, such views essentially provide a direct window onto a part of the SUM. To support this kind of view in a more efficient way, this paper presented a "lightweight" approach for projecting "subsetting" views based on the notion of filter expression in a dialect of OCL known as deep OCL. These filter expressions allow the contents of a view to be simply selected from the SUM without the need to define any complex mappings, since the mappings are by default one-to-one. To be compatible with, and enhance, the deep OSM approach "deep filters" are needed which, like deep transformations, are aware of the difference between linguistic and ontological classification levels and can select content from any one of the latter.

The prototype realization of the approach presented in this paper was therefore developed on top of the deep OCL platform implemented in the Melanee deep modeling environment.

By adding more options to the deep OSM toolkit, and allowing this important type of view to be projected from a SUM in a simple and efficient way, the deep OCL filter technology presented in this paper should enhance the usability of deep OSM approaches and thus, ultimately, promote the use of projectional, view-based modeling environments.

References

1. 5th International Workshop on Multi-Level Modelling - MULTI 2018. https://www.wi-inf.uni-duisburg-essen.de/MULTI2018/
2. ANTLR. https://www.antlr.org/
3. ISO/IEC/IEEE 42010:2011(E) (Revision of ISO/IEC 42010:2007 and IEEE Std 1471-2000). IEEE
4. Melanee 2.0—The deep-modeling domain-specific language workbench. http://www.melanee.org/
5. OMG Document - ormsc/01-07-01 (Model Driven Architecture (MDA)). https://www.omg.org/cgi-bin/doc?ormsc/2001-07-01, library Catalog: www.omg.org
6. Atkinson, C., Bayer, J., Bunse, C., et al.: Component-based software engineering. The KobrA Approach. In: CONQUEST 2001, 5th Conference on Quality Engineering in Software Technology. Proceedings, pp. 247–252 : Ill., Lit. (2001)
7. Atkinson, C., Gerbig, R.: Melanie: multi-level modeling and ontology engineering environment. In: Proceedings of the 2nd International Master Class on Model-Driven Engineering: Modeling Wizards, MW 2012, pp. 1–2. Association for Computing Machinery, Innsbruck, September 2012
8. Atkinson, C., Gerbig, R., Tunjic, C.: Towards multi-level aware model transformations. In: Hu, Z., de Lara, J. (eds.) ICMT 2012. LNCS, vol. 7307, pp. 208–223. Springer, Heidelberg (2012). https://doi.org/10.1007/978-3-642-30476-7_14

9. Atkinson, C., Gerbig, R., Tunjic, C.V.: Enhancing classic transformation languages to support multi-level modeling. Softw. Syst. Model. **14**(2), 645–666 (2015)

10. Atkinson, C., Stoll, D., Bostan, P.: Orthographic software modeling: a practical approach to view-based development. In: Maciaszek, L.A., González-Pérez, C., Jablonski, S. (eds.) ENASE 2008. CCIS, vol. 69, pp. 206–219. Springer, Heidelberg (2010). https://doi.org/10.1007/978-3-642-14819-4_15

11. Atkinson, C., Tunjic, C.: A deep view-point language for projective modeling. In: 2017 IEEE 21st International Enterprise Distributed Object Computing Conference (EDOC), pp. 133–142, October 2017. ISSN 2325–6362

12. Burger, E.: Flexible views for view-based model-driven development. Ph.D. thesis, KIT Scientific Publishing, Karlsruhe (2014)

13. Davis, J., Daniels, R.: Effective DevOps: Building a Culture of Collaboration, Affinity, and Tooling at Scale, 1s edn. O'Reilly Media, Beijing/Boston, June 2016

14. Gerbig, R.: Deep, seamless, multi-format, multi-notation definition and use of domain-specific languages. Ph.D. thesis, University Mannheim, Mannheim (2017). https://ub-madoc.bib.uni-mannheim.de/42010/

15. Kennel, B.: A unified framework for multi-level modeling. Dissertation, University Mannheim, Mannheim (2012). https://ub-madoc.bib.uni-mannheim.de/31906

16. Kramer, M.E., Burger, E., Langhammer, M.: View-centric engineering with synchronized heterogeneous models. In: Proceedings of the 1st Workshop on View-Based, Aspect-Oriented and Orthographic Software Modelling, VAO 2013, pp. 1–6. Association for Computing Machinery, Montpellier, July 2013

17. Lange, A.: dACL: the deep constraint and action language for static and dynamic semantic definition in Melanee. Master's thesis, University of Mannheim, Mannheim (2016). https://ub-madoc.bib.uni-mannheim.de/43490

18. Lange, A., Atkinson, C.: Multi-level modeling with MELANEE. In: CEUR Workshop Proceedings, pp. 653–662. RWTH, Aachen (2018)

19. Meier, J., et al.: Single underlying models for projectional, multi-view environments. In: Proceedings of the 7th International Conference on Model-Driven Engineering and Software Development. MODELSWARD 2019, pp. 117–128. SCITEPRESS - Science and Technology Publications, Lda, Portugal (2019). https://doi.org/10.5220/0007396401170128, event-place: Prague, Czech Republic

20. Meier, J., Winter, A.: Model consistency ensured by metamodel integration. In: MODELS Workshops (2018)

21. OMG: about the object constraint language specification version 2.4. https://www.omg.org/spec/OCL/2.4/PDF

22. Tunjic, C., Atkinson, C., Draheim, D.: Supporting the model-driven organization vision through deep, orthographic modeling. Enterp. Model. Inf. Syst. Architectures **13**(7), 1–39 (2018). https://doi.org/10.18417/emisa.13.7, https://www.emisa-journal.org/emisa/article/view/138

23. Warmer, J.B.: The object constraint language: precise modeling with UML. Object Techology Series. Addison Wesley, Reading, Mass.; Bonn [u.a.] (1999)

24. Werner, C., Assmann, U.: Model synchronization with the role-oriented single underlying model. In: MODELS Workshops (2018)

GrapeL: Combining Graph Pattern Matching and Complex Event Processing

Sebastian Ehmes[1][✉] [iD], Lars Fritsche[1] [iD], and Konrad Altenhofen[2] [iD]

[1] Real-Time Systems Lab at the Technical University of Darmstadt,
Darmstadt, Germany
{sebastian.ehmes,lars.fritsche,andy.schuerr}@es.tu-darmstadt.de
[2] Technical University of Darmstadt, Darmstadt, Germany
konrad.altenhofen@stud.tu-darmstadt.de

Abstract. Incremental Graph Pattern Matching (IGPM) offers an elegant approach to find patterns in graph-based models, reporting newly added and recently removed pattern matches. However, analyzing these matches w.r.t. temporal and causal dependencies can in general only be done by extending not just the IGPM engine but also the underlying model, which often is impractical and sometimes even impossible. Therefore, we transform the stream of pattern matches to a stream of events and employ Complex Event Processing (CEP) to detect such dependencies and derive more complex events from them. For this purpose, we introduce GrapeL as a textual language to specify and generate integrated solutions using both IGPM and CEP to benefit from the synergy of both approaches, which we present in the context of a flight and booking scenario. Finally, we show that our solution can compete with an optimized hand-crafted version without GrapeL and CEP while offering a specification that yields a less tedious and error-prone design process.

Keywords: Incremental graph pattern matching · Complex event processing · Model-driven development

1 Introduction

In the model-driven software engineering community, model transformation is a frequently used means to change models dynamically over time. Incremental Graph Pattern Matching (IGPM) tools offer an elegant approach to detect such changes in graph-based models. Whenever a change occurs in the model, an

This work has been funded by the German Federal Ministry of Education and Research within the Software Campus project MEMIK at TU Darmstadt, funding code 01IS12054.

Electronic supplementary material The online version of this chapter (https://doi.org/10.1007/978-3-030-58167-1_13) contains supplementary material, which is available to authorized users.

Ö. Babur et al. (Eds.): ICSMM 2020, CCIS 1262, pp. 180–196, 2020.
https://doi.org/10.1007/978-3-030-58167-1_13

IGPM tool produces notifications for each newly detected or recently vanished pattern match without needing to calculate all matches from scratch. However, in a dynamic system, it is often not only of interest to detect pattern matches but also to analyze them, e.g., w.r.t. the order in which they arrive. While IGPM is a proven approach to detect structural changes in graphs, it is not well-suited to detect temporal dependencies between model changes without extending the model by adding a notion of time that is detectable on a structural level. To solve this shortcoming, we employ a Complex Event Processing (CEP) engine, which analyses a stream of events in order to derive higher knowledge in the form of more complex events. In our case, newly detected or recently vanished matches, due to model changes, can be interpreted as events, which can be analysed w.r.t. temporal dependencies using a CEP engine. Industrial strength CEP engines such as Apama[1] are particularly suited for processing and analyzing individual events that occur over some time. Conversely, using CEP engines to detect structural changes on models can be a challenging task, which is especially true when the model itself is changed continuously [4,7,10,11]. Considering all possible atomic events in a graph-based model such as creation and deletion of arbitrary nodes and edges, the CEP engine would have to incrementally construct matches (complex events) from these events that can emerge in an arbitrary order and, furthermore, handle changes to the model that may render previously found matches invalid. While it is possible to mimic an IGPM tool using CEP, handcrafting such a solution is error-prone, expensive and not guaranteed to perform better than established IGPM frameworks [10]. Considering this, we aim to combine the benefits from both IGPM and CEP in one tool built around our novel specification language GrapeL (Graph Pattern Event Language)[2]. For this purpose, we use the general-purpose model transformation tool eMoflon[3] that integrates several state-of-the-art IGPM frameworks and offers pattern and model transformation specifications via a textual language. As a CEP engine, we use Apama a state-of-the-art CEP tool developed by Software AG that provides a textual language to define CEP queries. We demonstrate and evaluate our approach by implementing a flight and booking scenario, where structural changes such as flight delays are detected via IGPM, and CEP is used to detect unreachable connecting flights for individual passengers.

In Sect. 2.1, we introduce an illustrative example scenario, followed by background knowledge concerning graph pattern matching in Sect. 2.2 and complex event processing in Sect. 2.3. Section 3 and Sect. 4 explain the implementation of our approach and our newly developed domain specific language GrapeL, respectively. In Sect. 5, we present the evaluation of our approach with respect to performance and scalability. Following that, we discuss works that are related to our approach in Sect. 6. Finally, Sect. 7 sums up our contribution and gives a brief overview of planned future improvements as well as possible extensions to our approach.

---

[1] Apama - http://www.apamacommunity.com.

[2] GrapeL - https://github.com/eMoflon-CEP/GraPEL.

[3] eMoflon - https://emoflon.org/.

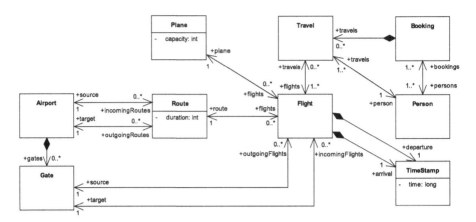

Fig. 1. Metamodel of a flight monitoring system

2   Preliminaries

2.1   Motivating Example: Flight Monitoring System

We chose a flight and booking monitoring system as a use case scenario to illustrate our newly developed approach. The system shall monitor booked flights and warn the traveller about, e.g., delays or cancellations. Additionally, our monitoring system will also look for alternative flights in case of delayed connecting flights and make suggestions for re-bookings. With a sufficiently large model such a system will have to cope with large amounts of events triggered by changes that correspond to, e.g., delays.

The metamodel of our flight monitoring system is shown in Fig. 1. In the figure, a traveller is represented by a `Person` that has some `Bookings`, possibly with other `Persons` s/he is traveling with. A `Booking` may contain several `Travels` and a `Travel` may consist of multiple `Flights`, which enable to model trips with several connecting `Flights`. `Flights` are assigned to a plane with a maximum passenger capacity as well as a source and target `Gate` belonging to their respective `Airports`. The duration of a `Flight` depends on the `Route` and is proportional to the travel distance and the airspeed of a certain `Plane`. Finally, `Timestamps` define the (expected) departure and arrival time or each `Flight`.

2.2   Graph Pattern Matching

In this work, models are represented by graphs with objects corresponding to typed nodes and references between objects corresponding to typed edges. Therefore, a key technology in our proposed approach is incremental graph pattern matching (IGPM), which we rely on heavily in order to detect structural changes in a graph-based model. IGPM tools find all occurrences of a structural dependency within a graph that are similar to a predefined graph pattern, where subgraphs of a model that fulfill a graph pattern are called (graph pattern) matches and consist of a mapping between graph pattern and model nodes. Given a graph pattern as depicted in Fig. 2, a graph pattern matcher searches through a model to find all `Flight objects` that reference a `Plane`, a `Route` and a `TimeStamp` object in the specified way. Hence, a valid match to the `FlightArrival` pattern will contain the defined pattern nodes `flight`, `plane`, `route` and `arrival` and the mappings to their corresponding graph pattern nodes.

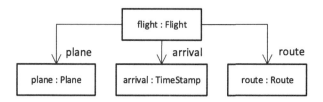

Fig. 2. Example: FlightArrival pattern

Graph Pattern Matching Approaches. Essentially, graph pattern matching approaches can be divided into two categories, namely batch and incremental approaches. In the first approach, batch pattern matching, matches are often obtained by solving a constraint satisfaction problem [8] or through local search algorithms using search plans [14]. However, these approaches often perform poorly when a model changes, which is caused by the fact that all previously found matches are discarded and the graph pattern matching process is restarted anew. The other approach, incremental graph pattern matching (IGPM), keeps track of individual model changes. This allows the sets of newly found or recently disappeared matches to be updated incrementally. Consequently, the runtime does not increase proportionally to the total size of the model, but is proportional to the magnitude of the model change. Looking at our example scenario, the flight and booking system, we can expect large amounts of small model changes over time. Re-collecting all previously gathered knowledge about a model every time a flight is cancelled or delayed would be grossly inefficient and would lead to potentially large reaction times. Therefore, IGPM-based tools seem to be the logical choice for this scenario to minimize the time between system updates. Forgy's Rete algorithm [3] is a widely known approach to incremental pattern matching. Besides the tool that Forgy developed himself, there are currently many other tools that implement Rete or derivatives of it, including tools such as Viatra [12], Democles [13] and the recently developed HiPE[4]. While Viatra, Democles and other well-known IGPM tools are mostly single-threaded, HiPE was developed with the goal to perform graph pattern matching massively in

---

[4] HiPE - https://github.com/HiPE-DevOps/HiPE-Updatesite.

parallel by reinterpreting Forgy's Rete-approach anew, using an actor system approach [6] based on the Akka[5] framework.

IGPM tools are well suited to search for any kind of substructure in graph-based models, such as the pattern in Fig. 3, which detects newly appearing connecting flights of specific travels as well as their disappearance, e.g., when a flight is canceled or has a delay. However, using IGPM to find an alternative connecting flight under the precondition that a connecting flight disappeared is impossible without changing the metamodel in Sect. 2.1 to incorporate a history of broken connecting flights, which is inefficient and may be undesirable in practical applications.

2.3   Complex Event Processing

To cope with the aforementioned weaknesses of IGPM approaches, we employ Complex Event Processing (CEP) techniques. In CEP, events are objects that represent records of activities in a system [9], for example, a graph pattern match that has appeared or disappeared. An event has a certain type and form. The form of an event contains so-called fields, which are similar to class attributes in object-oriented languages. When considering the appearance or disappearance of graph pattern matches as discrete events, the CEP paradigm naturally lends itself to correlate these pattern events to identify meaningful sub-sequences of events. Such specific sequences of events as well as event types are usually described in an event processing language (EPL), where a user may define a causal or temporal dependency inside an event pattern using different relational operators. The CEP engine will then constantly monitor streams of events and react whenever an event pattern is matched, e.g., by searching whether some event e1 precedes another e2. If such a sequence of events is detected by a CEP engine, the event pattern is matched and a new event is produced. Events derived from other events in such a way are called complex events. Additionally, events introducing unprocessed information from outside a CEP system into a CEP engine are commonly called first-level events. The example from

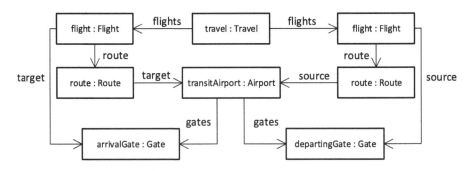

Fig. 3. ConnectingFlights pattern

---

[5] Akka - https://www.akka.io.

Sect. 2.2, where an alternative connecting flight has to be found if a match to the ConnectingFlights-pattern (Fig. 3) disappears, can now be solved by using a CEP engine. Furthermore, a CEP engine could report an alternative connecting flight whenever an event containing a flight is followed by an event signalling the disappearance of a match to the ConnectingFlights-pattern, sharing the same transit airport and target airport. The following section will present Apama as an example of a CEP engine, which we use in the tool presented in this paper.

Apama. is a commercially available industrial strength CEP engine developed by Software AG that comes with its proprietary event processing language called Apama EPL. In this tool, the typical notion of event patterns is implemented by event listeners, inside actions that are grouped within monitors.

Listing 1.1. Apama EPL - Example

```
1   monitor EventMonitor {
2       constant string channel = "channelName";
3       action onload() {
4           monitor.subscribe(channel);
5           on all EventOne as eventOne -> EventTwo {
6               userAction(eventOne);
7           }
8       }
9       action userAction(EventOne one) {
10          // user defined code
11      }
12  }
```

Listing 1.1 shows an illustrating example of such a monitor in the Apama EPL[6]. Actions (lines 3 and 9) are similar to functions in other programming languages and may have parameters (line 9) as well as return values. Monitors (line 1), on the other hand, are related to classes in object-oriented languages and may define attributes (line 2), as well as actions. Listeners (line 5) watch over streams of events, also called event channels, onto which the monitor has subscribed (line 4). Inside a listener a user defines event dependencies by using so-called relational operators, e.g., the arrow operator ->, which defines here that an Event of type EventOne has to precede another Event of type EventTwo. Whenever a listener detects an event of interest, a user defined action may be called or a nested listener may be spawned (line 6).

3   GrapeEngine

Remembering our motivating example from Sect. 2.1, we know that complex incremental structural changes such as the removal of several references, e.g, between flights, travels and bookings, can easily be detected by any IGPM

---

[6] Apama EPL reference - https://documentation.softwareag.com/onlinehelp/Rohan/ Apama/v10-3/apama10-3/apama-webhelp/.

tool but performing the same feat using a CEP tool requires major effort [10]. On the other hand, temporal dependencies between the appearance and disappearance of matches can be detected using a CEP tool, e.g, a flight has been cancelled (removed) and a possible alternative flight has appeared some time before. Relying solely on an IGPM tool scenarios like these can only be implemented by enriching the (meta-)model with history information. Motivated by these insights, we created a tool called **Graph pattern event Engine** (GrapeEngine) that combines the strengths of IGPM and CEP approaches. As a result GrapeEngine is able to do both, tracking structural changes incrementally and correlating appearing and vanishing graph pattern matches over time.

Model.pdf Model.pdf

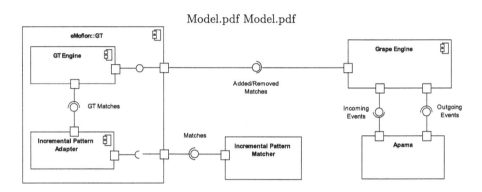

Fig. 4. GrapeEngine: software components

The main software components of GrapeEngine are depicted in Fig. 4. We use the Eclipse Modeling Framework[7] (EMF) to specify metamodels, such as our flight monitoring example, and create model instances that correspond to these metamodels. Our incremental graph pattern matching tool of choice is HiPE, which is integrated into the graph transformation tool eMoflon::IBeX-GT[8]. IBeX-GT operates on EMF-based models and can be used to find graph pattern matches or perform model transformations described by graph transformation rules. Furthermore, graph patterns or graph transformation rules are defined using the IBeX-GT textual language. Apama on the other hand, is a commercially available industrial strength CEP engine created by Software AG that comes with its proprietary event processing language called Apama EPL. GrapeEngine itself ties everything together by managing EMF-based models and by using IBeX-GT to find graph pattern matches, which are inserted into the Apama CEP engine as an event stream. The last missing component is our newly developed **Graph pattern event Language** (GrapeL), which is described further in Sect. 4. Via GrapeL, a user defines graph patterns and complex events that make use of appearing or vanishing graph pattern matches.

---

[7] EMF - https://www.eclipse.org/modeling/emf/.
[8] eMoflon::IBeX-GT - https://github.com/eMoflon/emoflon-ibex.

Hence, a GrapeL specification contains the necessary information to synthesize the required IBeX-GT pattern models, Apama EPL code and other software artifacts (e.g., adapters) that are required to connect Apama and eMoflon. This code generation process is illustrated in Fig. 5. After specifying events and patterns in GrapeL, the build process is executed, which transforms graph patterns written in GrapeL to a format conforming to the IBeX-GT pattern metamodel. Following that, those transformed models are passed to the eMoflon code generator, which generates a Java-API, required by any task related to IBeX-GT. Additionally, events defined in GrapeL are transformed into Apama EPL code, which is used to specify event monitors in the Apama engine and initialise them at runtime. In a final step, the actual GrapeEngine-API code is generated, which provides an interface to IBeX-GT, an adapter to the Apama engine, and an interface to control the GrapeEngine and alter the data.

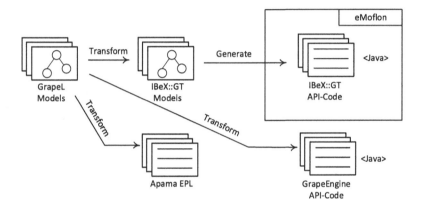

Fig. 5. GrapeEngine: code generation process

The basic idea behind GrapeEngine is to use IBeX-GT and in extension HiPE to track model changes incrementally by means of graph pattern matching. The resulting matches are transformed into events that are compatible with Apama, which in turn returns higher order events containing knowledge derived from correlating said pattern match events. This update process is repeated each time a user requests an update from the GrapeEngine tool and is illustrated by an example in Fig. 6. In this example, the flight monitor model underwent some changes, which lead to the cancellation of a flight (removal), before the update is performed. During the update step, the pattern matcher in IBeX-GT processes these changes (model deltas) and responds with a set of matches (FlightRemoved), which are (Flight) matches that vanished due to the modification of the model. The GrapeEngine-API converts these matches to corresponding types of events that signal their removal (FlightRemoved) and inserts them into the Apama engine. In this example, Apama reacts with events that signal possible alternative flights (FlightAlternativeEvent) if valid alternatives

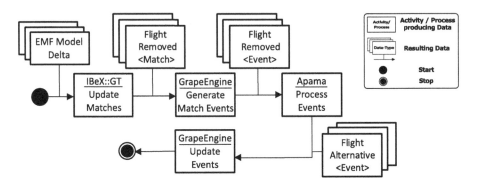

Fig. 6. GrapeEngine: update

(FlightAlternativeMatch) have been passed to Apama before. After the update step is completed, a user may request the results from the GrapeEngine-API.

4   Specification Through GrapeL

Connecting IBeX-GT with Apama can be a tedious and error-prone challenge as there are multiple tasks to work on that influence each other. First, graph patterns and Apama EPL patterns have to be specified in their respective frameworks. Given these specifications, a Java adapter has to be written that transforms each match of a graph pattern into an event that is sent to and recognized by Apama. Consequently, with increasing project size, the manual effort of specifying graph and EPL patterns as well as implementing the Java adapter becomes increasingly complex and time consuming. Hence, we propose the novel domain specific language GrapeL **Gra**ph pattern **e**vent **L**anguage that combines both graph pattern and EPL specification and from which we automatically generate graph pattern specification, EPL and Java adapter artifacts in the spirit of model-driven engineering. GrapeL is implemented with the Xtext framework[9], which offers extensive support for language specification and seamless integration into the Eclipse plugin-environment together with syntax checking and highlighting as well as code completion. In order to combine graph pattern matching and complex event processing in a single tool successfully, we needed to make some careful considerations on the necessary language features. First and foremost, GrapeL must offer a comfortable means to define graph patterns, events and event patterns and provide a way to import previously defined graph patterns. In addition to that, our language needs to support the import of metamodels, which is important to ensure type safety and enable type checking for events, event patterns and graph patterns. Furthermore, a user must be able to reference events as well as graph patterns within event patterns in order to correlate events and graph pattern matches. Therefore, GrapeL has to support such references as well as references to attributes and nodes within events and graph

---

[9] Xtext - https://www.eclipse.org/Xtext/.

patterns to allow the definition of attribute constraints. Finally, GrapeL must offer the usual CEP semantics, such as "Event e2 follows Event e1" or "Event e1 and Event e2 must be present", which in this case have to encompass events as well as graph pattern (events).

Graph Pattern Event Language. In the following, we introduce the syntax of GrapeL using our running example. A user defines events, graph patterns and event patterns, with `event`, `pattern` and `event_pattern` as their respective keywords. Events are defined as shown in an example in Listing 1.2, where the event is given a type name in line 1 and receives a list of typed attributes (`flight` and `flightArrivalTime`), which are often called fields in the CEP context and store values.

Listing 1.2. Example: FlightDelayedEvent (GrapeL)

```
1   event FlightDelayedEvent {
2       Flight flight
3       int flightArrivalTime
4   }
```

GrapeL supports all primitive types (e.g., `integer`, `char`, etc.) as well as complex types (e.g., `Flight`) that were defined in the imported metamodels, as shown in the example. Graph patterns as well as references to metamodels are defined as Ecore-models within Eclipse in the same fashion as in IBeX-GT[10], since GrapeL imports the IBeX-GT language metamodel. Within the limited space of this paper, we would like to show a glimpse of the expressivity of IBeX-GT using a simple example pattern and a metamodel reference in Listing 1.3.

Listing 1.3. Example: FlightArrivalPattern

```
1    import
2        "platform:/resource/.../FlightMetamodel.ecore"
3    pattern FlightArrivalPattern() {
4        plane  : Plane
5        route  : Route
6        arrival : TimeStamp
7        flight : Flight {
8            -plane->plane
9            -route->route
10           -arrival->arrival
11       }
12   }
```

The first two lines show a reference to an external metamodel, which makes it available in all patterns, events and event patterns through the `import` statement, using its uniform resource identifier (URI). The example pattern instructs the pattern matcher to find the set of matches, within a given model, that contains all flights, which are assigned to a route, a plane and have an arrival time

---

[10] IBeX-GT tutorial and documentation - https://bit.ly/2WjXGZI.

stamp. Whenever one of the nodes or references are removed or exchanged in the model (e.g., through a delay), a previously found match is discarded and a new match is created. Analogously to the event specification, line 3 defines the pattern type and allows for the definition of a set of parameters (round brackets) to parameterize attribute constraints, contained in the pattern. Line 4 through 7 specify nodes of the pattern along with their type. A returned match to this pattern will essentially contain these four nodes. Finally, lines 8 through 10 define references between two nodes, e.g., in this case between **plane** and **flight**.

Listing 1.4. Example: FlightDelayedEventPattern

```
1   event_pattern FlightDelayedEventPattern
2       spawns FlightDelayedEvent{
3       // event context
4       flightMatch : FlightPattern
5       arrivalMatch : FlightArrivalPattern
6       // context constraint
7       flightMatch.flight == arrivalMatch.flight
8       // temporal dependency
9       flightMatch -> arrivalMatch {
10          // attribute constraints
11          arrivalMatch.flight.arrival.time >
12          (arrivalMatch.flight.departure.time +
13          arrivalMatch.route.duration)
14      }
15      // create new event
16      spawn FlightDelayedEvent(flightMatch.flight,
17          arrivalMatch.flight.arrival.time)
18  }
```

The example in Listing 1.4 shows an event pattern that produces a new event of type **FlightDelayedEvent** if it is matched by the CEP engine, as indicated after the keyword **spawns** as a return type in line 2. This event pattern checks if the incoming match to FlightArrivalPattern (line 5) signals the delay of a flight and whether a match to FlightPattern (line 4) has appeared before. The -> operator expresses that **flightMatch** precedes **arrivalMatch**. To ensure that the flights in **flightMatch** and in **arrivalMatch** are the same, a context constraint can be introduced that checks both flights for equality (line 7). It produces (**spawn**) a new event if the attribute constraint defined in lines 11 through 13 is met. The constraint demands the departure time of the flight in combination with the planned flight duration to be smaller than the estimated time of arrival.

Constructing IBeX-GT Patterns and Apama EPL Code from GrapeL Specifications. Since GrapeL imports die IBeX-GT language metamodel, we can simply reuse the existing transformation implementations as well as the existing code generators to produce the IBeX-GT pattern model and generate the necessary eMoflon-API code. Generators for the Apama EPL description as well as the necessary API, which wraps the Apama Java-library, were implemented from scratch. An event definition as shown in Listing 1.2 leads to the Apama code in Listing 1.5, stored in a file along with the other event definitions.

Listing 1.5. Example: FlightDelayedEvent (Apama EPL)

```
1   event FlightDelayedEvent{
2       integer flight
3       integer flightArrivalTime
4   }
```

In contrast to the definition of `FlightDelayedEvent`, where `flight` is given a complex type `Flight`, line 2 defines an integer as type. This is done to circumvent the need to serialise objects contained within some model, which would increase the memory footprint needlessly. Instead, the generated Apama-API creates a unique identifier for each object of a certain type in order to allow for comparisons within context constraints and to distinguish and retrieve these objects later on in the process. A defined pattern also leads to the creation of an Apama EPL event description, such as the pattern in Listing 1.3. The creation of such a first level event is necessary since Apama can only take events as input. Again, in order to minimize the amount of memory required by Apama, we only define the absolute necessary fields within the event. By analysing the GrapeL description, we know exactly which class attributes are referenced and which pattern nodes are required by any event pattern.

Listing 1.6. Example: FlightArrivalMatchEvent (Apama EPL)

```
1   event FlightArrivalMatchEvent{
2       integer flight
3       integer flightArrivalTime
4       integer flightDepartureTime
5       integer routeDuration
6   }
```

In case of the example in Listing 1.6, only the flight node, the arrival and departure time as well as the flight duration are required in the event pattern in Listing 1.4, which is exactly what the generated example event contains. To prevent naming collisions dot-operators are removed and replaced by camel-case.

Each event pattern leads to the generation of an enclosing Apama-monitor, with the example in Listing 1.4 leading to the EPL code shown in Listing 1.7. The temporal dependency is checked in lines 5 and 6, where a listener is created whenever a `FlightPatternEvent` is received on channel `eMoflon` (lines 2 and 4), which waits until it receives a `FlightArrivalPatternEvent`. Whenever that is the case, the context constraint is evaluated, i.e., unique node ids are checked for equality (line 7). If node ids match, the attribute constraints are checked and if these evaluate true, a new `FlightDelayedMatchEvent` event is created inside the Apama engine.

Listing 1.7. Example: FlightDelayedEventPattern (Apama EPL)

```
 1  monitor FlightDelayedEventPattern {
 2      constant string channel = "eMoflon";
 3      action onload() {
 4          monitor.subscribe(channel);
 5          on all FlightPatternEvent as flightMatch
 6              -> FlightArrivalPatternEvent
 7                  (flight=flightMatch.flight)
 8                  as arrivalMatch {
 9                      if(constraint(arrivalMatch)) {
10                          spawnEvent(flightMath,
11                          arrivalMatch);
12                      }
13                  }
14          }
15      }
16
17      action
18      constraint(FlightArrivalPatternEvent arrivalMatch)
19          returns boolean {
20          return arrivalMatch.flightArrivalTime >
21              (arrivalMatch.flightDepartureTime +
22              arrivalMatch.routeDuration);
23      }
24
25      action spawnEvent(FlightMatchEvent flightMatch,
26          FlightDelayedMatchEvent arrivalMatch) {
27          route FlightDelayedEvent(flightMatch.flight,
28              arrivalMatch.flightArrivalTime);
29      }
30  }
31 }
```

5   Evaluation

While our model-driven approach might offer a more productive and less error-prone development experience, it might not be as good in terms of performance, when compared to a use case specific manually implemented solution that does not require a general-purpose tool such as Apama. To investigate this, we implemented two versions of a flight and booking monitoring system, as proposed in Sect. 2.1, which are functionally identical. One version is specified using GrapeL and, therefore, consists of automatically generated code that integrates both eMoflon and Apama. The second version makes use of eMoflon as well but does not rely on Apama to correlate sequences of matches over time. Instead, this alternative version uses a custom library to correlate matches in a similar way as Apama but is implemented for this specific use case only. We decided to implement the custom-solution without using Apama to avoid comparing near identical implementations. Using these two different implementations, we compared their performance and scalability to find out whether our approach generates code that matches up to a hand-optimized solution. For this purpose, we implemented a simulator for our flight and booking monitoring system, which operates on models that conform to the metamodel in Fig. 1. Using the simulator, we change the initial model over time and introduce, e.g., new flights and flight delays. The two variants of our monitoring system then observe the model and report on issues, e.g., unreachable connecting flights due to previous delays. We start our simulation with a model consisting of 56 flights and 14145 bookings spread equally over three days and expand this model linearly up to a factor of five reaching up to 280 flights and 70725 bookings over 15 days. For each model, we simulate 6 days where after each simulated day a new day is appended to keep a constant planning horizon while past flights and bookings are removed. We then measured the time it took for each approach to complete the simulation of a scenario. Figure 7 shows the results of our simulation runtime measurements, which were collected on an AMD Ryzen-7 1800x 8-core machine with 32 GB of DDR4-3200 MHz memory. The x-axis indicates the relative model size of a scenario compared to the initial model, whereas the y-axis indicates the measured runtime to complete the simulation of a scenario. Since both Apama and the employed pattern matcher HiPE are massively multi-threaded, we expected strong variations in runtime due to the non-deterministic runtime behaviour of multi-threaded applications. To combat this, we executed and measured each simulation scenario five times and calculated the median along with the maximal and minimal runtimes, which are plotted in Fig. 7. The strong similarity of the results show that the runtime overhead caused by the synchronization between eMoflon and Apama is almost negligible and massively outweighed by the advantages of our model driven approach. Generally speaking, graph pattern matching is the most costly operation and is responsible for 99% of the overall runtime of both approaches shown in Fig. 7. Note that the runtime behaviour depends heavily on the kind of patterns that a given IGPM tool has to search for in a model graph and its size. Keeping that in mind and looking at the plots, we can see that both approaches scale linearly with a growing model size in this

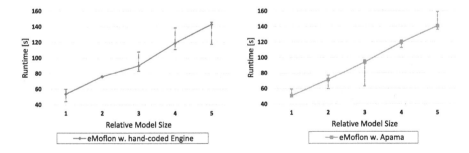

Fig. 7. Runtime measurements

example scenario, indicating that adding a general-purpose CEP engine to the mix does not affect the scalability negatively, which is still mostly influenced by the IGPM engine.

Threats to Validity. The results of our prototype give a first glimpse on the potential and capabilities of our approach. However, our evaluation was only performed using synthesized models that are inspired by real-world flight routes but are still rather simple in comparison. In addition, the used graph patterns and GrapeL specifications only cover the presented scenario. While it is only natural to extend the example and detect more useful information, this of course would also reduce the throughput of our tool, which we want to investigate in the near future. We, furthermore, like to point out that we do not yet cover nor use the full expressiveness offered by Apama. To sum up, we would like to increase the expressiveness of GrapeL by employing more advanced CEP features, increase the complexity of our graph patterns and GrapeL specifications to detect other useful information in the context of our example and, finally, use real-world flight data to show that our approach is indeed able to solve a realistic and non-trivial practical problem.

6   Related Work

In this paper, we introduced a novel approach to increase the expressiveness of classical graph transformations using a CEP engine. There are various other approaches that employ CEP in the context of graph-based model transformations, e.g., by using it to process complex event patterns. However, most related works have their origin in conjunction with the ACM DEBS 2016 Grand Challenge [5], in which a constantly changing social network graph was monitored and analysed in order to find the most important comments and communities within. This example has two major similarities compared to our flight and booking monitoring scenario in Sect. 2.1. Not only do we need to find patterns in a potentially large graph structure, but the found pattern matches need to be checked for correlations over time. Many works in the DEBS 2016 Grand Challenge (e.g., [7,10,11]) tried to implement some kind of batch graph pattern matcher using their CEP tool of choice, whereas only one work [4] presented a CEP-based incremental pattern matching approach. Most works came to the conclusion that such an approach is a complex and error prone task, which underlines the necessity of a model-driven approach, as proposed in this paper. Additionally, implementing graph pattern matching in a CEP engine must solve various problems, e.g., how to determine whether all matches have already been found by the multi-threaded CEP engine [10]. Our approach circumvents both problems by (i) using a model-driven approach, generating code automatically and (ii) using an IGPM tool to perform pattern matching on the graph-based model as a first step and then use the resulting matches as input for the CEP engine as a second step.

Other research aimed to extend CEP approaches for graph-structured information (e.g., [1]) as well, which resulted in a difficult and complex way to define rules and patterns, much like the above mentioned works since they lacked a specification language designed for exactly that purpose. Our approach alleviates the complexities of defining (or using external) graph patterns within CEP tools, by allowing a user to define events, event patterns as well as graph patterns textually with the help of a single domain-specific language, GrapeL.

Finally, Dávid et al. [2] also combine model transformations with CEP. Incremental changes to the model, detected by validation patterns, are fed to the CEP engine as atomic events to derive more complex events, which are used as inputs for their rule-based model transformation engine. Similar to our approach, they employ a domain-specific language to specify and generate integrated solutions, however, instead of using a proven industrial-strength CEP tool such as Apama, they build a custom CEP solution of their own.

7   Conclusion

While the specification of temporal dependencies is a hard task using graph patterns only, implementing an incremental graph pattern matching using complex event processing is an error-prone and time consuming task. Hence, we presented a novel approach to combine graph pattern matching and complex event processing in our paper. We use GrapeL as a textual language gluing IGPM and CEP together to generate solutions that integrate both approaches in order to benefit from their synergy. GrapeL is integrated into eMoflon, a state-of-the-art graph transformation tool, in which we implemented a flight and booking scenario as proof-of-concept that was used throughout our paper. We showed that the benefit of using GrapeL in comparison to a hand-crafted version is two-fold. First, GrapeL specifications promise to lower the complexity and error rate of the implementation significantly and we believe that this also has the potential to increase the efficiency during the implementation as a lot of usually hand-crafted code can be generated automatically. Second, we showed that our improvement of the implementation process is as efficient as an optimized and hand-crafted solution. In the future, we would like to extend our approach by closing the loop and feed information back to eMoflon in order to change models using the information derived from CEP. We, furthermore, want to improve GrapeL by integrating common CEP functions such as counting events and make it easier for users to implement specifications by offering more compact GrapeL expressions. Finally, using a CEP engine and HiPE as an actor-based pattern matcher has the advantage that we can distribute our process easily to different physical systems, which we also consider to be worth investigating.

References

1. Barquero, G., Burgueño, L., Troya, J., Vallecillo, A.: Extending complex event processing to graph-structured information. In: Proceedings of the 21th ACM/IEEE International Conference on Model Driven Engineering Languages and Systems. MODELS 2018, pp. 166–175. Association for Computing Machinery, New York (2018). https://doi.org/10.1145/3239372.3239402

2. Dávid, I., Ráth, I., Varró, D.: Foundations for streaming model transformations by complex event processing. Softw. Syst. Model. **17**(1), 135–162 (2016). https://doi.org/10.1007/s10270-016-0533-1

3. Forgy, C.L.: Rete: a fast algorithm for the many pattern/many object pattern match problem. Artif. Intell. **19**(1), 17–37 (1982). https://doi.org/10.1016/0004-3702(82)90020-0

4. Gillani, S., Picard, G., Laforest, F.: Continuous graph pattern matching over knowledge graph streams. In: Proceedings of the 10th ACM International Conference on Distributed and Event-Based Systems. DEBS 2016, pp. 214–225. Association for Computing Machinery, New York (2016). https://doi.org/10.1145/2933267.2933306

5. Gulisano, V., Jerzak, Z., Voulgaris, S., Ziekow, H.: The debs 2016 grand challenge. In: Proceedings of the 10th ACM International Conference on Distributed and Event-Based Systems. DEBS 2016, pp. 289–292. Association for Computing Machinery, New York (2016). https://doi.org/10.1145/2933267.2933519

6. Hewitt, C., Bishop, P., Steiger, R.: A universal modular actor formalism for artificial intelligence. In: Proceedings of the 3rd International Joint Conference on Artificial Intelligence. IJCAI 1973, pp. 235–245. Morgan Kaufmann Publishers Inc. (1973)

7. Jayasinghe, M., et al.: Continuous analytics on graph data streams using WSO2 complex event processor. In: Proceedings of the 10th ACM International Conference on Distributed and Event-Based Systems. DEBS 2016, pp. 301–308. Association for Computing Machinery, New York (2016). https://doi.org/10.1145/2933267.2933508

8. Larrosa, J., Valiente, G.: Constraint satisfaction algorithms for graph pattern matching. Math. Struct. Comput. Sci. **12**(4), 403–422 (2002). https://doi.org/10.1017/S0960129501003577

9. Luckham, D.: The Power of Events. 1 edn. Addison-Wesley, April 2002

10. Martin, A., Brito, A., Fetzer, C.: Real-time social network graph analysis using StreamMine3G. In: Proceedings of the 10th ACM International Conference on Distributed and Event-Based Systems. DEBS 2016, pp. 322–329. Association for Computing Machinery, New York (2016). https://doi.org/10.1145/2933267.2933514

11. Mayer, R., Mayer, C., Tariq, M.A., Rothermel, K.: Graphcep: real-time data analytics using parallel complex event and graph processing. In: Proceedings of the 10th ACM International Conference on Distributed and Event-Based Systems. DEBS 2016, pp. 309–316. Association for Computing Machinery, New York (2016). https://doi.org/10.1145/2933267.2933509

12. Varró, D., Bergmann, G., Hegedüs, Á., Horváth, Á., Ráth, I., Ujhelyi, Z.: Road to a reactive and incremental model transformation platform: three generations of the VIATRA framework. Softw. Syst. Model. **15**(3), 609–629 (2016). https://doi.org/10.1007/s10270-016-0530-4

13. Varró, G., Deckwerth, F.: A rete network construction algorithm for incremental pattern matching. In: Duddy, K., Kappel, G. (eds.) ICMT 2013. LNCS, vol. 7909, pp. 125–140. Springer, Heidelberg (2013). https://doi.org/10.1007/978-3-642-38883-5_13

14. Zündorf, A.: Graph pattern matching in PROGRES. In: Cuny, J., Ehrig, H., Engels, G., Rozenberg, G. (eds.) Graph Grammars 1994. LNCS, vol. 1073, pp. 454–468. Springer, Heidelberg (1996). https://doi.org/10.1007/3-540-61228-9_105

Author Index

Printed in the United States
By Bookmasters